KW-327-791

International Socialism 169

Winter 2021

Contributors

Baba Aye is a leading member of the Socialist Workers and Youth League in Nigeria. He is also co-convenor of the Coalition for Revolution.

Petros Constantinou is a member of the Greek Socialist Workers Party (SEK), a councillor in Athens municipality and coordinator of Movement Against Racism and the Fascist Threat (Keerfa).

Judy Cox is a teacher in East London. She is studying for a PhD in women and the Chartist movement at Leeds University. She is the author of *The Women's Revolution: Russia 1905-1917* (Haymarket, 2019) and *Rebellious Daughters of History* (Redwords, 2020).

Iannis Delatolas is a socialist and member of Marx21 in New York.

Clare Lemlich is a socialist in the United States and a member of Marx21.

Judy McVey is a Melbourne-based socialist, a member of Solidarity, and the author of a pamphlet, *Abortion: The Fight That's Still To Be Won* (2019). Currently, she is completing a PhD at the University of Sydney.

Ken Olende is researching a PhD on "Rethinking 'blackness' as a racial identity" at Brighton University. He has previously worked as a tutor for the Workers' Educational Association, a journalist on *Socialist Worker* and editor of Unite Against Fascism's *Unity* magazine.

Ilan Pappé is the Director of the European Centre for Palestine Studies at the University of Exeter and the author of *The Ethnic Cleansing of Palestine* (Oneworld, 2006). His latest book is *Ten Myths About Israel* (Verso, 2017).

Camilla Royle teaches at King's College London and is the author of *A Rebel's Guide to Engels* (Bookmarks, 2020).

Sabby Sagall is the author of *Final Solutions: Human Nature, Capitalism and Genocide* (Pluto, 2013) and of the forthcoming *Music and Capitalism: Melody, Harmony and Rhythm in the Modern World*.

Paul Simpson is a former university lecturer in the sociology of health who publishes mainly in the field of sexuality and gender in later life, with an emphasis on social class influences. Using analysis informed by socialism, he has also published on the health ideas and practices of working-class men.

Tomáš Tengely-Evans has worked as a journalist on *Socialist Worker* and is a member of the Socialist Workers Party (SWP) in North London.

Giles Ji Ungpakorn is a Thai socialist. He lives in exile in the Britain after being charged with lèse-majesté. He blogs about Thai politics at https://uglytruththailand.wordpress.com

Ben Windsor has worked as a graphic designer for the SWP since 2004. He is also an activist with the SWP in South London.

Colette Wymer is a socialist activist in South Yorkshire.

A year under the pandemic
Joseph Choonara

A year is a long time in pandemics.[1] It is a little over 12 months since the first victims succumbed to Covid-19. By the time of writing, the global death toll had reached 1.5 million, a figure likely to rise substantially over the winter months in the northern hemisphere. Vast numbers more have suffered ill health, sometimes lingering as the baffling array of symptoms dubbed "long Covid", alongside mental distress, the loss of a job or income, or the grief of losing loved ones.

The virus has dominated politics, absorbing the news agenda and reconfiguring the everyday lives of billions people. The two major breaks in the wall-to-wall coverage of Covid-19—the global Black Lives Matter movement last summer and the presidential election in the United States—were only partial exceptions; both were heavily inflected by the impact of the pandemic.

Yet with the turn of the year, there was hope in some quarters of a return to a semblance of normality. Furthermore, for some, the hope was not simply that newly developed vaccines would control the virus, but that the politics emerging in the post-pandemic era might restore the centre ground and stabilise capitalism. In this view "populism" (often little more than a label for radicalised politics of

---

1   Thanks to Richard Donnelly, Gareth Jenkins, Sheila McGregor and Camilla Royle for comments on earlier drafts.

the left or right that seeks mass support) has failed the test of the pandemic, and formerly restive populations now crave a return to mainstream politics.[2]

Adherents to this view could point to the US, where Donald Trump failed to win re-election. By early December, his opponent Joe Biden was constructing a cabinet centred on Obama-era neoliberals committed to defending US corporate interests at home and abroad. In Britain, Dominic Cummings, who has been identified as a key proponent of right-wing populism within the Boris Johnson administration, was driven from his positon in November, along with his ally, director of communications Lee Cain. Keir Starmer has not simply replaced the left-wing Jeremy Corbyn as Labour leader, but had by autumn made clear his intent to crush Corbynism.

Meanwhile in Germany Chancellor Angela Merkel saw support for her centre-right Christian Democratic Union rise from 30 percent at the start of the pandemic to 40 percent by June. Support for the radical right-wing AfD fell in the same period.[3] In France President Emmanuel Macron, if not exactly doing well, survived the Gilets Jaunes (Yellow Vests) protests and large-scale strikes that raged a year ago, and has seen his approval rating climb to 49 percent. By autumn he was seeking to bolster his support by significantly hardening official Islamophobia and imposing more draconian policing—though not without opposition on the streets.[4] In the Spanish state, after four inconclusive general elections, the radical left party Podemos agreed to lash itself to the centre-left Socialist Party (PSOE), entering a government coalition and alienating many of its supporters. Even chronically unstable Italy saw the radical right League replaced by the centre-left Democratic Party in the coalition led by the Five Star Movement and headed by the lawyer Giuseppe Conte. By April 2020, Conte had seen his approval rating rise to 71 percent.

Nevertheless, this apparent buttressing of the centre ground is superficial; it is unlikely to survive the deeper forces driving polarisation and crisis.

End in sight?

States facing outbreaks of pandemic disease are constrained by the capitalist logic of relentless profit-making and competitive accumulation. However, this does not mean that their responses are uniform or that there is a straightforward trade-off between lives and profits. In the absence of socialist solutions, the most effective responses have come where countries corralled their population, often in an authoritarian manner, into strict social distancing measures—then created

2 See Rachman, 2020; Watkins, 2020, p5, offers other examples.
3 *Strategic Survey*, 2020.
4 Mallet and Keohane, 2020; see Orr, 2020, for a discussion of recent events.

effective testing and contact-tracing regimes. Hence China is one of the few countries to experience something approximating a V-shaped recovery following the initial hit to its economy.[5]

For states unable or unwilling to pursue this course, the relationship between economic contraction and mortality rates depends on a multitude of factors—the country's size and geographical structure, its demographics, attitudes towards social distancing, how rapidly states responded to a rise in cases, and so on. Britain here represents a particularly dire example. The government did act in spring 2020, but only once a sharp increase in cases forced them to do so. The premature relaxation of the lockdown, followed by a confusing attempt to re-impose measures, the failure to implement effective testing and tracing systems, and reliance on outsourcing the public health response to private firms, meant an exceptionally high death toll and an especially bad economic collapse. The US, with its chaotic and uneven response to the pandemic, fared better economically; nevertheless, at the twilight of the Trump presidency, there were still high levels of infection and death, with evidence that jobs growth and the recovery were petering out.

To what extent might the development of new vaccines bring this horror show to an end?

Although the trials have been remarkably successful, there remains a gap between developing a vaccine and establishing sufficient immunity to quell the virus. One estimate, by management consultants McKinsey, suggests an "epidemiological end to the pandemic" in the US no earlier than autumn or winter 2021.[6] However, this relies on widespread uptake of the vaccine. A recent article in *The Lancet* estimates the level of immunity required, with a vaccine that is 80 percent effective, to be in the range of 75-90 percent of the population. This would include those who have acquired immunity after recovering from Covid-19 as well as those vaccinated, and many of the vaccines trialled appear to have an efficacy over 80 percent. Nonetheless, what the authors call "vaccine hesitancy" may yet prove an issue. In Britain, where 85 percent of people say they would be interested in taking a vaccine, reaching the threshold is plausible. However, that figure drops to 67 percent in Germany and the US, and just 59 percent in France.[7]

Moreover, the pandemic is a global affair. The firms planning to sell vaccines do not have the capacity to create enough for the world's population and are unlikely to waive their intellectual property rights to allow generic

5   Roberts, 2020.
6   Charumilind and others, 2020.
7   Anderson and others, 2020; World Economic Forum, 2020.

versions to be produced.[8] By September, rich countries with just 13 percent of the world's population had already cornered 51 percent of projected supplies.[9] Beyond their ranks, some countries, notably India, which has a huge domestic vaccine manufacturing infrastructure, will likely have access. However, many others, including the poorest and some middle-income countries, are likely to lose out in this upsurge of "vaccine nationalism".[10] Then there is the question of distribution. The vaccines being trialled require refrigeration, in some cases to -70C, and thus they would rely on cold-chain distribution systems that barely exist in many poorer countries and are inadequate in many others. The World Health Organisation estimates that broken cold-chain networks already lead to 1.5 million preventable deaths a year.[11] An additional question, still unresolved, is the degree to which immunity wanes over time, potentially necessitating repeated vaccinations.[12] These problems make it likely that the virus will remain endemic, resurfacing even in countries capable of vaccinating their populations.

The triple crisis

The pandemic is just one element in what I have described as a "triple crisis".[13] It cannot be understood in isolation from the broader ecological and economic disorder. Both of these reflect long-term tendencies, which now feed one another. Capitalism's long depressive phase does not simply generate repeated economic crises; it also pushes capital to make ever deeper incursions into fragile ecosystems in order to maximise profits. The ecological crisis in turn increasingly damages the capacity of capitalism to reproduce itself, for instance, through disruptive weather patterns, famines and wildfires.

The pandemic strikingly draws together these two long-term tendencies. Covid-19 emerged from animal populations into human society precisely through capital's penetration and commodification of nature. This then acted as a detonator for a new crisis phase within the long depression. We will see more such crises in the coming years. One warning sign was the outbreak of avian flu among poultry in late 2020, another viral hazard threatening to cross over into human populations and achieve pandemic take-off.[14]

---

8   This is despite the fact that these firms often received public money for their work. Moderna, for instance, received $2.48 billion.
9   Oxfam, 2020.
10 Bollyky and Bown, 2020.
11 Peters, 2020.
12 Anderson and others, 2020.
13 Choonara, 2020a.
14 For an introduction to the capitalist roots of pandemics, see Choonara, 2020b.

The relative weakness of capitalism in its current phase means, even if the pandemic recedes, the economic slump of 2020 will scar the system for years to come. Capitalism's long depression is ultimately rooted in an unresolved crisis of profitability that had emerged by the 1970s. As Marxist political economists have regularly pointed out, restoring profitability to high levels requires the destruction of unprofitable capital on a huge scale. However, each time this threatens to occur, it is met by interventions from states and their associated central banks that seek to avert the crisis. This, in turn, defers any resolution of the underlying problems—while also increasing capitalism's reliance on credit expansion and reinforcing its financial fragility.[15] The colossal state and central bank intervention of 2020 fits into this narrative—heralding another round of tepid growth that will eventually succumb to a new crisis. There will also be further pressure on workers. In Britain, for instance, we are seeing the first attempts to rein in government spending through a public sector pay freeze and projected cuts or tax rises of £27 billion by 2024.[16] This adds to the woe caused by mass job losses, particularly in retail.

The fragile centre

What does this mean for global politics? Across much of the Global South there is now an established pattern. Urbanisation and expansion of the working class tend to outpace the capacity of capitalism to deliver decent jobs, maintain infrastructure and improve living standards. To preserve their power and to enrich themselves further in conditions of growing inequality, ruling classes become increasingly repressive; cronyism and corruption become more glaring. The result, in 2019, was a series of explosions of popular anger.[17] By autumn 2020, after being briefly subdued by the pandemic, this pattern resumed, with outbursts in Belarus, Bolivia, Nigeria, Thailand and Guatemala.[18] Covid-19 was by now a factor driving revolt.

In the Global North, governments often won increased popularity when initial lockdowns and social distancing measures were introduced. Yet here too failure to control the virus has had a corrosive effect on this support. In Britain trust in the government's handling of the pandemic fell from 69 percent in April 2020 to 38 percent by late November. Only 13 percent of those polled took issue with the statement that the government's response was "confused and inconsistent".[19]

---

15   Choonara, 2018.
16   This is in line with the prediction in this journal, against the received wisdom of many on the left at the beginning of the pandemic crisis—see Choonara, 2020a, pp7-8.
17   Choonara 2020c.
18   See the articles by Baba Aye, Giles Ji Ungpakorn and Tomáš Tengely-Evans in this issue.
19   www.kcl.ac.uk/policy-institute/assets/the-handling-of-the-coronavirus-crisis.pdf

The degree of governmental failure and popular discontent does not correlate simplistically with the political stance of the government ("centre-ground" or "populist"). As Susan Watkins, editor of *New Left Review*, demonstrates, countries such as Peru (centre-right government), Spain (centre left-led coalition) and Belgium (a liberal-led coalition) have performed as badly as many with "populist" leaders.[20] The mishandling of Covid-19 contributed to Trump's downfall, but there is as yet no sign of the imminent departure of Brazil's Jair Bolsonaro or India's Narendra Modi.[21]

Even where "populists" do lose elections, the kind of neoliberal governance offered by figures such as Biden is unlikely to bring lasting stability.[22] The deep polarisation of politics reflects dissatisfaction towards the neoliberal consensus that developed under earlier generations of politicians, including such figures as Bill Clinton, George Bush, Tony Blair and David Cameron. Returning the political helm to their heirs, at a moment of far deeper crisis for the system, will not reverse this tendency. Rather, it will accelerate it. As Mike Davis argues about the US in the wake of the election:

> Trump's would-be successors—the current favourites include Tom Cotton, Josh Hawley, Nikki Haley and Ted Cruz—will be competing to feed red meat to the vengeful Trump faithful...the lynch-mob mood amongst Republicans will become even more dangerously anti-democratic and explosive.[23]

In the case of Britain, the problems are further compounded by Brexit. It remained unclear as we went to press whether a post-Brexit agreement would be reached with the European Union. Some of this reflects the Johnson government's incompetence. However, there are real political issues at play. These include tensions between the Thatcherite neoliberalism of sections of Johnson's party and a more "sovereigntist" impulse towards economic intervention, and between the desire to avoid the disruption feared by business and Johnson's embrace of his own nationalist rhetoric. On the EU side, there is intransigent opposition to Britain breaking free of the bloc's regulatory framework. There are also tensions between those such as Macron who hope the City of London's role as Europe's main financial hub will be supplanted, and those such as Merkel more concerned with market access for Germany's powerful manufacturing sector.[24]

---

20 Watkins, 2020.
21 Even in the US, as Mike Davis notes, in the absence of any alternative presented by the Democrats, many of Trump's 74 million voters accepted the "zero-sum choice" between jobs and health that he offered—Davis, 2020.
22 On prospects for Biden, see the piece by Iannis Delatolas and Clare Lemlich in this issue.
23 Davis, 2020.
24 Parker and Brunsden, 2020; Callinicos, 2020.

The radical left

The continued polarisation of politics poses two challenges for socialists. The first is to confront the radical right-wing forces that have entrenched themselves in the political landscape of most countries. The Black Lives Matter movement of 2020 demonstrates the potential that exists to beat back the right. The goal must be to use this dynamism to strengthen anti-racist and anti-fascist organisation that can disrupt the growth of far-right networks, along with the state racism feeding them, which is sharpening with the crisis. This is an essential lesson from the interview with Petros Constantinou in this issue of *International Socialism*, describing how the Greek fascist organisation Golden Dawn was broken.

No less challenging is finding a way to construct a socialist left capable of rising to the test of the current crisis. Repeated waves of radicalism in recent years have fed a resurgence of socialist politics. This was reflected in the rise of Syriza in Greece, Podemos in the Spanish state, Bernie Sanders and the Democratic Socialists of America in the US, along with Corbyn's capture of the Labour leadership in Britain. Each of these has been in essence a left reformist project, aiming at winning state power and wielding it to reform capitalism. Each has clashed with the nature of the capitalist state, the limits to the system's toleration of radical reforms, and the realities of electoralism.

Syriza won office only to confront a constellation of capitalist forces clustered around the EU, capitulating to the need to impose austerity before being defeated electorally. Podemos has gone from a party of indignant outsiders to a junior partner to PSOE, a party it once taught its followers to despise as part of the "caste" of career politicians. In the US, Sanders, along with allies such as Alexandria Ocasio-Cortez, find themselves prisoners of the Democratic Party machine, which has wasted little time in blaming them for the party's relatively poor electoral performance.[25]

Here in Britain, the left within the Labour Party has also come under attack since Corbyn's failure to win the 2019 general election. Starmer, having mounted only ineffectual opposition to the hapless Johnson, has been far more ferocious in dealing with Labour's former leader. Corbyn was suspended from membership of Labour for saying that the scale of antisemitism had been "dramatically overstated for political reasons by our opponents inside and outside the party" after the publication of the Equality and Human Rights Commission (EHRC) report into the party under his leadership. The report itself marks the latest phase in the weaponisation of the antisemitism accusation, serving both to undermine criticism of Israel and weaken the internationalist left, for which support for the

---

25   Kendi, 2020.

Palestinian cause is a touchstone.[26] Behind the scenes negotiations, and further concessions from Corbyn, secured his reinstatement to membership, only for Starmer to refuse to restore the Labour whip, forcing Corbyn to sit in parliament as an independent. In a Kafkaesque twist, Labour members were threatened with suspension if they expressed solidarity with, or even discussed, Corbyn at party meetings.[27]

The only way of extricating itself from the trap set by the EHRC report was for the left to mount a principled defence of its pro-Palestinian position, challenging the conflation of antisemitism with anti-Zionism. Unfortunately, the Labour left has not been able to develop such an approach, often placing a greater priority on party unity. This can take the form of capitulation, as with the journalist Paul Mason, who criticised Corbyn's response to the EHRC report and accused anyone daring to contemplate a break with Labour of plotting to form a "neo-Stalinist sect".[28] Others have pledged to stay and fight but with little idea of how such a fight can be won. Still others have begun drifting out of Labour, with an estimated 50,000 departing between April and November, even before Corbyn's suspension.

What these experiences imply is that prioritising the attainment of state power through the electoral system is, beyond a certain point, a barrier to the development of the left. Revolutionary socialists must insist that, whatever tactical use is made of elections, this work should be subordinated to struggles on the extra-parliamentary terrain. Any new party emerging from the calamity engulfing Corbynism would have to be based on that premise to avoid the pitfalls inherent in Labourism.[29] Moreover, the kinds of struggles required to renew the left are strengthened by the presence of a core of people who reject the idea that capitalism determines the outer limit of possible social transformation, and who ultimately wish to supplant the system altogether. Therefore, the growth and renewal of the revolutionary socialist tradition is essential to confronting the deepening crisis facing us.

---

26 Ferguson, 2020.

27 See Waugh, 2020.

28 Mason, 2020. Mason presumably knows a thing or two about sects, having spent his formative years in the Trotskyist groupuscule Workers' Power.

29 It is in this spirit that the Socialist Workers Party wrote an "open letter to socialists in the Labour Party" in November—https://swp.org.uk/an-open-letter-to-the-socialists-in-the-labour-party

References

Anderson, Roy, Carolin Vegvari, James Truscott and Benjamin Collyer, 2020, "Challenges in Creating Herd Immunity to SARS-CoV-2 Infection by Mass Vaccination", *Lancet*, volume 396, number 10263.

Bollyky, Thomas J, and Chad P Bown, 2020, "The Tragedy of Vaccine Nationalism", Foreign Affairs, volume 99, number 4.

Callinicos, Alex, 2020, "What Lies Behind the Divisions over Brexit?", *Socialist Worker* (7 December), www.socialistworker.co.uk/art/51030/What+lies+behind+the+divisions+over+Brexit

Charumilind, Sarun, Matt Craven, Jessica Lamb, Adam Sabow and Matt Wilson, 2020, "When Will the Covid-19 Pandemic End", McKinsey Insights (23 November), www.mckinsey.com/industries/healthcare-systems-and-services/our-insights/when-will-the-covid-19-pandemic-end

Choonara, Joseph, 2018, "The Political Economy of a Long Depression", *International Socialism 158* (spring), http://isj.org.uk/the-political-economy-of-a-long-depression

Choonara, Joseph, 2020a, "A Triple Crisis", *International Socialism 167* (summer), http://isj.org.uk/a-triple-crisis

Choonara, Joseph, 2020b, "Socialism in a Time of Pandemics", *International Socialism 166* (spring), http://isj.org.uk/socialism-in-a-time-of-pandemics

Choonara, Joseph, 2020c, "A New Cycle of Revolt", *International Socialism 165* (winter), http://isj.org.uk/a-new-cycle-of-revolt

Davis, Mike, 2020, "Trench Warfare", *New Left Review II/126* (November/December).

Ferguson, Rob, 2020, "Antisemitism and the Attack on the Left: What Do Socialists Say?", *Socialist Review*, issue 461 (October), https://socialistreview.org.uk/461/antisemitism-and-attack-left-what-do-socialists-say

Kendi, Ibram X, 2020, "Stop Scapegoating Progressives", *The Atlantic* (3 December), https://bit.ly/2K3alMi

Mallet, Victor, and David Keohane, 2020, "Emmanuel Macron Seeks Quick Escape from Security Law Fiasco", *Financial Times* (2 December).

Mason, Paul, 2020, "Labour's Mutually Destructive Civil War Should End Now", *New Statesman* (2 December).

Orr, Judith, 2020, "France, Islamophobia and the Right: An Update", *International Socialism* (26 November), http://isj.org.uk/france-islamophobia-update

Oxfam, 2020, "Small Group of Rich Nations Have Bought up More than Half the Future Supply of Leading COVID-19 Vaccine Contenders" (17 September), https://bit.ly/2Iykz7a

Parker, George, and Jim Brunsden, 2020, "'Insurgent' Boris Johnson Faces Moment of Truth on Brexit", *Financial Times* (6 December).

Peters, Toby, 2020, "How Can We Ensure Billions of People in the Global South Can Access a COVID-19 Vaccine?", Quest, https://bit.ly/2VSVkzj

Rachman, Gideon, 2020, "Coronavirus Can Kill Off Populism", *Financial Times* (29 June).

Roberts, Michael, 2020, "Covid and the Trade Off", Michael Roberts Blog (22 October), https://thenextrecession.wordpress.com/2020/10/22/covid-and-the-trade-off

Strategic Survey, 2020, "Europe", volume 120, number 1.

Watkins, Susan, 2020, "Politics and Pandemics", New Left Review II/125 (September/October), https://newleftreview.org/issues/ii125/articles/susan-watkins-politics-and-pandemics

Waugh, Paul, 2020, "Labour Bans Local Party Activists from Discussing Jeremy Corbyn's Reinstatement", HuffPost (26 November), www.huffingtonpost.co.uk/entry/labour-bans-corbyn-reinstatement-motions_uk_5fc00286c5b68ca87f82a356

World Economic Forum, 2020, "Three in Four Adults Globally Say They'd Get a Vaccine for Covid-19—But Is This Enough?" (31 October), https://bit.ly/3mZdMSL

New from Bookmarks • £3

Does Privilege Explain Racism?

Contemporary debates in anti-racism

Is racism explained by "white privilege"? Is oppression ultimately a systemic problem or one that emanates from "biased" individuals? How is racism linked to wider questions of inequality and power in society?

The new wave of Black Lives Matter protests in Britain and across the world have posed these questions and many others sharply.

On the streets and online, millions of people are grappling with how to turn the burning desire for change into concrete demands, and how to finally win freedom.

In this new collection of essays, **Esme Choonara**, **Yuri Prasad**, **Ken Olende** and **Weyman Bennett** critically examine the ideas of "privilege", "unconscious bias", "identity" and "intersectionality" and offer a socialist strategy for building a movement capable of confronting and defeating racism.

ISBN: 978-1-9129-2622-0
Published by Bookmarks Publications
c/o 1 Bloomsbury Street, London WC1B 3QE
020 7637 1848
www.bookmarksbookshop.co.uk
publications@bookmarksbookshop.co.uk

The end of a nightmare: where next after the US elections?
Iannis Delatolas and Clare Lemlich

Much of the United States breathed a collective sigh of relief on Saturday 7 November as Donald Trump's electoral defeat became clear. People posted reactions on social media immediately after the results were announced. In New York City, as in other Democrat-voting areas, people took to their balconies and windows as waves of celebration erupted across all the boroughs. People cheered and banged pots above the streets, while the cars below rhythmically honked to pedestrians who held their fists in the air. People danced in Times Square, celebrating the end of a nightmare. Some commented that it felt like we were living through the fall of a dictator.

The end of Trump's tenure in the White House is a blow to racists and the far right in the US and beyond. He is only the fifth president in the past century to fail to secure a second term. This article will argue that the outgoing president's defeat is a result of his catastrophic four years in office and the movements that fought relentlessly against Trumpism during this time. It will suggest that the future for the radical left lies in engaging with and developing such struggles. They hold the hope of posing an alternative to both the radical right, which is far from contained in the US, and the neoliberal centre-ground represented by the president-elect, Joe Biden.

The "Blue Wave" that never crested

Trump lost in large part because of his disastrous handling of the pandemic. A Pew Research Center study found that Biden voters tended to rate healthcare and the pandemic as their highest concerns; on the other hand, Trump voters overwhelmingly prioritised the economy, with less than a third rating the pandemic as "very important".[1] Counterposing the economy to saving lives may have worked for Trump among some voters, especially in rural areas and small towns, but was less effective among people living in urban centres that have witnessed the devastation caused by Covid-19. Trump also suffered in these areas because of the radicalisation produced by the struggles of the past four years, most importantly the 2020 Black Lives Matter rebellion.

Although Joe Biden, vice-presidential candidate Kamala Harris and the Democratic Party won the election, little credit for Trump's loss should go to them. His defeat was the result of poor people, working-class people and people of colour coming out to vote against him in numbers not seen for over a century.[2] This was astonishing, given how uninspiring Biden's campaign was. The Democrats should have beaten Trump by a landslide, and yet for several days after the vote the results were still neck and neck. A record 81 million people voted for Biden in spite of his lacklustre campaign, but turnout for Trump was also alarmingly high. Trump spent his term riling up his racist and right-wing base and was able to secure 74 million votes, the second highest number ever won by a presidential candidate after Biden and the highest number ever won by a losing candidate.[3] Beyond the presidential race, the Democrats underperformed in the House of Representatives, Senate and state elections held the same day. Despite nearly doubling their campaign spending compared with 2016, the Democrats actually lost seats in the House, although they still control it.[4] They did not flip a single state legislature and, unless the Democrats win two Senate run-off races in the state of Georgia in Janaury 2021, Republicans will retain control of the Senate.[5]

Trump's racism and authoritarianism, as well as his threat not to accept the election result if he lost, all contributed to the large turnout for Biden. However, unlike socialist senator Bernie Sanders's vibrant but ultimately unsuccessful campaigns to secure the Democratic Party nomination in 2016 and 2020, Biden failed to inspire people with bold, progressive policy proposals. When Trump and his media loyalists' attacked the Democrats as "socialists", this reinforced the rightward

---

1   Dunn, 2020.
2   Lauter and Hook, 2020.
3   Bryant, 2020; Riccardi, 2020.
4   Schwartz, 2020.
5   Nilson, 2020.

turn of the Democratic Party even further. The Democrat leadership bent over backwards to distance itself from any progressive agenda. The Biden-Harris ticket and the wider Democartic Party machine refused to tack left; instead, they invited Republicans to speak at their national convention in August, parading their willingness to "reach across the aisle". The party establishment's strategy was to appeal to the centre-ground and capture the votes of dissatisfied Republicans, rather than pursuing the millions who supported Sanders, a Green New Deal and universal healthcare. These and other such policies were considered too much of a liability in battleground states.

The right wing of the Democrats has wasted no time in blaming the left for their electoral failures, particularly at the state and local level.[6] However, in reality Democrats who campaigned on left-wing policies were often successful. The Medicare for All proposal, which would replace the country's catastrophic for-profit healthcare system with universal coverage funded by taxes rather than bloated insurance premiums, is in fact extremely popular. Every Democrat who ran on a platform for Medicare for All in the election retained their seat.[7] Some 72 percent of voters support socialising the US healthcare system. As left-wing journalist Luke Savage put it, "If you actively campaign against majority opinion on healthcare during a pandemic, don't be surprised that voters don't like it!"[8]

The election in Florida was another case in point. Trump won the state decisively, but Floridians also voted in a referendum held on the same day to increase the minimum wage to $15. The legislation was more popular than either presidential candidate and its passage marks the first move by a Southern state towards a $15 minimum wage. Biden quietly endorsed the measure, but the activists who fought and won the referendum argue that their bold, loud and left-wing campaign was the key to success. Richie Floyd, a member of the Democratic Socialists of America (DSA), the country's largest socialist organisation, in Florida's Pinellas County explains:

> The presidential election was largely about defeating Trump and not what Joe Biden would do for working people... This strategy completely failed as we can see from the results out of Miami-Dade [an area of Florida where Biden lost votes compared with Hilary Clinton's ill-fated 2016 campaign]... If the Florida and national Democratic Parties want to be successful here, then they need to realise that focusing on the economic plight of the multi-racial working class is the only

---

6   Broadwater and Fandos, 2020; Dixon and Fineout, 2020.
7   Marcertic, 2020. The author notes that "the only exceptions were lawmakers who retired, died, gave up their seats or were unseated in primaries."
8   Stancil, 2020.

way forward… To win, we have to focus on the needs of the working class, and not the donor class.[9]

The Black Lives Matter rebellion mobilised up to 26 million people in the US this summer, but building on this was not seen as an electoral priority either.[10] Biden did install Harris as his running mate, a progressive Democrat from California who is both a woman and a person of colour. Yet in truth this was an attempt to have it both ways: appealing to the right in policy terms, but simultaenously attempting to co-opt the anti-racist movement into the Democratic Party. Harris is the first woman, black and South Asian person to hold the position of vice president—not insignificant in a US context. However, the Democratic Party is less concerned with representation and more with taming Black Lives Matter. Harris said openly that she opposes defunding the police, a key radical demand emerging from the Black Lives Matter protests. This was entirely consistent with her record as a district attorney in San Francisco, where she built a career by increasing the felony conviction rate from 52 percent in 2003 to 67 percent in 2006. Convictions for drug-related offences increased from 56 percent to 74 percent over the same period. As California's attorney general, Harris continued a similar "tough-on-crime" trajectory. She opposed, for instance, a federal inquiry into California prisons that were so overcrowded that even the Supreme Court believed they inflicted cruel and unusual punishment.

The election results were thus, as Marxist economist Michael Roberts has suggested, the product of a decisive rejection of Trump that was based overwhelmingly on those in urban centres and city suburbs—especially women, the young, the poor and people of colour. These groups voted for Biden in large numbers, knowing all too well what a second Trump term would mean for them. There has been some consternation about Trump's increased support among black and Latinx voters this election, but as Roberts argues:

> The evidence for this is dubious and, even if true, the shift is tiny. According to the Edison exit poll, there was a fall-off in support among white men for Trump compared to 2012 from 62 percent to 57 percent, and a small rise among white women from 52 percent to 54 percent. The supposed rise in support for Trump among black men was 13 percent to 17 percent and among black women was from 4 percent to 8 percent. But considering that white voters were 75 percent of the vote and black voters were only 11 percent, the supposed shift to Trump from

---

9   Schueler, 2020.
10   Buchanan, Bui and Patel, 2020.

black voters is less than half the loss by Trump from white voters. More Hispanic voters backed Trump this time, it is claimed, but still around two-thirds did not.[11]

Nevertheless, this shift does warrant analysis. Even after four years of Trump's barrage of racism and attacks on immigrant communities, Biden still did slightly worse than Hilary Clinton among voters of colour across the board.[12] This reflects the Democrats' failed strategy more than support for Trump as such. It is true that in Florida right-wing Cubans and Venezuelans, whose families fled redistribution of land and wealth, helped hand Trump victory in the state. However the story is more complex in Texas, for instance, where Biden won the Latinx vote in urban centres, but not in southern communities on the US-Mexico border. Here, unlike in Florida, migration patterns do not offer obvious answers; it seems, rather, that socially conservative Mexican Americans, who traditionally vote Democrat, were decisive in Texas. For instance, in Hidalgo county, resident Barbara Ocañas told an interviewer that she ended up voting Trump because she felt that Democrats focussed too much on semantics, character and moral outrage toward the president, rather than actual policy.[13] Zapata county, a 93 percent Latinx border community in South Texas, had been solidly Democrat for over a century until Biden lost it in 2020; Trump voter Joe Gutierrez chalks this to the Democrats' neglect of an electorate they took for granted.[14] Similarly, Jessica Cisneros, a former Democrat primary candidate in South Texas, commented:

> In this area, people have been voting Democrat for so long that if they feel neglected, they might be interested in what other candidates have to offer... I think people wonder, "Well, maybe I should just try and vote for the Republican Party since I've been voting Democrat for so long and nothing changes."[15]

The racist claims Trump has made about them is not the only political issue for these voters. Unemployment and poverty matter to them too, and Biden failed to speak to their needs.[16] The Democrats ignored their traditional base

---

11 Roberts, 2020. Exit polls also probably exaggerate any swing towards Trump among particular groups because they do not include postal votes.

12 Wolf, Merril and Wolfe, 2020.

13 Villarreal, 2020.

14 Burnett, 2020.

15 Cardena, 2020. Indeed, the neglect that Latinx Texans describe from the Democrats was also a factor in Florida, where Biden campaign staffers warned that their Latinx outreach was lacking. As a result, it was not just ideologically committed communities of Cuban and Venezuelan emigres that voted for Trump there, but also networks of socially conservative Puerto Ricans—see Padró Ocasio and Wieder, 2020.

16 Cardena, 2020.

among communities of colour and took their votes for granted, believing that these voters have no political alternative.

Alongside these demographic trends in Southern states such as Florida and Texas, the electoral experience in the "rust belt" of the Midwestern states is also telling. In 2016 Hilary Clinton lost much of the working-class vote that Barack Obama had secured there for his 2008 victory. Clinton's career and campaign as a representative of the status quo contributed to voters abstaining or even voting for Trump. The fact that Biden's results in the rust belt were only slightly better than Clinton's underscores the conservative choice the Democratic Party made by picking Biden.

What to expect from Biden and Harris

When Biden and Harris take office in January 2021 they will be unable to offer solutions to the pressing issues such as climate change, institutional racism and the lack of access to healthcare faced by millions. Instead we will see increased collaboration with the Republicans around a neoliberal, pro-capitalist agenda. Biden's cabinet is expected to include a range of establishment figures, many of whom have strong links to US corporations, and even some Republican politicans.

According to Moody's Analytics, the policies Biden ran on included over $7 trillion in additional government spending over the next ten years, which outstrip Barack Obama and Bill Clinton's plans when they entered office.[17] He also promised to repeal some of Trump's worst tax breaks for the rich. In the context of the pandemic and economic crisis, this kind of Keynesian package would bring the US closer to what the International Monetary Fund currently advocates and to the practice of many European governments. However, it remains to be seen how much of even this package can be implemented by Biden; a Republican-controlled Senate will give him an easy excuse to avoid pushing progressive legislation and making cabinet appointments from the left of the Democrats.[18] Already Biden has shown his willingness to reach across the aisle, inviting Mitt Romney to head the Department of Health and Human Services. One of Trump's parting gifts was to nominate right-wing zealot Amy Coney Barrett to the Supreme Court, and Biden has made clear that he is against packing the court with more liberal judges to counter this. With abortion and the Affordable Care Act (commonly known as "Obamacare") on the chopping block, a Supreme Court dominated by the right could be

---

17   Zandi and Yaros, 2020.
18   Luce, 2020.

another obstacle for Biden—and a useful excuse for dissatisfaction with his administration.

A return to Obama-era neoliberalism may satisfy the Democratic Party establishment and big US corporations, whose leaders overwhelmingly backed Biden, but it will mean a continuation of misery for millions of people. This is reinforced by the deeply damaged US economy that Biden and Harris will inherit. The US has never fully recovered from the 2008 crash, and wealth inequality has increased to even more dizzying levels during the Covid-19 pandemic.[19] These problems are reflected in the world economy, which experienced a weak recovery after 2008, even before being hammered by the pandemic. As Joseph Choonara wrote in 2018:

> No region of the world is experiencing consistent growth at the rate enjoyed prior to 2008—even the more successful large economies of the Global South, some of which saw rapid growth prior to the crisis, have had to lower their expectations. For the established economies of the Global North, average growth rates of over 3 percent, as experienced in the 1960-80 period, now seem like a receding dream. Estimates of growth in 2016 put the US figure at 1.6 percent, the euro area at 1.8 percent and Japan at 1.1 percent.[20]

This has led in turn to low levels of investment, including in the US. A Green New Deal would have offered some meaningful reform, moving the US toward the creation of green jobs and a more sustainable economy. However, Biden has already ruled out the version of this policy long advocated by prominent left-wing Democrats such as Alexandria Ocasio-Cortez (known as AOC). At best, we can expect the US to return to the Paris climate agreement, which the ecological movement has long criticised as inadequate to addressing the urgent threat of catastrophic global warming.

The situation for foreign policy is volatile and hard to predict. Nevertheless, Biden's career to date suggests a return to a more traditional model of US imperialism, with the US reasserting itself in relation to Russia and, in particular, China. However, the isolationism of the Trump administration and the trade war with China mean that Biden will find the US increasingly isolated in Asia. One of Trump's first moves in office was to withdraw the US from the Trans-Pacific Partnership, a huge trade deal developed under the Obama administration in order to isolate China. In the absence of this, China has just announced the creation of the largest free trade area in the world, the Regional Comprehensive Economic Partnership. This pulls together 14 countries in the Asia-Pacific region including long-term US allies such as Japan, South Korea and

---

19 Fretz, 2020.
20 Choonara, 2018.

Australia.[21] Restoring US hegemony in the region will not be straightforward.[22] In the Middle East a similar picture emerges. The US has lost ground to Iran and Russia in Syria. Meanwhile, much of Afghanistan is back under Taliban control. Amid this instability it is worth noting that Biden voted for the disastrous 2003 US invasion of Iraq and that he has surrounded himself with advocates of US interventionism since the election.[23]

The limitations of the Democratic Party left

In the wake of the election, the party establishment sought to blame the Black Lives Matter movement, the Green New Deal and the left for its failures. This was all too predictable; the Democratic Party has consistently seen moving to the right as the best method for winning elections. Its long-term strategy has been to appeal to Republican voters and conservatives, while taking for granted the support of the left, progressives and oppressed groups. AOC, the de facto leader of the left inside the party, was interviewed by the *New York Times* and pointed out the obvious foolishness of this approach. If the Democratic Party only barely won this was precisely a consequence of its right-wing campaign and because it alienated young voters who had embraced the calls for a Green New Deal and Medicare for All. She also noted that left-wing activists mobilised millions of voters in decisive states such as Michigan, Georgia and Pennsylvania. These places were the key to getting Biden elected, and yet the Democratic Party will have few compunctions about selling out these same organisers once he takes office.[24]

AOC is right to criticise Biden's strategy but her solutions are less convincing. She argues that Democrats need to fund more campaigns like the one that took place in Georgia and engage in outreach among particular demographics. The problem with the AOC approach is that there are structural limitations that result from the left working inside the Democratic Party. Rather than using elections as a tactic to develop class struggle and strengthen social movements, elections become an end unto themselves, dragging left-wing activists into the party machine. Much has been written on this subject already, and it continues to be a live discussion across the left—particularly within the DSA, which has now grown into an organisation of over 80,000 members. As one of us argued in an earlier issue of *International Socialism*, the Democratic Party does not function like the British Labour Party and social democratic parties elsewhere.

---

21 Salmon, 2020.
22 Callinicos, 2018.
23 Callinicos, 2020a.
24 Herndon, 2020.

These parties have all kinds of limitations of their own, but they are at least membership-based, organically connected to trade unions and have contested political leaderships. This is not so with the Democrats:

> The Democratic Party is not a membership organisation; a person becomes a Democrat by registering as one in time to cast a ballot during a primary election. There is a party platform, but no accountability mechanisms or requirements for people who run as Democrats to campaign on or pursue policies consistent with that platform. There is also no elected or accountable party leadership other than the presidential candidate themselves and some congressional officials.[25]

For this reason, much of the US revolutionary left argues for a break from the Democratic Party and the formation of a new working-class party. However, the strategy that AOC and many in the DSA argue for is to elect more progressive Democrats at the state and local level—again reinforcing an electoral logic.

The challenges of operating in the context of the US electoral system are immense. In some places there is earnest discussion about how to break from the Democrats and form a new working-class party. Yet we must remember that social democratic parties in Europe were the result of broader processes of class struggle; they were not the fruit of a handful of far-left groups coming together and declaring a new party. A better strategy for the revolutionary left today lies in looking to the movements from below, rather than a singular focus on electoral politics. Even in the darkest days of Trumpism, people in the US have fought back. Struggle offers a way forward for building up independent working class activity and creating the context in which a political party with a revolutionary anti-capitalist perspective can develop. The remainder of this article will consider this perspective.

Crisis and polarisation

The Trump era has been one of polarisation, crisis and, above all, mass resistance. To mention only Trumpism and the growth of the far right would be to offer a mistaken and pessimistic assessment of the past four years. Trump faced protests from the moment he took office. A 2018 poll by the *Washington Post* and the Kaiser Family Foundation found that one in five people had been involved in political protests during the Trump administration. This is all the more astonishing because the poll was conducted before the marches against gun violence after the Stoneman Douglas High School mass shooting in Florida in 2018 and the Black Lives Matter rebellion in 2020.[26]

---

25 Lemlich, 2020. For a more detailed history of the Democrats, see Selfa, 2012.
26 Stewart, 2018.

Resistance to Trump was almost immediate. The 2017 women's marches that followed his inauguration were the largest mobilisation in the country since the movement against the Vietnam War. Millions marched across the country in defiance of Trump, who had won despite soundbites circulating of him gloating about his long history of sexual violence.[27] Next came a wave of teachers' strikes, which won increases to salaries, school budgets, healthcare coverage and support staff, as well as striking a blow against privatisation. The rebellion began in West Virginia in February 2018, quickly spreading to other Republican-controlled states and finally extending to California in early 2019.[28] Other workers in the school system took inspiration, with a strike among school bus drivers in Georgia, for instance, and smaller protests were held by school staff in Kentucky, North Carolina and Colorado, often supported by the teachers themselves. Victories for this heavily feminised workforce—in many places composed mostly of women of colour—in states regarded as "Trump country" set the tone for later eruptions.

These movements suggest encouraging starting points for potential struggles under Biden. However, struggle will not emerge automatically. The choices that the left makes in the coming months and years about what it prioritises, who it is willing to criticise and what kind of power it builds will be decisive.

Racism, fascism, and resistance

Under Trump's reign we have seen far-right and fascist groups emboldened by the racism coming from the top of society and the support Trump has repeatedly offered them. These groups have come a long way from the relatively disorganised mass of racists who participated in the anti-Obama "birther" movement and echoed Trump's "Build the Wall" slogan during the 2016 election.[29] Now we are beginning to see a large and organised fascist presence in the country for the first time in a long time. This may prove to be Trump's most enduring legacy.[30]

Trump's strategists, Steve Bannon and Stephen Miller, both of whom have links to white supremacist groups, worked from within the White House early in his administration to implement Executive Order 13769, the "Muslim ban". It blocked entry into the US for all refugees for 120 days, and Syrian refugees were blocked indefinitely. Also barred were citizens and green card holders

27   Trump now stands accused of 26 incidents of unwanted sexual contact and 43 instances of inappropriate behaviour—Mindock, 2020.

28   Blanc, 2020.

29   Birthers advocate the conspiracy theory that Obama was born outside the US and therefore was ineligible to be president. Such theories were often tinged with Islamophobia, with claims that Obama is secretly a Muslim and has a political relationship to Islamism.

30   Wilson, 2020.

from Iran, Iraq, Libya, Sudan and Yemen. Within hours of the ban's announcement, thousands of people across the country had rushed to airports to stage anti-racist pickets and demonstrations. Coming days after the gigantic women's marches, this was the first confrontation between the anti-racist movement and the Trump administration. At John F Kennedy International Airport in New York 7,000 people protested, holding signs with slogans such as "No Ban, No Wall" and "Let Them In". Protests spread to airports in Chicago, Los Angeles, San Francisco, Seattle, Indianapolis, Boston, Denver, Albuquerque, Hartford, Las Vegas, Orlando, Greenville and Philadelphia. Although some of those detained under the executive order were deported, many were freed under pressure from the movement. In some instances, riot police had to be called in to airports to disperse demonstrators.

Later came Trump's "zero tolerance" immigration policy, which ripped apart families by separating children and infants from their parents. Children were placed under the authority of the Department of Health and Human Services, while parents were detained in federal prisons or deported. According to the Southern Poverty Law Center, 4,368 children were separated from their families, and more than 500 are yet to be reunited. However, although this was one of the most hated anti-immigrant policies of the Trump era, it must be remembered that practices such as sealing the borders near San Diego, California, and El Paso, Texas, took effect under Bill Clinton's Democrat administration. Its aim was to force refugees and migrants to take the dangerous journey through the desert, where death was more likely due to heat and dehydration. Later Obama deported three million immigrants, and he is still referred to in the immigrant rights movement as the "deporter-in-chief". Trump may have separated the families, but Obama and Biden built the cages. The novel feature of Trump's immigration regime was not the policies themselves, but rather how aggressively Trump implemented his version of them and how blatantly he mobilised the racism of his political base to cultivate support for them. Open support for racist groups was one of the many taboos that he broke and was part of a deliberate attempt to solidify his radicalised right-wing base into a more coherent political bloc.

During Trump's presidency, our organisation, Marx21, argued that Trump was not a fascist and that full-blown fascism had not descended on the US.[31] Instead, the immediate threat was, and remains, Trump's use of racism to solidify his far-right base and his open support for fascists and far-right organisations such as the Proud Boys. At the debate with Biden, not only did he refuse to denounce fascists but he openly appealed to them to "stand down and stand by".

---

31   Marx21 is the affiliate of the International Socialist Tendency in the US and a sister
     organisation of the Socialist Workers Party in Britain.

There remains an urgent need for a united front, mobilising all those working-class forces threatened by fascism, to prevent fascist organisations from further expanding their activities and support. No matter what happens between now and January, when Biden is set to be inaugurated, anti-racism and anti-fascism have never been more urgent.

Here too it is important to recognise the resistance that took place under Trump and offers hope for the future. As early as August 2017, white suprema-cists and neo-Nazis gathered in Charlottesville, Virginia at a "Unite the Right" demonstration. Pictures emerged of torch-bearing crowds marching through the night, chanting the slogans "Jews Will not Replace Us" and "Blood and Soil", invoking imagery straight out of Nazi Germany. Over the course of two days clashes erupted with anti-fascist demonstrators and a white supremacist drove his car into counter-protesters, killing trade unionist Heather Heyer and seri-ously injuring others. Trump's subsequent claim that there were "good people" on both sides was not a slip but a calculated political response orchestrated by Bannon.[32] Yet it fed outrage and further anti-fascist demonstrations erupted across the country.[33] The protest in Boston, Massachusetts was a watershed moment, with 25,000 demonstrators completely surrounding a small number of fascists who were trying to hold a rally.[34] These protests helped pave the way for a series of later struggles, culminating with the Black Lives Matter rebellion.

The immediate post-election period has shown that the threat of the far-right remains. On 14 November, thousands of Trump supporters descended on Washington DC, running amok and stabbing three people. There is a large political space for the far right in the US today, framed by the QAnon conspiracy movement and far-right media personalities such as Alex Jones, and populated by Trump supporters mobilised under the slogan "Make America Great Again". This is the space that fascist groups—the Proud Boys, the Oath Keepers, American Guard and others—are seeking to exploit in order to grow and organise.

Class struggle under Covid-19

Another crisis that will not resolve as soon as Trump leaves the White House is, of course, the pandemic. Trump continually dismissed the threat of Covid-19, labelling it a hoax or referring to it as the "China virus". New York was the first US city to be hit hard by the novel coronavirus. Mayor Bill de Blasio and Governor Andrew Cuomo, both Democrats, were engaged in a political pissing contest at the start of the crisis, bickering about who would decide when schools

---

32 Kirk, 2020.
33 Ruder, 2017.
34 Roche, 2017.

would close and if there would even be a lockdown at all. They put profit before lives by prioritising the smooth functioning of the economy, and this criminal lack of action contributed to thousands of deaths. Ultimately, it fell to teaching unions to force the closure of schools in New York.[35]

A series of strikes and other actions by workers began in March 2020, and this has lead to struggles that are still ongoing at the time of writing. Nurses protested the lack of personal protective equipment. Then, as cases of Covid-19 were reported in Amazon logistical hubs (known as "fulfillment centers"), workers staged wildcat strikes along with protests at Amazon warehouses in New York. Waves of workers took similar actions, often on a small scale but still hugely significant. On 19-20 March, for instance, auto workers in Fraser, Michigan, refused to go to work and forced the plant to close after learning of an infection in their workplace. These are encouraging signs, even though this kind of activity is yet to be generalised across workplaces and industries.[36]

Due to Trump's criminal neglect, Democrat governors such as Cuomo continue to be seen as heroes. Yet during the initial peak of the pandemic in New York, it was found that the state was lacking an additional 20,000 hospital beds that would have been needed to deal with the sick—roughly the number of beds slashed over the past 20 years by Democrat state governments. Cuomo is responsible for much of this, and, incredibly, he continued to implement Medicaid cuts at the height of the pandemic.[37] No doubt Biden's pandemic response will be better than Trump's non-response, but the fight to protect lives rather than the economy—along with the broader underlying crisis driven by our for-profit medical system—will continue in 2021.

Black Lives Matter

An assessment of the resistance that developed under Trump would not be complete without looking at the vast social movement that developed under the banner of Black Lives Matter. On 25 May, the brutal murder of George Floyd by cop Derek Chauvin in Minneapolis, Minnesota, was captured in its entirety on video by horrified bystanders. Protests rapidly developed in Minneapolis, leading to clashes between hundreds of protesters and the police. Police cars were attacked and three days later a police station near the site where Floyd was murdered was set on fire. Demonstrations then spread across the country, with clashes in Portland, Los Angeles, Phoenix, Albuquerque, Denver, Columbus and New York.

---

35 Hummel, 2020.
36 Marx21 US, 2020.
37 Ferré-Sadurní and McKinley, 2020.

Workers responded to the brutal murder of George Floyd by joining the rebellion. Hundreds of postal workers in Minneapolis marched with a banner that read: "Postal Workers Demand Justice for George Floyd".[38] In New York bus drivers refused to collaborate with the police in the transfer of arrested protestors to the police precincts. Nurses in New York joined the anti-racist rebellion, with one placard stating: "We Fought Covid, Now we Will Fight the Police". In the wake of this movement from below, the SEIU service workers union, followed by others, responded to a call for action in support of Black Lives Matter. This was a tremendous step in the right direction, in spite of the limitations of a union bureaucracy that is often enmeshed in Democratic Party's electoralism.

Trump sought to split the movement by attacking Antifa, a loose network of anti-fascist organisations, but this was actually an attack on the entire anti-racist rebellion. Dismissing local authorities as soft in dealing with the uprising, he threatened to call in the military and the National Guard. This met with immediate resistance from the rank and file of these bodies as troops and guardsmen expressed their unwillingness to go and fight against protestors. Trump was also denounced by some generals. The attack on Antifa signaled an increasingly open ideological attack on the left from Trump, uncomfortably reminiscent of fascistic rhetoric of the past. At one conference in the wake of Black Lives Matter he argued, "Left-wing mobs have torn down statues of our founders, desecrated our memorials, and carried out a campaign of violence and anarchy... Far-left demonstrators have chanted the words, 'America Was Never Great.'" He linked this to the penetration of left-wing ideas into the US education system, singling out the late Marxist historian Howard Zinn and left-wing academic currents such as Critical Race Theory:

> Students in our universities are inundated with critical race theory. This is a Marxist doctrine holding that America is a wicked and racist nation, that even young children are complicit in oppression, and that our entire society must be radically transformed.[39]

In line with his threats, Trump deployed federal agents in Portland, Oregon, but ultimately he was forced to withdraw them in the face of mass opposition.[40] Parents came onto the streets to defend their children against thuggish attacks by federal forces, and the Proud Boys failed to gain any ground in the city. Many reluctant (and even some enthusiastic) Biden voters were part of this rebellion. There can be no place in such a movement for exclusion of activists based on whether or not

---

38 Cumming, 2020.
39 Callinicos, 2020b.
40 Cumming and Bacon, 2020.

they cast their ballot for the Democrats—the broadest possible unity is needed in the streets. However, this needs to be combined with a clear argument that neither Biden nor the Democratic Party can provide a solution to the social and political crisis in the US; instead, they are part of the problem. An attempt to restore the neoliberal centre-ground politics represented by the Clintons and Obama will simply lead to further polarisation and deepening discontent. The goal of socialists in this context cannot be to shore up the centre-ground. Instead, it has to combine forging unity in pursuit of its immediate goals, such as beating back the insurgent far-right, with a longer-term goal of winning broader forces to an anti-capitalist politics focused on working-class struggle.[41]

Conclusions

This article has emphasised the limits to Biden's campaign but also the enormous potential created by recent struggles in the US amid the horror of Trump's presidency. It is through an orientation on these struggles that the socialist left can best prepare to confront the incoming Biden administration and counter the far-right and fascist forces that have entrenched themselves in US politics during the Trump years.

However, in the context of these ongoing struggles, it is also necessary to offer an anti-capitalist politics that seeks a more fundamental transformation of society. This cannot be focused on the existing electoral terrain, accepting that the outer limits of radical politics should be the less repugnant of two pro-capitalist parties. Social movements should not be corralled into the task of bolstering the left in the Democratic Party, dissipating their vitality in the process. The two Sanders campaigns, the growth of the DSA and the rise of figures such as AOC have demonstrated the resonance of socialist ideas in the US, but they have not yet offered a clear means of escaping the gravitational pull of the Democrats. If a break with two-party politics is to happen, it will not come through clever organisational manoeuvres or a rearrangement of the existing radical left, but rather through mass struggle that draws millions of workers into activity and into contact with socialist ideas. That is why the socialist left must place itself at the heart of those struggles.

---

41 Despite its modest numbers, Marx21 is seeking to do this—combining activity within the various struggles with an attempt to rebuild a socialist and anti-capitalist current in the US. Members are active in United Against Racism and Fascism (UARF) in New York City, where, for instance, the recent attempt of the Proud Boys to drive a car convoy to Trump Tower in Manhattan was derailed by anti-fascists. Members in California are involved in the movement for immigrant rights. In Portland, members were part of the protests against the Proud Boys and organise among unemployed workers.

References

Blanc, Eric, 2020, "The Teachers' "Red for Ed" Movement Is Far From Dead" (13 October), *Jacobin*, https://jacobinmag.com/2020/10/red-for-ed-movement-teachers-unions-covid-19

Broadwater, Luke, and Nicholas Fandos, 2020 "Amid Tears and Anger, House Democrats Promise 'Deep Dive' on Election Losses" (5 November), *New York Times*, www.nytimes.com/2020/11/05/us/house-democrats-election-losses.html

Bryant, Nick, 2020, "US election 2020: Why Donald Trump lost", BBC News (7 November), www.bbc.com/news/election-us-2020-54788636

Buchanan, Larry, Quoctrung Bui, and Jugal K Patel, 2020 "Black Lives Matter May Be the Largest Movement in U.S. History" (3 July), *New York Times*, https://nyti.ms/36jAZto

Burnett, John, 2020, "How Texas' Longtime Democratic And Heavily Latino County Flipped Red", National Public Radio (5 November), www.npr.org/2020/11/05/931836590/how-texas-longtime-democratic-and-heavily-latino-county-flipped-red

Callinicos, Alex, 2018, "US is Trying to Slow Down China's Rise", *Socialist Worker* (13 November), https://socialistworker.co.uk/art/47479/US+is+trying+to+slow+down+Chinas+rise

Callinicos, Alex, 2020a, "Biden Heralds Return to US 'Forever Wars'" (23 November), *Socialist Worker*, https://socialistworker.co.uk/art/50951/Biden+heralds+return+to+US+forever+wars

Callinicos, Alex, 2020b, "Trump is Escalating an Ideological War", *Socialist Worker* (22 September), https://socialistworker.co.uk/art/50670/Trump+is+escalating+an+ideological+war

Cardenas, Cat, 2020 "Why Did Joe Biden Lose Ground With Latinos in South Texas?" (11 November), *Texas Monthly*, www.texasmonthly.com/politics/latinos-biden-trump-south-texas

Choonara, Joseph, 2018, "The Political Economy of a Long Depression", *International Socialism* 158 (spring), http://isj.org.uk/the-political-economy-of-a-long-depression

Cumming, Sean, 2020 "Labor in the Black Lives Matter Movement", Marx21 US (12 June), https://marx21us.org/2020/06/12/labor-in-the-black-lives-matter-movement

Cumming, Sean, and Bob Bacon, 2020 "Police and Feds: Two Cheeks of the Same Arse", Marx21 US (28 July), https://marx21us.org/2020/07/28/police-and-feds-two-cheeks-of-the-same-arse

Dixon, Matt, and Gary Fineout, 2020, "'I'm Not a F---ing Socialist': Florida Democrats Are Having a Postelection Meltdown", Politico (18 November), https://politi.co/3meWwJ7

Dunn, Amina, 2020 "Only 24% of Trump Supporters View the Coronavirus Outbreak as a 'Very Important' Voting Issue" (21 October), Pew Research Center, www.pewresearch.org/fact-tank/2020/10/21/only-24-of-trump-supporters-view-the-coronavirus-outbreak-as-a-very-important-voting-issue

Ferré-Sadurní, Luis, and Jesse McKinley, 2020, "NY Hospitals Face $400 Million in Cuts Even as Virus Battle Rages" (30 March), *New York Times*, www.nytimes.com/2020/03/30/nyregion/coronavirus-hospitals-medicaid-budget.html

Fretz, Eric, 2020, "Covid Recession Casts 100 Million into Extreme Poverty, While World's Richest Gain Record Trillions" (2 November), Marx21 US, https://marx21us.org/2020/11/02/covid-recession-casts-100-million-into-extreme-poverty

Herndon, Astead W, 2020, "Alexandria Ocasio-Cortez on Biden's Win, House Losses, and What's Next for the Left", *New York Times* (16 November), www.nytimes.com/2020/11/07/us/politics/aoc-biden-progressives.html

Hummel, Thomas, 2020, "How We Shut Down the Schools: Interview with NYC Teacher" (13 April), Marx21 US, https://marx21us.org/2020/04/13/how-we-shut-down-the-schools

Kirk, Michael, 2020 "America's Great Divide: From Obama to Trump" (14 January), PBS, www.pbs.org/wgbh/frontline/film/americas-great-divide-from-obama-to-trump/#video-2

Lauter, David, and Janet Hook, 2020, "Americans Broke a 120-year-old Turnout Record—and Are More Divided Than Ever" (4 November), *Los Angeles Times*, www.latimes.com/politics/story/2020-11-04/2020-election-trump-biden-count-analysis

Lemlich, Clare, 2020, "Bernie Sanders, the Democratic Socialists of America and the New US Left", *International Socialism 167* (summer), http://isj.org.uk/bernie-sanders-the-democratic-socialists-of-america-and-the-new-us-left

Luce, Edward, 2020, "US Gridlock: 'Biden Will Have One Hand Tied Behind His Back From the Start'", *Financial Times* (7 November).

Marcetic, Branko, 2020, "No, Medicare for All Didn't Sink the Democrats in 2020", *Jacobin* (16 November), www.jacobinmag.com/2020/11/medicare-for-all-democratic-party-down-ballot-2020-election

Marx21 US, 2020, "COVID Class Struggle: One Month of US Workplace Actions" (17 April), https://bit.ly/2KZEw7z

Mindock, Clark, 2020 "Trump Sexual Assault Allegations: How Many Women Have Accused the President?", *Independent* (6 November), www.independent.co.uk/news/world/americas/us-politics/trump-sexual-assault-allegations-all-list-misconduct-karen-johnson-how-many-a9149216.html

Nilson, Ella, 2020, "House Democrats Will Keep Their Majority for Two More Years", Vox (8 November), www.vox.com/2020/11/8/21539959/election-2020-house-democrats-control-majority

Padró Ocasio, Bianca, and Ben Wieder, 2020, "Trump Saw Gains Among Florida Puerto Ricans. They Say Democrats 'Don't Hear Us'", *Miami Herald* (12 November), http://hrld.us/3mjfZbt

Riccardi, Nicolas, 2020, "Referendum on Trump Shatters Turnout Records" (9 November), AP News, https://apnews.com/article/referendum-on-trump-shatter-voter-record-c5c61a8d280123a1d340a3f633077800

Roberts, Michael, 2020, "US Election: Women, the Young, the Working Class, the Cities and Ethnic Minorities Get Rid of Trump" (8 November), Michael Roberts Blog, https://thenextrecession.wordpress.com/2020/11/08/us-election-women-the-young-the-working-class-the-cities-and-ethnic-minorities-get-rid-of-trump

Roche, Ryan, 2017, "How Boston Turned the Tide on the Far Right" (21 August), SocialistWorker.org, https://socialistworker.org/2017/08/21/how-boston-turned-the-tide-on-the-far-right

Ruder, Eric, 2017, "An Avalanche Of Anti-Nazi Resistance", SocialistWorker.org (29 August), https://socialistworker.org/2017/08/29/an-avalanche-of-anti-nazi-resistance

Salmon, Felix, 2020, "China's New World Order", AXIOS (16 November), www.axios.com/rcep-trade-bloc-china-new-world-order-4993564c-ca57-411f-aca4-15250869f762.html

Schueler, McKenna, 2020 "The $15 Minimum Wage Won in Florida, But Biden Didn't. Here's Why", *In These Times* (13 November), https://inthesetimes.com/article/fight-for-15-minimum-wage-workers-seiu-labor-joe-biden-election

Schwartz, Brian, 2020 "Total 2020 Election Spending to Hit Nearly $14 Billion, More Than Double 2016's Sum" (28 October), CNBC, www.cnbc.com/2020/10/28/2020-election-spending-to-hit-nearly-14-billion-a-record.html

Selfa, Lance, 2012, *The Democrats: A Critical History* (Haymarket).

Stancil, Kenny, 2020, "As Centrist House Democrats Attack Medicare for All, Fox News Poll Shows 72% of Voters Want 'Government-run Healthcare Plan'", Common Dreams (6 November), www.commondreams.org/news/2020/11/06/centrist-house-democrats-attack-medicare-all-fox-news-poll-shows-72-voters-want

Stewart, Emily, 2018, "Poll: More Americans are Hitting the Streets to Protest in the Era of Trump", Vox (7 April), https://bit.ly/3lAQ7GT

Villarreal, Alexandra, 2020 "Why Democrats Lost Latino Voters Along Texas Border: 'They Relied on Loyalty'", Guardian (November 7), www.theguardian.com/us-news/2020/nov/07/how-democrats-latino-voters-texas-border-towns

Wilson, Jason, 2020, "White Nationalist Hate Groups Have Grown 55% in Trump Era, Report Finds", Guardian (18 March), www.theguardian.com/world/2020/mar/18/white-nationalist-hate-groups-southern-poverty-law-center

Wolf, Zachary B, Curt Merrill, and Daniel Wolfe, 2020, "How Voters Shifted During Four Years of Trump", CNN (7 November), www.cnn.com/interactive/2020/11/politics/election-analysis-exit-polls-2016-2020

Zandi, Mark, and Bernard Yaros, 2020, "The Macroeconomic Consequences: Trump vs. Biden" (23 September), Moody's Analytics, www.moodysanalytics.com/-/media/article/2020/the-macroeconomic-consequences-trump-vs-biden.pdf

Revolutionary pressures in Nigeria
Baba Aye

For several weeks in October 2020, tens of thousands of people took to the streets of Nigeria to protest against police brutality. The protests came after news circulated that the federal Special Anti-Robbery Squad (SARS) had killed a young man named Ochuko in Ughelli, a town in the Niger Delta region. In fact, Ochuko had been brutalised by a local police unit and not SARS, and had not been killed. However, the genie of mass anger was already out of the bottle—and the anger would extend beyond its initial #EndSARS demand and become, in the words of one journalist, "almost a revolution".[1]

After several attempts to break the peaceful protests with hired thugs, the state ultimately attempted to drown them in blood in order to avert a full-blown challenge to its power. This set in motion five days of rage, driven by a combination of social forces, which have dismissively been described as "hoodlums" by the ruling class and mainstream media. More than 200 police stations were burned down and 22 police officers killed. There were four jail-breaks, as hundreds of young people tore down prison gates and prisoners rose up. Malls were looted and businesses, particularly those owned by key supporters of the regime, were looted and set ablaze. Warehouses where the government kept

---

1   Abati, 2020.

food items that were meant to ameliorate the burden of the pandemic for poor people were also raided by tens of thousands of people in several states.

The first act of an unfolding revolutionary drama now appears to have run its course. There have been a few efforts to reignite the embers of the movement; demonstrations were called in Lagos and Abuja at the beginning of November. However, these were brutally snuffed out by the police, who launched a crackdown on organisers. Nevertheless, worsening living conditions, political uncertainty and a renewal of mass confidence in struggle point to a deepening of revolutionary pressures in Nigeria.

Background to a rebellion

SARS is the most notorious among the 14 units forming the federal police. It was established in 1992 to combat a sharp spike in crime that developed in the wake of the imposition of an IMF-backed structural adjustment programme in the 1980s. However, SARS' operatives were better known for brutalisation, torture and killing with impunity than for crime reduction. Amnesty International has documented some of the atrocities of the squad in a series of reports.[2]

With increases in online scams at the turn of the century, SARS turned its focus more to apprehending internet fraudsters than armed robbers. Young people with laptops and recent iPhone models were considered suspicious. Profiling also played a role in their arrests—having dreadlocks or tattoos made one a suspect. Their victims had to pay huge sums of money to regain their freedom, and they were the lucky ones; others would be tortured into making "confessions". These nefarious activities were so rampant that most young people in urban areas had either had some bitter personal SARS experience or knew someone who had.

The barbarity of SARS alone does not explain October's explosion of discontent. There is a long history of police brutality in Nigeria, stretching all the way back to the colonial era. There had also been earlier protests against police violence, though none as significant as #EndSARS. The #EndSARS hashtag rallied resistance to police brutality for the first time in 2016, leading to a series of localised demonstrations. The deepening of resistance has occurred against the backdrop of life becoming increasingly nasty and brutish for working-class people. In 2018 Nigeria overtook India as the country with the largest number of extremely poor people in the world—and the situation has since worsened. By the second quarter of 2019, 105 million of the country's population of 214 million people were living below the poverty line, compared with 90 million in 2018.

---

2   See Amnesty International, 2016 and 2020. See also Amnesty International, 2009, for an earlier broader treatment of police killings.

Petroleum accounts for two-thirds of Nigeria's revenue and so the global economic slowdown in 2020 had a severe impact; the country was pushed towards its second recession in five years, following an earlier contraction in 2016. The Covid-19 pandemic made a terrible situation for workers even worse. Tens of thousands in both the public and private sector were laid off or had their wages cut. A third of states are yet to pay the new national minimum wage of $77, over a year after it was legislated.[3] The unemployment rate increased from 23.1 percent in the third quarter of 2019 to 27.1 percent by the end of the second quarter of 2020. Underemployment rose from 20.1 percent to 28.6 percent over the same period.[4] Young people have borne the brunt of this sorry experience, with 13.9 million unemployed by the second quarter of 2020.[5]

Workers have fought back with a wave of strikes, particularly in the health and education sectors. This started with rank and file mobilisations, often against the diktats of the trade union bureaucracy.[6] Some concessions were won by doctors as result of this, but the government has not acceded to the demands of university lecturers who have been protesting since March. To rub salt in an open wound, the government increased both fuel prices at the pump and electricity tariffs at the beginning of September. After much dithering, the Nigeria Labour Congress (NLC) and Trade Union Congress (TUC), the country's two national trade union centres, called a general strike on 28 September, demanding a reversal of these increases. However, the strike was called off at the 11th hour. In response to the loud outcry against the betrayal, the NLC's general secretary, Emma Ugboaja, made it clear that the unions were not a revolutionary movement and would not be used "to cause destabilisation".[7] Stressing the unions' commitment to dialogue, he added that those who felt the need to fight should go ahead and do so without the labour movement. Musa Lawal, the TUC general secretary, echoed this view, saying that unions were "wiser" and stood in defence of "the national interest", against those outside the trade unions who wanted to capitalise on a general strike for more radical struggle.[8]

While the trade unions picked their battles, the ruling All Progressive Congress (APC) party has waged an all-out war against human rights and the poor. Taking a stand against the regime's "lawlessness" in December 2019, *The Punch*, a major daily newspaper, declared it would henceforth address President

---

3   Indeed, the new minimum is effectively a cut in real wages. In Nigerian nairas, $77 is N30,000, but when the 2011 minimum wage of N18,000 was passed into law this amounted to $120.

4   Trading Economics, 2020.

5   Nairametrics, 2020.

6   See Ogidan, 2020.

7   Ugboaja, 2020.

8   Ozigi, 2020.

Muhammadu Buhari as "major-general"—his rank as head of one of the vicious military juntas that ruled the country in the 1980s.[9] APC became the first opposition party to win federal elections in 2015, with Major-General Buhari (retd) as president. Buhari's APC is a merger of five regional bourgeois parties that had come together after a general strike and mass protests shook the ruling People's Democratic Party (PDP) in 2012.[10] In the absence of a left-wing alternative to the PDP, which had governed since the return of civilian rule in 1999, APC rode on the waves of the 2012 uprising, promising change.

Buhari's APC managed to hold on to power in the February-March 2019 general elections, which were marred by violence and vote-buying. However, for the first time this century, a radical left formation was on the ballot paper—the African Action Congress. This left-reformist party was formed in mid-2018 and came tenth out of the more than 70 parties that ran, winning almost 34,000 votes (0.12 percent) for its candidate in the presidential election. It is a party that places priority on extra-parliamentary mass mobilisation, and it became further radicalised after the elections as it organised a series of community campaigns against erratic power supply and for democratic rights. The party was pivotal to forming the Coalition for Revolution (CORE) along with socialist organisations such as the Socialist Workers and Youth League and the Federation of Informal Workers Organisation. This was the first time in a long time that Nigeria has seen the creation of a left-wing formation with any significant mass base.

On 5 August 2020, CORE launched a "RevolutionNow" campaign. Five million people in the country searched for the word "revolution" online that day. Since then, the coalition has organised a series of nationwide "Days of Rage". The most recent of these was on 1 October, the 60th anniversary of Nigerian indepedence. CORE and its affiliates formed the main section of the left that was not caught off guard when the recent protests started, taking its place in the thick of the revolt.

Thirteen days that shook Nigeria

A video of Ochuko drenched in his own blood and assumed dead went viral on 3 October. By the next day calls were issued online for a nationwide protest by notable musicians and Omoyele Sowore, national chair of the African Action Congress. The revolt started on 8 October in Abuja, the capital city, and Lagos, the major commercial city. By the following day it had spread to about a dozen of the country's 36 states—and continued spreading until over 20 states were engulfed. In Lagos, no fewer than 2,000 people occupied the entrance to Lagos state's House of Assembly in the Alausa district. Hundreds of them would spend

---

9   *The Punch*, 2020.
10 Aye, 2012.

their nights there until 20 October. By the following day thousands also took over the main Lekki Toll Gate Plaza. Two towns on the outskirts of Lagos also became outlying centres for the revolt. In Abuja the city centre became the point of convergence, as would be the case elsewhere.

CORE activists argued from the beginning that police brutality is inherent in the exploitative capitalist system and raised more radical demands, such as for the end of the regime. They faced attacks from the liberal wing of the movement, which blackmailed the coalition, claiming that it wanted to "hijack" the mass movement for its RevolutionNow agenda. This was one of two main reasons for an insistence on the movement being "leaderless", along with a desire to avoid empowering leaders who could compromise as the trade union bureaucracy had. The debate on how far the movement's demands should go led to the liberals pulling out of the centre of Alausa in Lagos state within 72 hours. CORE activists then took over coordination of the movement, as they also did in the outlying cities of Ikorodu and Badagry. Generally, CORE activists were more active in providing leadership within working-class areas. The liberal wing of the movement, which included celebrities and a feminist coalition of a dozen "exceptional women", were much more active on Twitter, dominating the online narrative. They were also central to raising funds; the feminist coalition in particular had raised over $200,000 by the time the movement was repressed. This went into providing legal and medical aid for protesters, as well as food. Many other people, including restauranteurs in various cities, supported the movement with food and drinks.

Within days, the regime had realised it had a rebellion on its hands. The mood on the streets was electrifying, even carnival-like in many places, with popular musicians singing. Young workers, professionals, artisans and others could feel the power they wielded with collective action as they chanted "End SARS Now!" On 11 October the government announced what appeared to be a concession, declaring SARS banned and urging the protesters to go home. But once beaten, twice shy—the government had made such announcements three times in the past four years. The following day, the protests continued, and the state responded with tear gas, water cannons, batons and the arrest of demonstrators, particularly in Abuja. Nevertheless, protesters regrouped and, in defiance, presented a five-point set of demands. They dubbed these demands "5for5", meaning all five points had to be addressed: immediate release of all protesters; justice for all deceased victims of police brutality and compensation for their families; an independent body to oversee the investigation and prosecution of all reports of police misconduct; psychological evaluation and retraining of all officers from the disbanded SARS; and an increase in the police salary.[11]

---

11   See Vanguard, 2020.

In an attempt to regain control of the situation, a hurriedly constituted presidential panel on police reforms summoned a "stakeholders' forum" on 13 October. This included philanthropic capitalist bodies and international NGOs such as the MacArthur Foundation and the Open Society Foundations, as well as local NGOs. They were joined by some liberal figures within the "leaderless" movement such as the popular musician Folarin "Falz" Falana. The police's inspector general, who organised the meeting in conjunction with the National Human Rights Commission, accepted the 5for5 demands. Nonetheless, a few hours later he announced that SARS was being replaced with a Special Weapons and Tactics (SWAT) unit. This replacement of six with half a dozen simply increased the determination of protesters to carry on the struggle. More radical demands than #EndSARS now found popular resonance, including calls to slash, rather than increase, public officers' remunerations and to #EndInjustice as a whole.

At this stage the state became both more repressive and more insidious. State-hired thugs attacked demonstrators in several locations. In Abuja, dozens of protesters' cars were burnt. Ethno-regional narratives were invented, presenting #EndSARS as a Southern project that aimed to overthrow a president from the North of the country. Particular attention was paid to stopping demonstrations from spreading to Northern states, where protesters had not gathered in the same numbers.

By the 12th day, over a dozen protesters had been killed in various parts of the country. These included two CORE activists, killed in Osun state by the thugs of the ruling party in the presence of the governor. The governor's entourage was attacked by enraged young people as he left. In the mid-western Edo state two prisons were sacked and prisoners freed. In Lagos, a major police station notorious for torture was torched. Police officers were also hounded in several parts of the state. The "Buhari Must Go" call, initiated by RevolutionNow activists, had started to echo within demonstrations. The rebellion was shedding the "almost revolutionary" label and starting to fully stamp "revolution" on its banner.

Bloodbath and aftermath

The state drowned the budding revolution in blood on 20 October. The state of Lagos was the centre of the massacre. At about noon, the governor of Lagos state, Babajide Sanwo-Olu, declared a 24-hour curfew. It was to come into effect by 4pm, but this was later shifted back to 9pm. By 4.30pm, a combined team of soldiers and police surveyed the situation at Alausa. Reading the signs, CORE activists began coordinating an orderly retreat of protesters before the anticipated return of security forces at 7pm.

CCTV cameras beside the Lekki Toll Gate were disabled.[12] The floodlights were also switched off. By 6.45pm soldiers moved in. Their clear intent was to kill in order to send a message of fear to the movement. Fires were set up at the two entrances and at exit points. Then they started shooting. This was captured on camera and streamed on social media. Calls were made by protesters for ambulances but the soldiers prevented these from coming in.

These events sparked the following days of rage in which police stations, prisons and several government buildings were set ablaze. The television station and newspaper offices of Ahmed Tinubu, a former Lagos state governor and APC leader, were also burned down. Covid-19 palliatives were expropriated from government warehouses by the crowds, which in some states now dwarfed the numbers on the streets during the earlier peaceful protests. The action extended into the North where the police had earlier been able to stop demonstrations. At least 500 people were subsequently arrested for "looting". Most of these, arrested during house-to-house searches, were guilty only of taking the Covid-19 palliatives that those in power had kept from them. The National Broadcasting Commission, which is chaired by an APC stalwart, also fined three television stations for their reporting of the protests. Identified organisers and volunteers from the protests have not been spared. The bank accounts of 20 people were frozen and a "no-fly" list was issued to the airports, which came to light when the passport of a lawyer who had offered free legal services was seized at Lagos's international airport as she tried to travel to the Maldives for a holiday. CORE activists were arrested at the National Assembly in Abuja for painting graffiti, and another was arrested in Lagos after being tracked through the phone number on a flyer.

Although repression is the main strategy of the regime, it also dangled the carrot of judicial panels of inquiry and restitution of abuses perpetrated by SARS. Revelations of the extent of these abuses have been pouring into these panels.

It will be impossible for the regime to force the genie of revolt back into the bottle of suppression. On the one hand, government is set to implement further anti-poor measures related to the conditions attached to a $3.4 billion loan from the International Monetary Fund that it received in March. On the other, the October revolt was a defining moment that has renewed the spirit of struggle among a pauperised populace. The trade union bureaucracy will not be able to hold back organised labour, the missing social force in the fire this time round, as revolutionary pressures intensify among the rank and file and on the streets.[13]

---

12 Authorities later claimed it was the licensing plate verification cameras that been disabled, which makes no sense given a curfew was in place.

13 Aye, 2020 .

This will likely lead to a condensed version of what transpired in 2012. Back then, the trade union bureaucracy was forced to hurriedly call for a general strike when state-level union officials said they would be stoned if they went back to their states without a concrete resolve to fight.

The question is how ready the revolutionary left will be to fan the embers of revolt into the fires of revolution.

References

Abati, Reuben, 2020, "#EndSARS: Almost a Revolution", *Sahara Reporters* (13 October), http://saharareporters. com/2020/10/13/endsars-almost-revolution-reuben-abati

Amnesty International, 2009, "Killing at Will: Extrajudicial Executions and Other Unlawful Killings by the Police in Nigeria" (Amnesty International Publications), www.amnesty.org/download/ Documents/44000/afr440382009en.pdf

Amnesty International, 2016, "'You Have Signed Your Death Warrant': Torture and Other Ill Treatment by Nigeria's Special Anti-Robbery Squad (SARS)", www. amnesty.org/download/Documents/ AFR4448682016ENGLISH.PDF

Amnesty International, 2020, "Nigeria: Time to End Impunity. Torture and Other Violations by Special Anti-Robbery Squad (SARS)", www.amnesty.org/download/Documents/ AFR4495052020ENGLISH.PDF

Aye, Baba, 2012, *Era of Crises and Revolts, Perspectives for Workers and Youth* (Solaf Publishers), www.academia.edu/7947545/ Era_of_Crises_and_Revolts

Aye, Baba, 2020, "#EndSARS Revolt and the Bloodbath in Nigeria—Part 2: The Missing Social Force", Global Labour Column, https://globallabourcolumn. org/2020/10/26/endsars-revolt-and-the-bloodbath-in-nigeria-part-2-the-missing-social-force/?fbclid=IwAR1vuUvmkG-cYg aB6a3LHLTjYehvAne6qt8qEQ9VyibRVA UFYxcmx8L71yc

Nairametrics, 2020, "13.9 Million Nigeria Youth Are Unemployed—NBS", Nairametrics (14 August), https://nairametrics. com/2020/08/14/13-9-million-nigerian-youth-are-unemployed-as-at-q2-2020-nbs

Ogidan, Muda, 2020, "Strike Waves Hit Health Sector", *Socialist Worker*, (August-September), https:// socialistworkersleague.org/2020/08/25/ strike-waves-hit-health-sector

Ozigi, Musa-Lawal, 2020, "Why We Suspended Strike, Accepted Deregulation", National Record (9 October), https://nationalrecord.com. ng/why-we-suspended-strike-accepted-deregulation-comrade-musa-lawal-ozigi

The Punch, 2019, "Buhari's Lawlessness: Our Stand", *The Punch* (11 December), https://punchng.com/buharis-lawlessness-our-stand

Trading Economics, 2020, "Nigeria Unemployment Rate", https:// tradingeconomics.com/nigeria/ unemployment-rate

Ugboaja, Emma, 2020, "Labour did not Call Off Any Pain that Nigerians are Feeling", National Record, (12 October), https://nationalrecord.com.ng/ labour-did-not-call-off-any-pain-that-nigerians-are-feeling-nlc

Vanguard, 2020, "Five Demands from #EndSARS Protesters" (12 October), www. vanguardngr.com/2020/10/five-demands-from-endsars-protesters

Thailand: return of the mass movement for democracy
Giles Ji Ungpakorn

Large, youth-led pro-democracy protests hit the Thai military junta in autumn 2020. Crowds of up to 50,000 started to gather around the Democracy Monument in central Bangkok in August. By 19 September—an important anniversary marking a military coup against an elected government in 2006—crowds had swelled to over 100,000. Then, on the 14 October, the 47th anniversary of a mass uprising against an earlier military dictatorship, crowds gathered in similar numbers and marched on Government House, demanding the resignation of the dictator Prayut Chan-ocha, the writing of a new constitution and reform of the monarchy.

By then, the stakes had been raised by the military government, which insisted that protests should be cancelled because the king had decided to visit a nearby temple in Bangkok. Protesters ignored this and, again, the numbers had swelled to 100,000 by nightfall as people joined after work. The government conscripted state municipal employees, wearing yellow shirts, symbolising support for the monarchy, to line the roads and welcome the royal cavalcade. They treated these conscripts like dirt—many were transported in open trucks and some literally had to sit in dust carts. Many voiced their displeasure and some were seen making the three-fingered salute used by pro-democracy protesters. Police allowed the queen to be driven through the demonstrating crowds, where she was met with more three-fingered salutes and even a few middle finger gestures. The crowd shouted "my taxes!" at her.

In the days that followed, protesters continued to defy the government, which announced emergency powers in a futile attempt to stop demonstrations. The police also used water cannon mixed with a chemical irritant on one occasion.[1] Yet this merely angered people, swelling the protests in the capital, and in towns and cities up and down the country. At one site in Bangkok organisers distributed a truckload of crash helmets, masks and raincoats to the crowd in case the police attacked. Reports from many areas tell of an impressive organisation by rank and file activists. Some leading activists have been arrested, but this seems to have had little effect, demonstrating the strength of the movement.

At the time of writing, it looks as if Prayut and his gang of military thugs are unlikely to go easily. They have spent the years since their 2014 coup putting in place measures to maintain their power, rewriting the constitution, appointing a senate, designing a national strategy and fixing last year's elections. Prayut already has blood on his hands. When he was commander-in-chief of the army in 2010, he and the military-appointed government of the time ordered the shooting down of unarmed pro-democracy "Red Shirts". The military have also used death squads against dissidents sheltering in neighbouring countries.

Relatively little has been said by Western governments about any of this. The Thai state was closely allied to the United States during the Cold War but has gradually moved away from this alliance since the end of the Vietnam War. Today the government seeks to balance its relationship between the two main imperialist powers that influence the region: China and the US. It has warm relations with China, from which the military often buys equipment. In an effort to maintain its influence, the US has been reluctant to make any real criticism of the Thai government over its lack of democracy, even during Barack Obama's presidency. The British government and the European Union also want to maintain cordial relations with the junta so that they can sell arms and access Thai markets. As prime minister, Theresa May had a friendly meeting with Prayut as recently as 2018.

This article will look at the context and challenges for the new movement in Thailand. At the time of writing, early November 2020, the movement had reached a crossroads. Organising flash mobs over and over again risked tiring out protesters, and these actions were insufficient to make the country ungovernable. Either the movement will advance, drawing on more militant and powerful action such as strikes, or the momentum will be lost. Given the high level of public support for the protests, it is important that activists seize the moment, building the basis for workplace stoppages, which would add strength to the movement.

---

1   Khaosod English, 2020.

The nature of the movement

The recent protests have been composed primarily of students and workers. They were organised by a group formed mainly of young people and university students, which initially called itself the "Free People". They originally had three major demands: stop intimidating activists, rewrite the constitution and dissolve parliament. A further set of radical demands were raised by the human rights lawyer Anon Nampa in an attempt to reform the discredited monarchy, and these have now been supported by the movement. People are scandalised and fed up with the behaviour of the new king, Wachiralongkorn.[2] For the first time in decades, people have had the confidence to criticise the monarchy in public, despite the fact that there are draconian laws against this. From the platform at a recent rally in the north east of Thailand, a leading student activist asked why the former king, Pumipon, who died in 2016, had supported military coups.[3]

The Free People has now created a coalition called the "Peoples' Party", named after a movement that led a revolution in 1932, toppling the absolute monarchy. The new generation of protest leaders has become acutely aware of the importance of the historical struggle for democracy. This latest movement is marked out from the earlier Red Shirt democracy movement, which emerged ten years ago, by its independence from existing political parties.[4] In fact, the mainstream opposition, which wants to divert the struggle into parliamentary reform, has been unable to keep up with the movement—unlike the mobile meatball vendors who turn up at protest sites as soon as people start arriving.

Secondary school students up and down the country have staged three-fingered salute protests during the compulsory flag raising ceremony before the start of the school day. They have argued with and defied their teachers. Often young women have been the most militant. At one point, a group of school students left their classes to protest outside the Ministry of Education because the junta-appointed minister had made threats against them. As the minister tried in vain to address the students, he was sent packing with shouts of "lackey of the dictatorship!" There are even reports of a primary school student speaking at one rally.

The three-fingered salute used by the protesters was borrowed from the *Hunger Games* series of books and movies, becoming a symbol of opposition to the military dictatorship during anti-coup protests in 2014. Thai demonstrations are always full of symbolism. A few student protests have involved "taking the

---

2   This name is often Romanised as "Vajiralongkorn", althought there is actually no "V" sound in the Thai language.

3   Pumipon is often Romanised as "Bhumibol" in the mainstream media, leading to gross mispronunciation.

4   See Ungpakorn, 2010, 2014.

knee". Similarly, the mass democracy protests of a decade ago used the red shirt as their symbol, while royalist supporters of the military wore yellow shirts. Indeed, the same pro-military reactionaries later tried to pretend that they were non-partisan by simply donning different coloured shirts. They were immediately branded as "salim", after a multicoloured noodle dessert. "Salim" has now become a widely used derogatory term to describe reactionaries. It was through a middle-class salim-backed coup in 2014 that the present junta came to power. This putsch followed a brutal crackdown against the Red Shirt movement and democratic elections in 2011 that brought to office a Red Shirt-backed government, with Yingluck Shinawat as Thailand's first woman prime minister.[5] Her government was repeatedly undermined by the military and the conservative courts before finally being overthrown by Prayut's coup.

After Prayut seized power, elections were eventually held in 2019, but under anti-democratic rules and a reactionary constitution. Despite losing the popular vote to anti-junta parties, the military-appointed senate helped to propel the junta back into government, with Prayut as prime minister. The junta's courts also dissolved two opposition parties. Even the so-called National Human Rights Commission was packed with soldiers and police officers.

Students and young people have managed to enliven and expand pro-democracy protests, which have occurred sporadically since 2014, because the new generation sees that pushing for reforms within the military-controlled parliamentary system has not worked. They are fed up with the entrenched conservatism in society, especially in the education system. The economy is a mess due to the Covid-19 crisis and youth have little hope for their future. Although their feelings of anger and frustration are shared with the majority of the adult population who voted against the military, the youth do not share the fear that is common among older activists who have been through brutal military crackdowns. This is a phenomenon among many young people internationally today—we see it, for instance, in recent protests in Hong Kong, Chile, Lebanon and Nigeria. Protest leaders in Thailand are being intimidated by security officers, who visit their homes. Activists are continually being charged by police with a number of supposed offences. Yet, they are becoming less and less afraid of this intimidation.

Two or three years ago, anti-junta protests were staged by small fragmented groups of university students who claimed that mass movements were no longer necessary in an age of social media. This feeling too has been radically changed by the younger generation who are now convinced of the need to build large protests

---

5   Yingluck Shinawat (often unhelpfully spelt as Shinawatra) is Taksin Shinawat's sister. See the
    section "Roots of the Present Political Crisis" below.

by using face to face networks of activists.[6] The demands of the movement are also expanding as it evolves. LGBT+ and abortion rights activists have joined in, along with activists campaigning for self-determination in the Muslim Malay region of Patani. Older Red Shirt activists have also been drawn back into protests for the first time since the movement was suppressed in 2010.

All ruling classes throughout the world are capable of brutality. Buddhist Thailand is no exception, and the country's history of repression makes the fearlessness of the protesters more remarkable. Unarmed pro-democracy protesters have been shot down in cold blood on four separate occasions in the past 50 years: during uprisings in 1973 and 1992 and as part of crackdowns against democracy movements in 1976 and 2010.[7] The massacre at a university in Bangkok on 6 October 1976 was particularly brutal, and the killing of young Malay Muslims in Patani by suffocation during transportation in military trucks in 2004 was equally horrifying.[8] To this day no member of the security forces or government has been punished for these state crimes. Significantly, school students have been attending pro-democracy meetings that highlight some of these past massacres. There is a thirst to learn about history.

In some ways the flowering of student activism today is similar to the political mood among young Thai people in the early 1970s, when the influence from the 1968 movements in the West and the defeat of the US in Vietnam sparked a huge rebellion against the military dictatorship of that era. This led to a massive expansion of the Communist Party of Thailand (CPT). However, the influence of the Maoist CPT had negative as well as positive elements. It made a shift to guerrilla warfare in the countryside instead of attempting to build strong urban struggles. Nevertheless, the Communists did organise many workers, and their influence among students helped to bring down the military regime in 1973.

The Thai monarchy

Since the activist lawyer Anon Nampa raised a number of criticisms of King Wachiralongkorn, anger over the arrogance of this thuggish and rather foolish monarch has emerged into the open. The king spends his time with his harem in Germany and has changed the constitution in order to preserve this lifestyle, for instance, by allowing him to live abroad. When his consorts fall out of favour they can often end up in jail. People are angry about laws that prevent

---

6   Twitter, 2020. The Thai state has also been using social media to hit back. Twitter uncovered a network of 926 accounts taking part in "information operations" linked to the army. These accounts were amplifying pro-military and pro-government content, as well as targeting prominent political opposition figures.

7   Ungpakorn, 2010, 2014; Sopranzetti, 2012.

8   Ungpakorn, Giles Ji, 2010.

the monarchy being subject to criticism or even accountability, and they are also infuriated that he amended the constitution to bring all wealth associated with the monarchy under his personal control. The demands to reform the monarchy reflect a feeling that its influence and privileges should be checked.

Many activists in Thailand believe that they live under an absolute monarchy, but nothing could be further from the truth. Since the 1932 Revolution the monarchy has had little power in itself. Instead, it acts as a willing tool of the military and conservatives. Although criticism of the monarchy can weaken the junta and hasten the long overdue day that Thailand becomes a republic, the military dictatorship remains the main enemy.

Elites have ruled Thailand for decades through a conservative-royalist network that cultivates an image of the king as an all-powerful god.[9] Yet the previous king, Pumipon, was always weak and characterless, and his power a fiction. Over the years, Pumipon was happy to play this role, benefitting from all regimes, whether military dictatorships or elected governments. Under the elected Taksin Shinawat government (2001-6), for instance, the king praised the government's extra-judiciary killings in its "war on drugs", in which many hundreds of people were murdered. Pumipon's rambling speeches used obscure language and were reproduced by the elites like sacred texts, but the words contained little substance until they were interpreted in the media by the conservative members of the ruling class in order to suit their own interests. The people with real power among the Thai elites are the army, high-ranking state officials and business leaders. They prostrate themselves on the ground and pay homage to the king on televison, but it is they themselves that exercise the real power, using it to enrich themselves. This is ideological theatre, acted out in order to fool the public. The fact that it is in any way believable is a good example of what Karl Marx called alienation. When people feel powerless, it is easier to believe the nonsense fed to them by their rulers.[10]

According to ruling class ideologues, the Thai monarchy is an ancient "Sakdina-Absolutist" institution, yet it is simultaneously argued that the country is a constitutional monarchy.[11] Students of Thai history will know from the works of historian Thongchai Winichakul, political scientist Thak Chaloemtiarana and journalist Paul Handley that the Thai monarchy evolved in a constantly changing environment full of political tensions.[12] It cannot be claimed that the

---

9   Duncan McCargo has termed this a "network monarchy", although he implies that the king is more powerful than I believe to be the case. See McCargo, 2005.
10 See Lukács, 1971.
11 The Sakdina system was the local form of feudalism.
12 See Winichakul, 2005; Chaloemtiarana, 1979; Handley, 2006.

institution remains the same as that which existed centuries ago. What all modern monarchies throughout the world have in common is their ideological role in supporting the status quo. After the Thai absolute monarchy was overthrown in the 1932 Revolution the country was ruled for a period by anti-monarchy civilians and generals. In the 1950s, during the Cold War, the monarchy was revived and promoted by military dictatorships. This "return" of the monarchy mirrors Christopher Hill's description of the restoration of Charles II in England after the English Revolution: "Charles was called 'king by the grace of God', but he was really king by the grace of the merchants and squires".[13] Similarly one could say that the Thai king is king by the grace of the generals and capitalists.

Many intellectuals rely, consciously or unconsciously, on the old Maoist analysis, originating with the CPT, that underdeveloped countries such as Thailand have yet to complete their "bourgeois revolutions", which would pave the way for the full development of capitalism. According to this view, these countries are therefore "semi-feudal".[14] However, as Neil Davidson has explained, bourgeois revolutions can take two main forms. There are revolutions from below, as was the case of England, America and France, and revolutions from above, led by a section of the old feudal order and common in late-developing countries such as Germany, Italy, Scotland and Japan.[15] Thailand's revolution can be counted among the latter and took place in response to European colonial encroachment into South East Asia. This process includes, but did not end with, King Rama V's revolutionary transformations in the 1870s. However, the absolute monarchy stage of this transition proved to be an unstable one, leading to the 1932 Revolution and the establishment of a constitutional monarchy under capitalist control.[16]

Roots of the present political crisis

The roots of the present crisis lie in the events leading up to the earlier 2006 coup against the elected Taksin Shinawat government. Many commentators try to explain the ruling-class conflict between the conservatives and Taksin in terms of "the old feudal order" fighting back against "the modern capitalist class", but this is not what that conflict was really about. Both Taksin and his conservative opponents were royalists. The conservatives are not feudal, but rather authoritarian neoliberals. In supporting the monarchy, they are also supporting one of the largest capitalist corporations in Thailand. The present military junta is the

---

13   Hill, 1959.
14   Ungpakorn, 1998.
15   Davidson, 2004; Davidson, 2012.
16   Kesboonchoo Mead, 2004.

strongest faction among these conservatives. They used force in order to seize power in the interests of capital, personally enriching themselves in the process. The Thai military itself owns a large bank, various media outlets and a network of other companies.

Taksin is also a wealthy capitalist who started out in the computing sector and became the owner of one of Thailand's leading telecommunications networks. At one point he owned Manchester City Football Club. Taksin was prepared to use "grassroots Keynesianism" in combination with free-market policies at a national level to modernise the country. He called this his "dual-track" approach. In the early years of his government, he received widespread support from all sections of the elite because he pulled the economy out of the Asian economic crisis, which began in Thailand in 1997 before spreading to other countries in East and South East Asia.

What gradually turned the conservatives against Taksin was their fear that they would lose their privileges in the face of his widespread modernisation project. His programme involved large infrastructure projects and pro-poor policies. The power of Taksin's political machine came from the fact that his Thai Rak Thai (TRT) party could win the hearts and minds of the electorate through genuine anti-poverty policies. His government introduced the first ever universal healthcare scheme, created funds for job creation in rural areas and offered debt relief for farmers. Taksin had mass support from the electorate, and the conservatives' neoliberal ideas could not challenge this strong political base at the polls. That is what drove the conservatives eventual recourse to a military coup.

Prior to Taksin's TRT, mainstream parties had not relied on real policies in order to win elections. They merely claimed that they would "work hard" for the benefit of the nation and relied on buying influence among local bosses who could bring in the votes. Taksin was threatening old networks of money politics, which had resulted in weak political parties that governed the country through corrupt and unstable coalition governments. He upset the apple cart by proving that the electorate were responsive to genuine pro-poor policies. Other governments had used massive amounts of public funds to prop up the banks and financial firms in order to protect the rich after the 1997 economic crisis. The unemployed were told to "go back to their villages" and depend on their already poor relatives. Those in work were expected to take pay cuts. The elites also ignored the crying need to develop Thailand's chaotic transport and communications infrastructure and to improve healthcare and education for the majority. Taksin was neither a socialist nor a principled democrat and advocate of human rights; his vision was to build a modern society where the state and big business could incorporate the majority of the population in a capitalist development project. He looked to countries such as Singapore for inspiration.

As the conflict between Taksin and the conservatives developed, a parallel war emerged at grassroots level between those who had voted for Taksin's government and the conservatives. In the wake of Taksin's overthrow, thousands of ordinary Red Shirt farmers and workers struggled for democracy, dignity and social justice, while Taksin and his political allies waged a very different campaign to regain the political influence that they had enjoyed before the 2006 coup. The present mass movement against Prayut's junta is independent of Taksin's political apparatus and, like that earlier grassroots movement, aspires to equality, freedom and social justice. Taksin himself has been permanently exiled since 2008 and has no intention of supporting a mass uprising. Since the 2006 military coup, the military have been firmly in the driving seat, aside from a brief interlude when Taksin's sister, Yingluck, won democratic elections and formed a government from 2011 to 2014.

Classes and movements

There is a mainstream myth that "civil society", centred on the middle classes and non-governmental organisations (NGOs), is a necessary force to build and maintain democracy in countries such as Thailand.[17] From this viewpoint, only the "educated classes" have the ability to think independently, unlike poor peasants and workers, and NGOs are required to empower the poor because they are unable to organise themselves. Many among the Thai middle classes felt uncomfortable that Taksin was favouring the poor and were worried that their advantageous position in society would be undermined. The NGO activists were worried that the government's pro-poor policies were diminishing their influence with villagers. Thus the middle classes and some NGOs took part in anti-democratic protests and welcomed two military coups.[18] Marxists have long seen the middle classes as being a potential base for fascism and dictatorship.[19] We saw this in the 1930s and also in 1976 in Thailand. However, the middle classes can also join pro-democracy movements at other times and support working-class demands. What is consistent is the fragmentation and weakness of the middle classes, which are unable to set their own class agenda. Instead, they flip flop between the interests of the business and bureaucratic elites and the interests of the working class and the poor.

Throughout the recent development of capitalism in Thailand there has been a steady decline in the peasantry and a corresponding increase in the

---

17 Pye, 1990; Clarke, 1998; Cohen and Arato, 1997; Laothamatas, 1996.
18 Ungpakorn, 2004. See also, Ungpakorn, 2009.
19 Trotsky, 1975.

modern working class. This is a phenomenon found in all developing countries, especially those in South East Asia.[20] Since the mid-1990s, less than half the Thai population has been engaged in agriculture and by 2019 urban settings accounted for over half of the population.[21] The working class is rapidly becoming the largest class in Thai society.

Of course, the potential power of the working class is only expressed through its organisation into bodies such as trade unions and political parties. At present there are no political parties of the working class, although the mainstream opposition Future Forward Party has tried to co-opt more militant trade unionists into its "worker section".[22] Thai trade union membership stands at less than 5 percent of the workforce. However, such an average figure can be misleading. Most state enterprises and large factories in the private sector do have active unions. This includes some offices, especially in the banking sector. Unionised workers are mainly concentrated in Bangkok and the surrounding provinces of the central region and the eastern industrial seaboard. These concentrations of working-class organisation indicate greater influence than might be inferred from the national union density figures. Strikes occur on a regular basis and trade union membership has expanded in manufacturing on the eastern coast, especially in auto parts and auto assembly factories.

Trade unions and strikes have been part of Thai society for many years. Nonetheless, a number of ideological factors have held back the working class. Firstly, there is the historical influence of the CPT, which organised urban workers in the 1940s and 1950s, but which, as noted above, took a Maoist turn away from the working class and towards the peasantry in the 1960s. This legacy means that there have been few left-wing activists willing to agitate among workers. Unlike in South Korea, where student activists had a long tradition of going to work in urban settings with the aim of strengthening trade unions, Thai student activists headed for the countryside after graduation.

Secondly, since the the collapse of the CPT, the influence of NGOs has grown. These often use funds from US and German foundations, although more recently Thailand has seen the arrival of representatives of large international union federations, dominated by union bureaucrats with little rank and file involvement. These NGOs and international unions have a number of commonly held beliefs. They actively support trade unions so long as they stay within the law. Thai labour law stipulates that trade unions must remain

20 Elson, 1997.
21 World Bank, 2019.
22 For more on the Future Forward Party, which renamed itself the "Move Forward Party" after being dissolved by the junta's courts, see Ungpakorn, 2018.

apolitical and most NGOs are opposed to trade unionists taking up socialist politics and forming political parties. Thai labour law also makes it hard to organise official strikes.

NGO activists are often referred to as "pi-lieng" (nannies), helping supposedly childlike workers to organise unions, to know their rights under the labour laws and to conduct themselves properly in labour disputes. When a dispute arises at a workplace, pi-lieng are sent out to stay with the workers in their picket tents. On some occasions, more rebellious workers will be scolded like children. NGO and international union activity has resulted in more trade unions being established; nevertehless, it also breeds worker dependency on external funding and socialises union representatives into a lifestyle of seminars in luxury hotels and trips to overseas conferences.[23]

In Thailand, as in other countries, trade union bureaucrats enjoy a better standard of living than their members. However, networks of independent unofficial rank and file activists are organised in "klum yarn" ("area groups"). These exist in many industrial areas in and around Bangkok, for example, in Rungsit, Nawanakorn, Saraburi, Ayuttaya, Prapadaeng and Omnoi-Omyai, and also in the industrial estates of the eastern seaboard. These area groups are considerably more democratic than the leading union bodies and their congresses. The entire committee of each group is usually elected every year and made up of lay representatives, men and women, who cover different workplaces and industries. Area groups were initially established in the mid-1970s by activists from the CPT and, later, by NGO workers. Along with these networks, official groupings such as the Federation of Textile, Garment and Leather Workers' Unions are able to bring together different unions at rank and file level, independent of the various bureaucratised leaderships.

Many active trade unionists who wish to fight in a more politicised manner have turned towards militant syndicalism. In the present day Thai context this means engaging in the class struggle, supporting and organising strikes and opposing cooperation with the state and the elites. These militants, who are mainly in the private sector workplaces, oppose the military and the royalist Yellow Shirts. Although syndicalists are characteristically wary of forming political organisations—preferring to use unions as the primary vehicle for struggle—some have been wooed by the Future Forward Party, rather than seeking to build an independent revolutionary party of the working class.

---

23 The royalist Yellow Shirts also gained some influence in the trade union movement, although this was strictly limited to sections of workers in state enterprises. Here a mentality of putting more faith in talking to sympathetic managers or politicians, rather than organising and building a mass base, helped to entrench right-wing views.

In recent months syndicalist militants have turned up to support the youth-led pro-democracy demonstrations as individuals and as part of trade union groups. On the eastern seaboard, with its automobile assembly, vehicle parts and electrical machinery plants, the Eastern Relations of Labour Group, a rank and file trade union organisation, has coordinated worker rallies against the junta. Textile workers in Sarabury, just north of Bangkok, have also organised a rally. But the influence of these militants remains limited.

The Thai working class is much more than factory workers in the textiles and auto industries. There are white collar workers in offices, banks and universities. There are transport and hospital workers. To build for strike action against the junta, youth activists need to link up with worker activists and visit workplaces to discuss how to get rid of the dictatorship.

Lessons from the 1970s and from the defeated Red Shirt protests ten years ago show that the expansion the movement into the organised working class is urgently needed. The working class is the main location of our side's power. The lack of a significant organisation of the left in Thailand will make the task of mobilising workers more difficult, but it is hoped that militants will step forward to try and achieve this. A call for a general strike on 14 October was made without any concrete work being done among the working class. Socialists know only too well that it is far easier to make abstract calls for general strikes than to actually do the necessary organisational work to bring one about. A few individual socialists do exist in Thailand and it is the job of such people, no matter how small in number, to encourage the spread of radical ideas in the working class and to strengthen workers' struggles. This work will be all the more effective if combined with attempts to build the beginnings of a revolutionary socialist party.

References

Chaloemtiarana, Thak, 1979, *The Politics of Despotic Paternalism* (SEAP Publications).

Clarke, Gerard, 1998, *The Politics of NGOs in South-East Asia* (Routledge).

Cohen, Jean L, and Andrew Arato, 1997, *Civil Society and Political Theory* (MIT Press).

Davidson, Neil, 2004, "The Prophet, his Biographer and the Watchtower", *International Socialism 104* (winter).

Davidson, Neil, 2012, *How Revolutionary Were the Bourgeois Revolutions?* (Haymarket).

Elson, Robert Edward, 1997, *The End of the Peasantry in Southeast Asia* (Macmillan).

Handley, Paul, 2006, *The King Never Smiles: A Biography of Thailand's Bhumibol Adulyadej* (Yale University Press).

Hill, Christopher, 1959, *The English Revolution 1640: An Essay* (Lawrence and Wishart).

Kesboonchoo Mead, Kullada, 2004, *The Rise and Decline of Thai Absolutism* (Routledge).

Khaosod English, 2020, "Police Admit Teargas Was Used in Protest Crackdown" (9 November), https://bit.ly/2JSMzTh

Laothamatas, Anek, 1996, "A Tale of Two Democracies: Conflicting Perceptions of Elections and Democracy in Thailand", in Robert H Taylor (ed), *The Politics of Elections in Southeast Asia* (Cambridge University Press).

Lukács, Georg, 1971, *History and Class Consciousness* (Merlin Press).

McCargo, Duncan, 2005, "Network Monarchy and Legitimacy Crises in Thailand", *The Pacific Review*, volume 18, issue 4.

Pye, Lucien W, 1990, "Political Science and the Crisis of Authoritarianism", *American Political Science Review*, volume 84, number 1.

Sopranzetti, Claudio, 2012, *Red Journeys: Inside the Thai Red-shirt Movement* (Silkworm Books).

Trotsky, Leon, 1975, *The Struggle Against Fascism in Germany* (Pelican).

Twitter, 2020, "Disclosing Networks to Our State-linked Information Operations Archive" (8 October), https://blog.twitter.com/en_us/topics/company/2020/disclosing-removed-networks-to-our-archive-of-state-linked-information.html

Ungpakorn, Ji Giles, 1998, "The Failure of Stalinist Ideology and the Communist Parties of Southeast Asia", *Thammasat Review*, volume 3, issue 1.

Ungpakorn, Ji Giles, 2004, "NGOs: Enemies or Allies?" *International Socialism 104* (winter), http://isj.org.uk/ngos-enemies-or-allies

Ungpakorn, Giles Ji, 2009, "Why Have Most Thai NGOs Chosen to Side with the Conservative Royalists, Against Democracy and the Poor?", *Interface: A Journal For And About Social Movements*, volume 1, issue 2.

Ungpakorn, Giles Ji, 2010, *Thailand's Crisis and the Fight for Democracy* (WD Press), http://bit.ly/1TdKKYs

Ungpakorn, Giles Ji, 2014, "Thailand's Red Shirts", *International Socialism 141* (winter).

Ungpakorn, Giles Ji, 2018, "Future Forward Party Fails to Move Beyond the Mainstream", Ugly Truth Thailand blog (3 June), https://uglytruththailand.wordpress.com/2018/06/03/future-forward-party-fails-to-move-beyond-the-mainstream

Winichakul, Thongchai, 2005, "Stepping Beyond the 14th October Model of Democracy", Prachatai, https://prachatai.com/journal/2005/11/6468

World Bank, 2019, "Urban Population—Thailand", https://data.worldbank.org/indicator/SP.URB.TOTL.IN.ZS?locations=TH

ALEXANDRA KOLLONTAI
Writings from the Struggle

ALEXANDRA KOLLONTAI was a major figure in the Russian revolutionary movement, a pioneer of women's liberation and one of the founders of International Women's Day.

This selection of her writings from the revolutionary struggle is edited and translated by Cathy Porter, author of *Alexandra Kollontai: A Biography*. The collection includes articles translated for the first time into English.

Available from:
www.bookmarksbookshop.co.uk
publications@bookmarks.uk.com
+44 (0)20 7637 1848

£12

the socialist ∎ bookshop
bookmarks

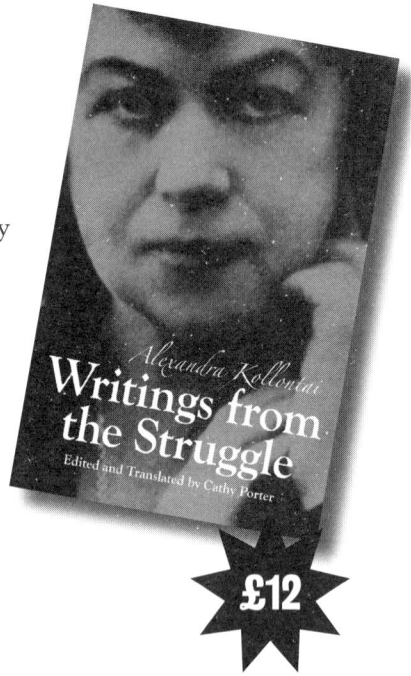

Migration in an era
of climate catastrophe
Camilla Royle

The new decade started with the news of flooding in Jakarta, Indonesia
that killed more than 60 people and displaced tens of thousands. Caused
by extremely heavy rainfall, the effects of the floods were exacerbated by poor
infrastructure and the ongoing sinking of the city due to groundwater extraction.
Homes were inundated with filthy water; one mother described trying to raise
her baby in an emergency shelter full of wet garbage: "My baby is not sleeping as
the rain comes in and the wind comes in... It is disgusting here, but we are stuck".[1]
The response of the ruling class is to move the capital city to Borneo, but this
will provide little comfort to the poorest inhabitants of Jakarta.[2] Disasters like
this can bring into sharp relief all the existing relations of class exploitation and
oppression within a society. They reveal that the human relationship with the
natural environment under capitalism is already irrational and destructive, even
in "normal" times.

People around the world are responding to these events already by trying to
find safer places to live and we can expect to see greater numbers of refugees

---

1   Associated Press, 2020. Thanks to Majed Akhter, Simon Behrman, Erica Borg, Alex Callinicos,
    Diego Macias Woitrin, Phil Marfleet, John Narayan and Lucia Pradella for their generous
    comments on this article in draft. The views expressed here are my own.
2   Varagur, 2020.

and migrants in future due to climate change. The Intergovernmental Panel on Climate Change (IPCC) has stated that "the greatest single impact of climate change might be on human migration".[3] This means there is an urgent need for socialists to consider how to respond. It is a complex issue that affects huge numbers of people on every continent on Earth. Therefore, this article will not discuss every example of people moving due to climate change in detail. Instead, the aim is to provide an overview of the scale of environmental migration, an explanation of the arguments around the ongoing conflict in Syria, which is sometimes discussed as an example of a climate war, and some suggestions as to how Marxists can approach the issue. Some accounts have supposed that there is a linear relationship between increased climate change and more conflict (and therefore more refugees) in places such as the Middle East and sub-Saharan Africa. However, this discussion will caution against some of these mechanistic interpretations, arguing that it is not inevitable that people will turn to violence in response to a warming world. The article concludes with some thoughts on the importance of raising anti-racist arguments in the environmental movement.

Unnatural disasters

People moving from one part of the world to another due to ecological breakdown is not new. Indeed, climatic changes thousands of years ago played a role in the development of agriculture and the establishment of settled societies and cities. The Irish Great Hunger in the 1840s saw one million deaths, and a further one million people leaving Ireland, many of them settling in Britain, the United States and Canada. Although the immediate cause was ecological—the failure of the potato harvest due to a fungal disease—the scale of the suffering was made immeasurably worse due to the actions of the British government.[4] Karl Marx outlined in *Capital* how British colonial policies had laid the ground for the disaster in the first place by moulding Irish agriculture to the requirements of the colonial power: "For a century and a half England has indirectly exported the soil of Ireland".[5] Similarly, anyone who has read John Steinbeck's classic *The Grapes of Wrath* will also be aware of the suffering experienced by Americans in the 1930s trying to escape the dustbowl and searching for work elsewhere.

Environmental migration will undoubtedly become more of a political issue in the coming decades. There are various estimates of how many climate-related refugees and migrants there will be. The most widely cited study suggests that around 200 million people will be displaced due to climate change by 2050,

3   See Brown, 2008, p11.
4   Newsinger, 2006, pp34-38.
5   Marx, 1976, p860.

Figure 1: New displacements associated with conflict/violence and disasters in millions (2008-2019)

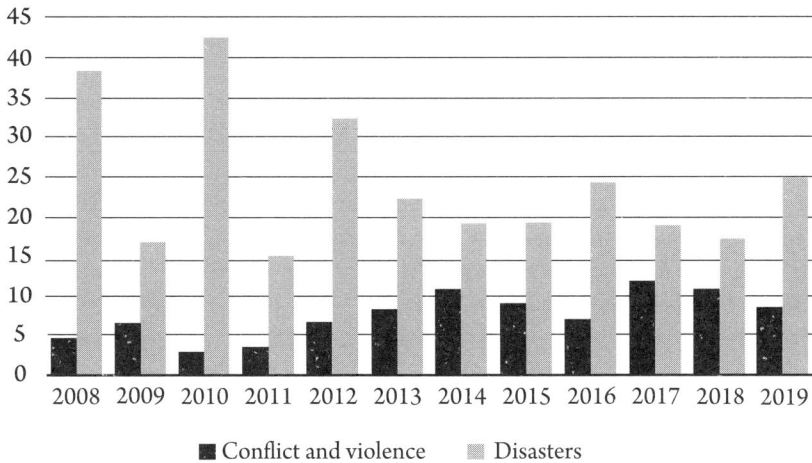

Source: Internal Displacement Monitoring Centre, 2019; 2020.

around a ten-fold increase on current rates, although the academic who came up with this figure admits it is only an estimate. Another study from academics at Cornell University talks about 2 billion climate refugees by 2100, a staggering figure that would amount to a fifth of the global population.[6]

As figure 1 demonstrates, "disasters" have consistently been a bigger reason for internal displacement than conflict or violence in the past ten years. This category includes geophysical events such as earthquakes and volcanoes. But the vast majority of displacements of people are due to weather-related events such as storms, floods, fires and drought (table 1). It is these weather-related disasters that are likely to become more common with increased climate change. Warmer temperatures mean more moisture in the air. This is likely to contribute to "extreme precipitation events", particularly in South East Asia. The risk of wildfires increases with warming, flooding is likely to become more common as sea levels rise and it is probable that tropical storms will be more frequent, intense and devastating, hitting coastal regions especially hard when combined with sea level rise.[7]

These will be unnatural disasters in several senses. Firstly, because dangerous climate change could have been avoided. As this journal has argued, the profit

6   Brown, 2008, p10; Friedlander, 2017.
7   Berlemann and Steinhardt, 2017.

motives of a tiny proportion of the world's population have been put before the survival of the many. Global capitalism has become dependent on fossil fuels and the industry and their supporters are powerful and influential. The science of climate change has been understood for several decades, yet governments have stuck to business as usual, failing to put in place the urgent measures needed to turn back from catastrophe and spreading doubt about the reality or seriousness of climate change.

Secondly, the effect that ecological breakdown has on people and the response of states is also shaped by the interests of capitalism. Indeed, the outcome of any disaster, whether climate-related or not, will be influenced by the type of society in which it takes place. For example, Cyclone Gorky in Bangladesh in 1991 left at least 138,000 people dead. The following year, Hurricane Andrew hit Florida and Louisiana. Despite being a stronger storm, the death count of 65 was much lower.[8] The way in which social forces shape the outcomes of disasters (including the Covid-19 pandemic) has led many to conclude that the degree to which an event such as a storm becomes a disaster depends on how vulnerable the population is; there is no such thing as a "natural" disaster.[9] Some scholars have also used the terminology of "hazards", in recognition of the fact that facing extremes of environmental variation is an integral aspect of how societies relate to their surroundings. This also implies a longer-term perspective of how people understand and cope with risk rather than a focus only on a particular destructive event such as a fire or hurricane.[10]

Environmental hazards can force people from their homes, but the experience of being a refugee can itself make someone more vulnerable to the effects of climate change due to inadequate accommodation, resources or social support networks. Areesha camp in northern Syria has flooded several times, with heavy rainfall destroying people's tented accommodation.[11] This has also been illustrated recently by Covid-19—refugees and their supporters fear the consequences of an outbreak in refugee camps where people will not be able to self-isolate and may not even have access to adequate washing facilities.[12]

One of the most striking illustrations of the effects of a warming climate on human migration is the plight of people on low-lying islands. For example,

8   Brown, 2008, pp17-18. Sometimes measures of financial loss are used instead of death counts, which perversely implies that disasters are more damaging if they affect rich people—Mustafa, 2009.
9   See Pelling, 2001, for an overview of theoretical approaches to "natural disasters" and Choonara, 2020, on Covid-19.
10 Mustafa, 2009.
11 Save the Children, 2019.
12 KEERFA, 2020.

Table 1: Causes of disaster-related internal displacement in 2019

Disaster type		Number displaced
Geophysical	Earthquakes	922,500
	Volcanic eurptions	24,500
Weather related	Cyclones, hurricanes and typhoons	11,900,000
	Other storms	1,100,000
	Floods	10,000,000
	Wildfires	528,500
	Droughts	276,700
	Landslides	65,800
	Extreme temperatures	24,500

Source: Internal Displacement Monitoring Centre, 2020.

Kiribati in the Pacific Ocean could become entirely uninhabitable in a matter of decades. Rising sea levels and storm surges are combining with biodiversity loss, warmer temperatures and the contamination of freshwater supplies with saltwater. Its government has already purchased an area of land in Fiji of over 6,000 acres to rehome the population and is encouraging people to leave.[13]

India and the Philippines currently account for huge numbers of displacements, with 5 million people displaced in India in 2019, mostly due to monsoons and cyclones (figure 2).[14] Riverbank erosion, which is predicted to worsen in the coming years, displaced thousands of people in Bangladesh in 2018. The country has one of the highest rates of displacement due to flooding in the world, with 1.8 million displaced people in any given year. Many of them are expected to move to the capital, Dhaka.[15] In Southern Africa, the unusually powerful Cyclone Idai displaced hundreds of thousands of people in 2019, mostly in Mozambique.

A series of reports in the *Guardian* have argued that climate change has played a role in the recent movements of people from Central to North America, forcing them to join the "migrant caravans" trying to cross the border into the US. Changing weather and drought are proving devastating for people who rely on their crops to have enough food to eat, with some farmers reporting that there has

13   Ives, 2016.
14   Internal Displacement Monitoring Centre, 2020, p48.
15   Internal Displacement Monitoring Centre, 2019, pp34-35.

been no maize crop at all in some years.[16] As in other zones of mass displacement around the world, this is likely to be an example of mixed migration, with people trying to cross the border due to conflict or repression mixing with those forced to move due to the collapse of local food markets. In many cases the drought is likely to be the final factor in causing people to move who have already faced the crushing impact of trade deals such as the North American Free Trade Agreement (NAFTA), which undermined domestic agriculture in Mexico.[17]

In the Western hemisphere it is the US itself that consistently experiences the most internal displacement due to disasters (at least in terms of absolute numbers of people). In 2018, more than 1.2 million people were forced to leave their homes. This included more than 350,000 people in California, which experienced the most destructive wildfires in its history in that year.[18] The devastating fires in Australia over the past year and the effects of storms and fires in the US demonstrate that even the so-called "high-income" countries are ill-equipped to cope with climate change.

Although it seems clear from these examples that climate change will have an effect on migration, it has been fiendishly difficult to try to find an overall pattern at a global scale. In 2017, the *New York Times* published a world map showing forcible displacements of people and temperature change alongside an article suggesting that there is some correlation between the two.[19] However, as we might expect, the map reveals many exceptions to the trend. There is a complex array of different factors involved. As we know, the issue is not generally one of high temperatures as such, but their effects in terms of oceanic warming or reduced or less predictable rainfall. Therefore, temperature change is only a proxy, and not an ideal one, for climate-related extreme weather events. This is before we even start to look at the social reasons why some populations are more vulnerable and why some people choose to move while others stay where they are.

The Internal Displacement Monitoring Centre treats "conflict" and "disasters" as two separate causes. However, commentators are increasingly concerned that climate change might lead to conflict. The United Nations has stated that: "While not in themselves causes of refugee movements, climate, environmental degradation and natural disasters increasingly interact with the drivers of refugee movements".[20] In particular, the 2003 conflict in Darfur marked a turning point in official interest in the link between climate and conflict. In the Darfur conflict,

---

16   Milman, Holden and Agren, 2018; Markham, 2019.
17   Weisbrot, 2014.
18   Internal Displacement Monitoring Centre, 2019, pp42-43.
19   Benko, 2017.
20   United Nations, 2018, p2. The UN currently does not include environmental migrants within the legal definition of "refugees", an issue that will be discussed further below.

Figure 2: Ten countries with most new displacements associated with disasters in 2019 (numbers of people displaced in millions)

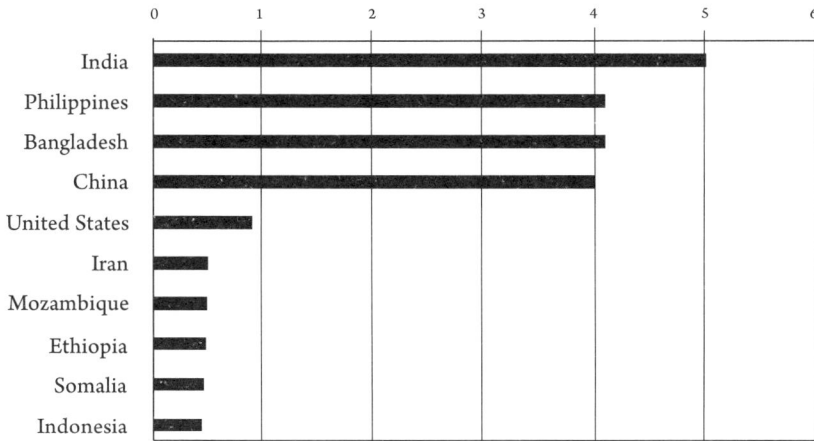

Source: Internal Displacement Monitoring Centre, 2020.

which followed a severe and long-lasting drought, hundreds of thousands of people died and more than 2 million were internally displaced.[21] Although accepting that the causes of the war were extremely complex, Jonathan Neale points to the role of climate change:

> Abrupt climate change will create famine and refugees on a massive scale. It will also mean war. Change the balance of economic and geographical power, and governments will use military might to grab it back. If you want to see that future, look at Darfur.[22]

More recently, some have looked at the role of drought as one factor in the Syrian civil war. To understand how environmental change, neoliberalism and political power struggles have fuelled the conflict it is necessary to understand a little about Syria's recent history.

Revolution and war in Syria

Colonialism had a divisive influence in Syria. Established by the Sykes-Picot agreement in 1916, during the collapse of the Ottoman Empire, it was a French colony until 1946. The French Mandate authorities divided up Syria (and Lebanon) along religious lines, establishing distinct statelets for the Alawite

---

21 Ban, 2007.

22 Neale, 2010.

and Druze populations and dividing the rest of the country into two, with one state centred on Damascus and the other centred on Aleppo. However, as Anne Alexander and Jad Bouharoun have described, there were repeated revolts against French rule in the 1920s that were often able to unite people across sectarian divisions.[23]

After independence, Syria was a deeply unequal state; a tiny elite dominated land ownership and played a disproportionate role in political life while landless sharecroppers made up two-thirds of the peasantry. Yet by the second half of the 20th century, a new political class had come to prominence. The Ba'ath Party, led by Hafez al-Assad, rose to power in a coup in 1970. The party drew on the new middle class for part of its support.[24] In 2000, Bashar al-Assad succeeded his father as president. Assad junior instituted a series of neoliberal measures that resulted in the liberalisation of trade, cuts and privatisation of sections of the welfare state and the abolition of rent controls. Overall, real wages declined and poverty and youth unemployment increased.

Perhaps most significantly for this discussion of climate refugees, these measures also affected agriculture. Land in arid regions was privatised and used for growing wheat and cotton commercially, but the effect of this, combined with mismanaged irrigation, was a long-term decline in freshwater supplies, making rural Syrians particularly vulnerable to drought.[25] Syrian oil production peaked and started to decline in the 1990s, leading to a cut in fuel subsidies in 2008. This had further consequences for water supply and agriculture because fuel is needed to work water pumps.[26]

Also, beginning in the 1970s, rainfall from the Mediterranean became less predictable, leading to what are thought to be the driest conditions in Syria in 900 years. Between 2006 and 2010 the drought was particularly intense and livestock farming and harvests of wheat and barley collapsed.[27] As Alexander and Bouharoun explain:

> The social consequences of the combination of natural disaster with neoliberal agricultural policies were profound. Up to 3 million small-scale farmers and herders lost their livelihood and were driven off their lands and into poverty.

Many of them migrated to the south and west of the country, to places such as Deraa in the south or to the periphery of Damascus. This fed into a growing

23 Alexander and Bouharoun, 2016, pp2-4.
24 Alexander and Bouharoun, 2016, pp5-10.
25 Fröhlich, 2016.
26 Fröhlich, 2016, p42.
27 Malm, 2016.

population in these cities, which faced both poverty and political repression at a time when the Assad government and its cronies were continuing to enrich themselves, investing in golf courses and luxury apartments.[28]

The Syrian Revolution that began in March 2011 has been discussed at greater length elsewhere in this journal than is possible here.[29] Starting as a popular uprising inspired by the revolts in Egypt, Tunisia and elsewhere that became known as the Arab Spring, the revolution drew its support from the urban peripheries, including among those who had migrated from rural areas. So, the anger among farmers who had lost their livelihoods may have played a role. Deraa, mentioned above, was one of the centres of the revolt after a group of teenagers were arrested and tortured for writing "the people want to overthrow the regime" on a wall, which sparked militant protests in the city.[30] At its high point, the revolution brought up to one million people onto the streets and saw the beginnings of alternative modes of government in the form of revolutionary councils. In Idlib and Aleppo it inflicted military defeats, and at times it looked close to toppling the government.[31] However, the Assad regime's forces were able to contain the movement, responding to the protests with brutal force and using artillery, barrel bombs and chlorine gas against civilian populations.[32] Both sides in the ensuing civil war gained the support of regional and international powers. The Lebanese Shia militia Hizbollah, the Iranian Revolutionary Guards and the Russian state all backed Assad at various points in the conflict, while armed anti-government forces attracted funding from the Gulf states, Turkey and the US. Islamist rebels such as Jabhat al-Nusra, whose politics are far from those of the initial uprising, became more prominent among the anti-government forces.[33] The actions of the state and the intervention of the various regional actors rapidly polarised the war along sectarian lines, although this must be understood in the context of sectarian divisions that were already present in the Ba'athist state.[34]

Around 500,000 people have died in the Syrian civil war.[35] Many more have been forced to move, with 6.6 million internally displaced and 5.6 million leaving Syria, making this the biggest movement of refugees in recent times. Although some Syrian refugees have come to Europe, the vast majority of those displaced

---

28 Alexander and Bouharoun, 2016, pp11-12; Malm, 2016.
29 Maunder, 2012; Alexander, 2016; Naisse, 2016; Hearn and Dallal, 2019.
30 Alexander and Bouharoun,2016, p14.
31 Hearn and Dallal, 2019.
32 Alexander, 2016.
33 Alexander and Bouharoun, 2016, pp22-23.
34 Alexander, 2016.
35 Hearn and Dallal, 2019.

by the fighting have remained within the region: there are 3.6 million Syrian refugees in Turkey, around one million in Lebanon, 655,000 in Jordan, 246,00 in Iraq and at least 126,000 in Egypt.[36] Some of these people will have migrated twice—moving into urban areas during the period of drought and then fleeing again several years later as the war intensified.

Is Syria a source of climate refugees?

Naomi Klein argues that the impact of the drought on rural to urban migration was significant for the uprising and subsequent war and refugee crisis in Syria. She notes that the revolution started in areas that had experienced migration into cities:

> Deraa is where Syria's deepest drought on record brought huge numbers of displaced farmers in the years leading up to the outbreak of Syria's civil war, and it is where the Syrian uprising broke out in 2011. Drought was not the only factor in bringing tensions to a head. But the fact that 1.5 million people were internally displaced in Syria as a result of the drought clearly played a role.[37]

Klein, drawing on the theories of Israeli architect Eyal Weizman, refers to the aridity line in trying to find a correlation between climate change and conflict. This line designates areas where the average rainfall is 200 millimetres per year. Populations on the aridity line will be able to grow cereal crops without irrigation but will be at risk of drought and desertification. A map in one of Klein's articles shows how the aridity line circles the Sahara Desert and extends eastwards through the Middle East and into Afghanistan, Pakistan and the west of India. She intriguingly shows how many of the sites of Western drone strikes—taken as a proxy for conflict—including in Mali, Libya, Gaza, Yemen, Somalia, Afghanistan, Pakistan and Iraq, were on or close to the aridity line. Klein concludes: "Just as bombs follow oil, and drones follow drought, so boats follow both: boats filled with refugees fleeing homes on the aridity line ravaged by war and drought".[38]

One advantage of accounts of climate wars is that they are a corrective to the type of analysis that blames religion and ethnicity for outbreaks of violence. The Assad regime and their supporters have tried to paint the Syrian uprising as a "terrorist conspiracy".[39] By contrast, those who point to the drought as a

---

36   All figures from www.unhcr.org/uk/syria-emergency.html
37   Klein, 2016.
38   Klein, 2016. The association of conflict with arid regions seems somewhat speculative.
     The attack on Gaza in 2014, in the context of decades of Israeli occupation and Palestinian
     resistance, is one example that sits uneasily with the narrative of a climate change war
     (although water rights certainly play a role).
39   Alexander and Bouharoun, 2016.

factor in the conflict make clear that Syrians had a genuine grievance against their government's policies. It is a materialist explanation, rather than one that sees conflict as arising due to the invasion of "jihadist" ideas.

However, there are reasons to be cautious about the suggestion that conflict is bound to follow climate change. Some progressive thinkers are concerned that climate change is being "securitised" as it is adopted by militaries and linked to issues of conflict and terrorism.[40] Indeed, the US Department of Defense has taken more of an interest in climate change in recent years. Its 2014 Climate Change Adaptation Roadmap made its concerns explicit:

> The impacts of climate change may cause instability in other countries by impairing access to food and water, damaging infrastructure, spreading disease, *uprooting and displacing large numbers of people, compelling mass migration,* interrupting commercial activity, or restricting electricity availability. These developments could undermine already-fragile governments that are unable to respond effectively or challenge currently stable governments, as well as increasing competition and tension between countries vying for limited resources. These gaps in governance can create an avenue for extremist ideologies and conditions that foster terrorism.[41]

For the US military establishment, the prospect of "societal breakdown" and conflict in a warming world is a threat that calls for new strategies of counter-insurgency.[42] This continued during Donald Trump's presidency, despite his denial of climate change. As John Sinha argues, even far-right figures in the mould of Trump might switch their strategy in the future from climate denial to imposing their own solutions to climate change in the form of more walls and barbed wire.[43]

When employed by organisations such as the UN, arguments about climate refugees can be used as justification for intervention by international development bodies and non-governmental organisations (NGOs). This can obscure discussion of the often detrimental consequences of Western intervention in the first place, whether in the form of military intervention or structural adjustment policies mandated by the World Bank and International Monetary Fund.[44] In the case of Syria, Jan Selby and Mike Hulme have criticised the securitised narrative around climate refugees, arguing that trying to link climate change

40 Selby and Hulme, 2015.

41   Department of Defense, 2014, p4, quoted in Callinicos, 2019, emphasis added.

42 Malm, 2016.

43 Sinha, 2020.

44 Writing in this journal, Julie Hearn and Abdulsalam Dallal make a strong case that NGOs have also played a damaging role in the case of Syria—see Hearn and Dallal, 2019.

to conflict is "sensationalist".[45] Similarly, some argue that the term "climate migrant" is misleading or even dangerous due to its association with alarmist calls for greater migration controls and because it conceals the economic and social reasons for migration.[46]

Betsy Hartmann adds that the narrative of a security threat from climate refugees builds on problematic ideas originating with colonialism such as the "degradation narrative".[47] This assumes that people in the Global South degrade the natural environment due to their farming and herding practices, causing soil depletion and desertification in response to the pressures of a growing population, which in turn causes migration. This interpretation overlooks other potential causes of damage to the environment, including those related to agricultural reform and the influence of extractive industries. Hartmann argues that the narrative of degradation has little basis in fact. It draws on racist "fears and stereotypes of the dark-skinned, over-breeding, dangerous poor" and old arguments that environmental problems are really caused by overpopulation.[48]

In the case of Syria it is difficult to tease out the specific influence of climate change, especially as the environmental factor was a drought that took place over a long time period, rather than a sudden onset event such as a flood or storm that caused people to migrate. For authors such as Christiane Fröhlich, climate change is certainly a real concern, but its effects cannot be understood without also addressing the economic and political context, including the neoliberal and authoritarian agricultural policies of the Syrian government.[49]

It is one thing to say that climate change will lead to hardship, another to argue further that this will result in conflict. Some have argued that such an analysis grossly oversimplifies the situation by playing down the role of political factors in conflict situations.[50] Political rivalries certainly did play a role in the case of Syria. Our analysis of the roots of conflict and displacement should not absolve political forces such as the Assad regime of blame.[51]

Hartmann provides several examples from research in Africa that challenge the assumption that extreme weather might lead to conflict. For example, research in northern Kenya has shown that drought actually led to less violence among

---

45 Selby and Hulme, 2015. They doubt that 1.5 million people were displaced due to the drought in Syria and find that it was closer to 250,000.
46 Goodfellow, 2020.
47 Hartmann, 2010.
48 Hartmann, 2010, p238.
49 Fröhlich, 2016, pp40-41.
50 On Darfur, see Butler, 2007.
51 Malm, 2016.

herders rather than more. This is because herders establish their own systems to negotiate and govern access to water and are not inclined to start fights during droughts. Where conflict does occur, Hartmann concludes that this is more often due to the detrimental effects of outside intervention, it is a sign that "local resource users themselves have been made powerless and that their negotiating system has been paralysed, either by external agencies or local elites".[52]

However, Hartmann seems too dismissive of the very notion of a climate refugee. She suggests that accounts of climate refugees "depoliticise the causes of displacement" as they place the blame on an external environmental factor.[53] Yet climate change is very much a political issue. In Latin America, South Asia, Syria and many other places, people have been made vulnerable to the effects of extreme weather by neoliberal agricultural and trade policies. A more radical analysis could address how the global expansion of fossil fuel extraction that is ultimately the cause of climate change is also a feature of the same aggressive drive towards neoliberalism. Research by Lucia Pradella and Rossana Cillo on Libya has outlined how oil extraction and the system of detention and militarised borders are interlinked. From 2014, Italy's main oil and gas company, ENI (Ente Nazionale Idrocarburi), collaborated with the Al-Ammu and Brigade 48 militias in Libya in order to maintain its supplies. The resulting drain of Libya's resources led to further impoverishment within the country and there was an increase in migrants being pushed towards Europe. These authors argue that the migrants acted as a reserve army of labour that was easily exploited in an Italian agricultural industry that also benefitted from energy imports from Libya. They point to a link between poverty and environmental degradation in the Global South and in the North.[54]

Andreas Malm is more sympathetic to the argument that drought played a role in Syria. However, he cautions that temperature rise will not act as a cause of unrest in a *linear* manner. This will depend on the levels of anger and discontent already present within a society.[55] Responses to climate change might also involve people revolting against those at the top of society or even the kind of revolutionary upheavals seen in Syria. The degree of political organisation our side can draw on will undoubtedly play a role in determining these outcomes. The possibility of revolution has been little understood in much of the mainstream discussion of this topic. For instance, Selby and Hulme state that, in the case of rural to urban migrants in Syria, there is "no evidence that any of the early unrest was directed

52 Witsenburg and Roba, 2007, quoted in Hartmann, 2010, p237.
53 Hartmann, 2010, p236.
54 Pradella and Cillo, in press.
55 Malm, 2016.

against these migrants".[56] But why should there have been? The Syrian civil war began as a revolution that, at least temporarily, united migrants from rural areas and urban dwellers against their government. Selby and Hulme seem to assume that it was a case of stressed poor people attacking each other.

There is strong evidence that climate change will lead to more extreme weather events and more movements of people. However, we should also accept that it is not inevitable that events such as droughts will be followed by conflict and consequently by flights of refugees. This downplays people's own agency in coping with and adapting to the ecological circumstances in which they find themselves.

Climate justice and solidarity

Climate refugees are already being discussed as part of a growing movement around climate change. In recent years increasingly alarming reports about the extent and rapidity of climate and ecological breakdown have been met with mass, radical protest. In late September 2019 an estimated 7 million people around the world took part in some form of climate protest after the global movement of school strikers inspired by Greta Thunberg called for adults to walk out of work in solidarity.[57] In Britain, this was almost certainly the biggest ever protest over the issue of climate change by working class people, organised in their unions as workers. It is a global movement. School strikes took place in 161 countries, with big protests in India, the Philippines, South Africa, Kenya, Brazil, Mexico, Australia, the US and many other places.[58]

Having declared a state of emergency in autumn 2018, Extinction Rebellion (XR) has embarked on a mass campaign of civil disobedience, blocking streets in Central London in two huge rebellions as well as organising numerous other actions around Britain and elsewhere. XR has been incredibly impressive and successful in mobilising people scared and angry about our government's lack of action on climate change (and ecology more broadly) and in putting these issues on the media agenda. Alex Callinicos is right to say that there is a need for humility when socialists engage with this movement.[59]

However, more than two years on, there are intense debates within the movement, many of which concern issues of race and social justice. In 2019, a high-profile open letter to XR made several criticisms of the group, including that,

---

56 Selby and Hulme, 2015.
57 Marches took place on either 20 September or 27 September, depending on local arrangements.
58 *Socialist Worker*, 2019.
59 Callinicos, 2019.

by encouraging activists to get arrested as a central tactic, XR lacked awareness of black people's experiences of police violence. The letter made the key point that the rhetoric of much of the environmental movement assumes that ecological breakdown is a looming threat that will happen in the future. For many people, especially in the Global South, ecological violence is already a present day reality.[60]

The founders of XR in the UK set out to make the organisation as broad as possible. Although they are not resistant to talking about social justice as such, they also wanted to make the group appealing to conservatives in an effort to recruit from beyond the left and those already involved in political activism.[61] According to their line of reasoning, the struggle against climate change will be so monumental that it will need a movement on an unprecedented scale, and therefore it should include as many people as possible—XR has sometimes talked in terms of 3.5 percent of the population being needed to make the necessary change. Some therefore suggest that talking about race might alienate those with more conservative views. XR founder Roger Hallam has said that "identity politics" has significant drawbacks, in that "it can't appeal to everyone".[62]

In the US, XR has split over such issues. Although XR US had the need to prioritise "black people, indigenous people, people of color and poor communities" embedded within its demands, a group called XR America split away from XR US, removed this demand and replaced it with wording that talked about "one people, one planet, one future".[63] According to XR America founder Jonathan Logan, climate change is just too urgent to take on social justice demands:

> If we don't solve climate change, black lives don't matter. If we don't solve climate change now, LGBT+ people don't matter. If we don't solve climate change right now, all of us together in one big group, the #MeToo movement doesn't matter... I can't say it hard enough. We don't have time to argue about social justice.[64]

Prominent XR member Rupert Read has written in the past that environmentalists should be in favour of halting mass immigration and that this would put us on the side of "working-class Britons".[65] However, aside from the obvious point that plenty of working class British people are from migrant backgrounds, this assumes that people's ideas are static. Experience shows that people's ideas change, especially when they are engaged with others in mass movements. Read's

60 Wretched of the Earth, 2019.

61 Taylor, 2020.

62 See Roger Hallam's comments in Dembicki, 2020.

63 Dembicki, 2020.

64 Quoted in Dembicki, 2020. This quote is from before the dramatic recent re-emergence of Black Lives Matter protests in the US.

65 Read, 2014.

position also ignores research that suggests that people from black and ethnic minority backgrounds are more likely to be concerned about environmental issues than white people.[66] Playing down discussions of race in order to appeal to an (imagined) white conservative milieu ignores a big potential audience among people who are being drawn into political activity by their anger about racism.

The other reason to build an internationalist and anti-racist movement is that it is the best way to fight climate change. As Klein has argued, the "othering" or dehumanisation of many of the people most affected is, in part, what has allowed climate change to go on for so long in the first place. Environmental racism has allowed governments in the Global North to downplay the effect of their inaction and to treat parts of the world such as the Niger Delta as sacrifice zones for the extraction of fossil fuels. Klein talks about the Global South but also mentions rural poverty in the US, referring to the neglect of communities affected by mountain-top removal coal mining: "If you are a 'hillbilly', who cares about your hills?"[67]

However, it should be emphasised that environmentalists who want to limit discussions of social justice are in the minority, both in the US and Britain. There are ongoing discussions in XR groups across Britain about adopting a "fourth demand" in order to make climate justice a more explicit part of what the group stands for (the existing three demands of XR are "tell the truth", "act now" and "beyond politics"). A recent online poll of XR supporters found that 77 percent of respondents were in favour of a fourth demand, with 60 percent strongly in favour. Rather than seeing these demands as unattractive, more people than not thought that such a demand would be popular with the public and most said that it would make them more contented to continue to be involved with XR.[68]

Debates about climate justice are refracted and magnified in discussions of climate refugees. It is tempting for those who say we do not have time to talk about social justice to also treat climate-related migration as a problem that must be solved by first addressing climate change. For others, discussions about migration are a distraction from these efforts. According to Read, one of the most effective and humane ways to limit migration is to tackle climate change, therefore removing a push factor that causes people to move.[69] From a more sympathetic perspective,

---

66 Dembicki, 2020.

67 Klein, 2016.

68 The poll was initiated by Global Justice Rebellion and shared on their Facebook page on 2 July 2020. Go to https://bit.ly/34HwxDF

69 Read, 2014.

but with an argument that leads in the same direction, Lauren Markham argues in *The Guardian* that:

> Migration is a natural human phenomenon and, many argue, should be a fundamental right, but forced migration—being run out of home against one's will and with threat to one's life—is not natural at all... If we want people to be able to stay in their homes, we have to tackle the issue of our changing global climate, and we have to do it fast.[70]

Few would argue in favour of people being forced from their homes. However, tackling climate change cannot be the end of the discussion on climate refugees. This again treats climate change as a calamity that will face us in the future. It ignores the role of colonial policies of the past and neoliberal capitalism in creating the conditions for both climate change and migration. As this article has shown, extreme weather is already displacing millions of people. Moreover, states around the world are already erecting borders and trying to prevent people from fleeing ecological breakdown that those selfsame states have played a role in causing.

Socialists need, therefore, to have a view on climate refugees. We should put anti-racist arguments against borders and controls on migration. Borders have not always existed but arose with the modern state and the colonial carve up of the world in the 19th and 20th centuries (including in Syria). They cause immediate suffering to those trying to cross them. As Klein puts it: "The same capacity for dehumanising the other that justified the bombs and drones is now being trained on these migrants, casting their need for security as a threat to ours, their desperate flight some sort of invading army".[71] National borders also foster racism, creating a division between those who are included within the nation-state and those derided as aliens or outsiders. This divides people against each other and ultimately serves the interests of capitalists in exploiting and oppressing ordinary people.[72] Socialists should try to convince others of these arguments, including those who see nation-states and borders as necessary or inevitable. It is hardly surprising that people think this way; in Britain all the mainstream political parties and most of the media argue for some kind of controls on migration. However, if any of the predictions of the numbers of climate refugees are accurate it will become more and more difficult to justify controls on migration in the decades to come. Bringing anti-racist ideas into the environmental movement provides an

---

70 Markham, 2019.

71 Klein, 2016. One of the demands in the Wretched of the Earth's open letter is also for an end to the hostile environment.

72 Marfleet, 2016.

opportunity to discuss these ideas with a newly radicalised group of people who have been drawn into the climate movement.

We can also put arguments about migration that acknowledge the agency of the refugees and migrants themselves. We can point to the many examples of the contributions migrants and refugees make in the societies that they move to as well as the positive role that migration can play in the lives of migrants themselves. In Britain, migrants have staffed public services, including the NHS. They have organised in some key trade union struggles, from the strikes of Asian workers in the 1970s to the fight for decent pay for cleaners in more recent times. They have sometimes brought militant traditions with them. Refugees from Syria who were part of the revolution have been part of anti-racist protests in Greece, for example.[73]

Our solidarity with refugees should not be conditional on them "making a contribution". All migrants and refugees should be welcome as a point of principle. Nevertheless, it is important to point to some positive examples of migrants playing an active role in working class movements. This is because there is a tendency for some environmentalists to treat the displacement of refugees as just another addition to the long list of terrible things that will happen if we do not address climate change. It is almost as if the "threat" of refugees is being used to try to force our governments to act on climate change. This is why Minnie Rahman of the Joint Council for the Welfare of Immigrants says that "the way forward is to ensure that any organising around climate migration has to be done in a way that does not treat movement as a threat".[74] The securitisation discourse described above likewise treats refugees as a potential danger for national security. On this point Selby and Hulme are right to say that there are strong enough reasons for acting on climate change already without trying to turn it into a security issue.[75]

Some participants in discussions around climate refugees have been tempted to use metaphors of natural disasters to refer to the refugees themselves, for instance, referring to "waves" or "floods" of people. Anti-racists should avoid such dehumanising language.[76]

A legal status for climate refugees?

Where people cross borders in an attempt to escape disasters, they will not be recognised as refugees by international law.[77] The 1951 Refugee Convention states

---

73 Constantinou, 2016.
74 Goodfellow, 2020.
75 Selby and Hulme, 2015.
76 Markham, 2019.
77 Benko, 2017.

that a refugee is someone who, due to a "a well-founded fear of being persecuted for reasons of race, religion, nationality, membership of a particular social group, or political opinion, is outside the country of his nationality, and is unable to or, owing to such fear, is unwilling to avail himself of the protection of that country". Written in the aftermath of the Second World War, this convention was shaped by the Cold War agenda and intended to attract defectors from the Soviet bloc towards the West. By defining refugees solely in terms of persecution, it has always excluded people moving due to ecological degeneration, economic collapse or the effects of new infrastructure such as mineral extraction, dams or plantations.[78] Although people who move within a state do receive some support from the UN High Commissioner for Refugees (UNHCR), they are not legally defined as refugees.

So, should the definition of a refugee be expanded? There are arguments from migrant and refugee advocates on both sides. Michael Doyle of Columbia University points out that people escaping the effects of climate change are migrating against their will. They are just as much "forcibly displaced" as those escaping persecution:

> If your farm has been dried to a crisp or your home has been inundated with water and you're fleeing for your life, you're not much different from any other refugee... The problem is that other refugees fleeing war qualify for that status, while you don't.[79]

Avidan Kent and Simon Behrman further argue that climate refugees are faced with structural violence in the form of climate change, which might cause suffering comparable to the interpersonal violence feared by those escaping persecution.[80]

However, some point out that the reasons for leaving somewhere are complex and interrelated, and so it will be very difficult for people to prove in practice that climate change was a factor and therefore attain the status of a climate refugee. Richer countries are, unsurprisingly, unwilling to extend the definition of a refugee and the UNHCR is also resistant to the idea because it is already stretched and lacks the financial resources to cope with the huge rise in refugee numbers that would potentially result.[81]

The UN also points out that people fleeing from the effects of climate change will often stay within the same country. If drought, tropical storms and sea level rise cause more people to leave their homes in the coming decades, we

78 Thanks to Phil Marfleet for this point.
79 Quoted in Markham, 2019.
80 Kent and Behrman, 2018, p56.
81 Brown, 2008, pp13-15.

might expect to see more people moving from rural to urban areas within the same country, or leaving coastal areas to head inland.[82] Farmers in rural Nigeria affected by drought, for example, might lack the means or the inclination to travel to Europe, but may be able to move to a town or city. In many cases the poorest people will be "trapped" without the resources to migrate to another country, even if they want to.[83] In this respect they differ from those escaping political persecution who may need to cross borders and cannot turn to their own state for support.

However, it is worth remembering that the vast majority of people who are displaced—for any reason—tend to move within a state (58 percent of forcibly displaced people) or to travel to a neighbouring state (a further 80 percent), so the existing legal protection is already inadequate. At present, the three countries that host the most refugees are Turkey, Pakistan and Uganda. With the exception of Germany, all of the world's top eight refugee hosting countries share a border with a country of refugee origin.[84] There has never been a huge exodus of people heading from the South to the North—at least not yet. If climate change makes large parts of the globe completely uninhabitable then there is likely to be a rerouting of global flows of refugees. However, even then this is unlikely to be a straightforward case of people leaving the Global South and heading to the Global North en masse.[85]

An end to controls on migration in their entirety would make debates about the legal distinction between refugees and migrants irrelevant. There would no longer be any need to justify moving from one part of the world to another. It could be accepted that everyone who moves does so for a number of reasons, including reasons to leave one place and the attractions of another. Kent and Behrman make this argument in their book on the legal aspects of climate and migration. However, they also make a compelling argument that, in the here and now, people crossing borders due to climate change should be defined as refugees. At least then their legal status would qualify them for more protection. In response to those who argue that talk of climate refugees deflects attention from solving climate change in the first place, these authors point out that the term "climate refugees" is actually more political than other terms such as "climate-induced migration". Using the term "refugee" implies that someone is to blame, in this case the fossil fuel industry and the states that back it.[86]

---

82 Internal Displacement Monitoring Centre, 2019.
83 Brown, 2008, p22. Kent and Behrman, 2018, pp4-5.
84 Go to www.unhcr.org/uk/figures-at-a-glance.html
85 Brown, 2008, p9.
86 Kent and Behrman, 2018, pp44-59. These authors point out that the definition of a refugee has in practice been extended to include other types of forced migrants not included in the 1951

Conclusion

In a welcome development, there have been some initial attempts to bring together anti-racist and environmental struggles over the past few years. The Campaign against Climate Change (CaCC) held a one-day conference in February 2017 with speakers from trade unions as well as anti-racist and environmental organisations.[87] As part of XR's first rebellion event in spring 2019, Stand up to Racism (SUTR), organised a rally with trade union banners and anti-racist speeches and some XR groups have incorporated an inflatable boat at their events in order to symbolise the issue of climate refugees. CaCC and others supported SUTR's annual march in 2020 in order to make a clear link between climate change and refugees (although the demonstration unfortunately had to be turned into an online event due to the Covid-19 pandemic). A group called Global Justice Bloc (formerly Global Justice Rebellion) played a significant role during the 2019 and 2020 XR rebellions. In September 2020 they led a march from Parliament Square, where XR supporters had gathered, to the Home Office with the slogan "Climate Justice is Migrant Justice". Protestors sat down and blocked the road and heard from a range of speakers on different aspects of climate justice. The group describes itself as anti-capitalist as well as anti-racist and anti-imperialist.[88] Activists from the Global South have spoken out at climate events including a group of African women refugees at XR's blockade of the BBC in December 2018, and an Ecuadorean striker from the PCS civil service union spoke on a picket line at the Department for Business, Energy and Industrial Strategy on 20 September 2019. The SUTR banner and placards and demands to welcome climate refugees have also been a regular and popular feature on school climate strikes. There are undoubtedly other examples like this. These modest initiatives show that there is much potential to link anti-racist arguments around refugees with the broader demands of the climate movement.

This article has argued that the world is already seeing the effects of climate and ecological breakdown in the form of disasters such as floods, fires and hurricanes. We know that these will lead to displacements of people—they already do—and they are likely to get worse in future. However, the effects of any disaster will be shaped by the social, political and economic context in which it happens. As Neale concludes in his discussion of Darfur, the tragedy was not a "*simple* climate change disaster", but a process that must be seen in the context of competition rooted in the capitalist drive for profit on a global scale.[89]

---

convention and so it could in principle be further extended.

87　See www.cacctu.org.uk/climaterefugees

88　See www.facebook.com/GlobalJusticeBloc

89　Neale, 2008, p233.

The root cause of climate change is a global system based on profit. People are already feeling the catastrophic effects, and the worst affected tend to be the least responsible. However, this article has tried to put an account of climate refugees that recognises the agency of refugees themselves, rather than taking a liberal view that treats them as either passive victims or objects of charity. Climate change is a problem to be solved; people moving from one part of the world to another is not.

References

Alexander, Anne, 2016, "ISIS, Imperialism and the War in Syria", *International Socialism* 149 (winter), http://isj.org.uk/isis-imperialism-and-the-war-in-syria

Alexander, Anne, and Jad Bouharoun, 2016, *Syria: Revolution, Counter-revolution and War* (Socialist Worker).

Associated Press, 2020, "Jakarta Floods: Recovery Effort Begins as City Counts Cost of Worst Deluge in a Decade", *Guardian* (6 January), https://bit.ly/35M9YOC

Ban Ki-Moon, 2007, "A Climate Culprit in Darfur", *Washington Post* (16 June), https://wapo.st/3lMwCvW

Benko, Jessica, 2017, "How a Warming Planet Drives Human Migration", *New York Times* (19 April), https://nyti.ms/2K7jzan

Berlemann, Michael, and Max Friedrich Steinhardt, 2017, "Climate Change, Natural Disasters, and Migration—A Survey of the Empirical Evidence", *CESifo Economic Studies*, volume 63, issue 4.

Brown, Oli, 2008, "Migration and Climate Change", IOM Migration Research Series, no. 31, International Organization for Migration (15 February), www.iom.int/news/iom-migration-research-series-no-31-migration-and-climate-change

Butler, Declan, 2007, "Darfur's Climate Roots Challenged", *Nature*, issue 447.

Callinicos, 2019, "Betting on Infinite Loss", *International Socialism* 163 (summer), http://isj.org.uk/betting-on-infinite-loss

Choonara, Joseph, 2020, "Socialism in a Time of Pandemics", *International Socialism* 166 (spring), http://isj.org.uk/socialism-in-a-time-of-pandemics

Constantinou, Petros, 2016, "Anti-racists Will March in 17 Countries on Saturday: Greece Will See Eight Demos", *Socialist Worker* (15 March), https://socialistworker.co.uk/art/42362/Anti+racists+will+march+in+17+countries+on+Saturday%3A+Greece+will+see+eight+demos

Dembicki, Geoff, 2020, "A Debate Over Racism Has Split One of the World's Most Famous Climate Groups", Vice (28 April), www.vice.com/en_us/article/jgey8k/a-debate-over-racism-has-split-one-of-the-worlds-most-famous-climate-groups

Department of Defense, 2014, "FY 2014 Climate Change Adaptation Roadmap" (June), www.acq.osd.mil/eie/downloads/CCARprint_wForward_e.pdf

Friedlander, Blaine, 2017, "Rising Seas Could Result in 2 Billion Refugees by 2100", *Cornell Chronicle* (19 June), https://news.cornell.edu/stories/2017/06/rising-seas-could-result-2-billion-refugees-2100

Fröhlich, Christiane J, 2016, "Climate migrants as protestors? Dispelling Misconceptions about Global Environmental Change in Pre-revolutionary Syria", *Contemporary Levant*, volume 1, issue 1.

Goodfellow, Maya, "How Helpful is the Term 'Climate Refugee'?", Guardian (31 August), www.theguardian.com/world/2020/aug/31/how-helpful-is-the-term-climate-refugee

Hartmann, Betsy, 2010, "Rethinking Climate Refugees and Climate Conflict: Rhetoric, Reality and the Politics of Policy Discourse", *Journal of International Development*, volume 22, issue 2.

Hearn, Julie, and Abdulsalam Dallal, 2019, "The 'NGOisation' of the Syrian Revolution", *International Socialism* 164 (autumn), http://isj.org.uk/the-ngoisation-of-the-syrian-revolution

Internal Displacement Monitoring Centre, 2019, "Global Report on Internal Displacement" (May), www.internal-displacement.org/sites/default/files/publications/documents/2019-IDMC-GRID.pdf

Internal Displacement Monitoring Centre, 2020, "Global Report on Internal Displacement" (April), www.internal-displacement.org/sites/default/files/publications/documents/2020-IDMC-GRID.pdf

Ives, Mike, 2016, "A Remote Pacific Nation, Threatened by Rising Seas", *New York Times* (3 July), www.nytimes.com/2016/07/03/world/asia/climate-change-kiribati.html

KEERFA, 2020, "Statement from Greek Anti-racists: Protect Refugees from Coronavirus", Marx21 (14 March), https://marx21us.org/2020/03/14/statement-greek-anti-racists-coronavirus

Kent, Avidan, and Simon Behrman, 2018, *Facilitating the Resettlement and Rights of Climate Refugees: An Argument for Developing Existing Principles and Practices* (Routledge).

Klein, Naomi, 2016, "Let them Drown: The Violence of Othering in a Warming World", *London Review of Books*, volume 38, number 11, www.lrb.co.uk/the-paper/v38/n11/naomi-klein/let-them-drown

Malm, Andreas, 2016, "Revolution in a Warming World: Lessons from the Russian to the Syrian Revolutions", *Socialist Register 2017: Rethinking Revolution*, https://climateandcapitalism.com/2018/03/17/malm-revolutionary-strategy

Marfleet, Phil, 2016, "States of Exclusion", *Socialist Review* (November), https://socialistreview.org.uk/418/states-exclusion

Markham, Lauren, 2019, "How climate change is pushing Central American migrants to the US", *Guardian* (6 April), https://bit.ly/3lOmfrn

Marx, Karl, 1976 [1867], *Capital*, volume 1 (Penguin).

Maunder, Jonathan, 2012, "The Syrian Crucible", *International Socialism* 135 (summer), http://isj.org.uk/the-syrian-crucible

Milman, Oliver, Emily Holden and David Agren, 2018, "The Unseen Driver behind the Migrant Caravan: Climate Change", *Guardian* (30 October), www.theguardian.com/world/2018/oct/30/migrant-caravan-causes-climate-change-central-america

Mustafa, Daanish, 2009, "Natural Hazards", in Noel Castree, David Demeritt, Diana Liverman and Bruce Rhoads (eds), *A Companion to Environmental Geography* (Blackwell Publishing).

Naisse, Ghayath, 2016, "Interview: Lessons of the Syrian Revolution", *International Socialism* 153 (winter), http://isj.org.uk/interview-lessons-of-the-syrian-revolution

Neale, Jonathan, 2008, *Stop Global Warming: Change the World* (Bookmarks).

Neale, Jonathan, 2010, "Climate Politics After Copenhagen", *International Socialism* 126 (spring), http://isj.org.uk/climate-politics-after-copenhagen

Newsinger, John, 2006, *The Blood Never Dried: A People's History of the British Empire* (Bookmarks).

Pelling, Mark, 2001, "Natural Disasters?", in Noel Castree and Bruce Braun (eds), *Social Nature: Theory, Practice and Politics* (Blackwell).

Pradella, Lucia and Rossana Cillo, in press, "Bordering the Surplus Population across the Mediterranean: Imperialism and Unfree Labour in Libya and the Italian Countryside", *Geoforum*.

Read, Rupert, 2014, "Love Immigrants, Rather Than Large-scale Immigration", *Ecologist* (19 June).

Save the Children, 2019, "Northern Syria Flooding: Thousands of Children at Risk of Further Displacement" (20 December), www.savethechildren.net/news/northern-syria-flooding-thousands-children-risk-further-displacement

Selby, Jan, and Mike Hulme, 2015, "Is Climate Change Really to Blame for Syria's Civil War?", *Guardian* (29 November), www.theguardian.com/commentisfree/2015/nov/29/climate-change-syria-civil-war-prince-charles

Sinha, John, 2020, "Notes on the Climate Crisis: Racism", *Socialist Review* (March), http://socialistreview.org.uk/455/notes-climate-crisis-racism

Socialist Worker, 2019, "Millions Join Worldwide Protests to Save Planet" (24 September), https://socialistworker.co.uk/art/48974/Millions+join+worldwide+protests+to+save+planet

Taylor, Matthew, 2020, "The Long Read: The Evolution of Extinction Rebellion", *Guardian* (4 August), www.theguardian.com/environment/2020/aug/04/evolution-of-extinction-rebellion-climate-emergency-protest-coronavirus-pandemic

United Nations, 2018, "Report of the United Nations High Commissioner for Refugees: Part II, Global Compact on Refugees" (13 September), https://bit.ly/36Sp3NU

Varagur, Krithika, 2020, "Death Toll Rises in Indonesia's Sinking Capital as Flood Defences Struggle", *Guardian* (4 January), https://bit.ly/37rrnvJ

Weisbrot, Mark, 2014, "NAFTA: 20 Years of Regret for Mexico", *Guardian* (4 January), https://bit.ly/37rrl75

Witsenburg, Karen, and Adano Wario Roba, 2007, "The Use and Management of Water Sources in Kenya's Drylands: Is There a Link Between Scarcity and Violent Conflicts?", in Bill Derman, Rie Odgaard and Espen Sjaastad (eds), *Conflicts Over Land and Water in Africa* (Currey).

Wretched of the Earth, 2019, "An Open Letter to Extinction Rebellion", *Red Pepper* (3 May), www.redpepper.org.uk/an-open-letter-to-extinction-rebellion

Anti-fascism in Greece: how we smashed Golden Dawn
Petros Constantinou

On 7 October 2020, following a trial lasting more than five years, a Greek court found the leaders of Golden Dawn guilty of forming and running a criminal organisation. Heralded as the biggest trial of Nazis since the post-war Nuremberg tribunals, in total 68 members of Golden Dawn faced prosecution. Seven former Golden Dawn MPs, including party leader Nikos Michaloliakos, were convicted of leading a criminal organisation. Others were convicted of participating in it.

Further guilty verdicts were given for the murder of the anti-fascist rapper Pavlos Fyssas by Golden Dawn members in September 2013, the attempted murder of Abouzid Embarak and three other Egyptian fishermen in June 2012, and a brutal attack on Communist Party trade unionists just days before the murder of Fyssas.

The outcome of the trial was a final devastating blow to Golden Dawn. In 2012, amid the huge economic and political crisis that gripped Greece after the global financial crash of 2008-9, Golden Dawn had made a dramatic electoral breakthrough in the two general elections of May and June 2012, winning 7 percent of the vote and 18 MPs. Yet by the 2019 general election Golden Dawn fell below the 3 percent threshold required to enter parliament, resulting in the loss of all its MPs.

However, even as the long history of complicity between the Greek state, the ruling conservative party New Democracy and Golden Dawn was being exposed, it was argued that the crushing of the fascists was a demonstration of the robustness *of liberal democratic institutions. Mainstream political forces were celebrated for having seen off "extremists".*

The real story was very different. It was a mass anti-fascist movement that broke Golden Dawn. This movement was increasingly able to isolate Golden Dawn, driving it out of the public arena and thus denying it the opportunity to present a "respectable" face in the wake of its election breakthrough. Simultaneously, the anti-fascist movement placed huge pressure on New Democracy and the state to distance themselves from the Nazis and to launch a legal crackdown.

At the centre of the anti-fascist movement was the organisation Keerfa (United Movement Against Racism and the Fascist Threat). Petros Constantinou is coordinator for Keerfa and a member of the Greek Socialist Workers Party (SEK). Petros spoke to Mark L Thomas about the danger that Golden Dawn represented, Keerfa's strategy and the lessons for the international fight against the far right.

MT: In the 1980s and 1990s we saw the growth of the fascists in France with Jean-Marie Le Pen's Front National, the gains by the British National Party in Britain, the rise of the Freedom Party in Austria and so on. But there was an argument that Greece was immune to fascism due to its experiences of the Nazi occupation during the Second World War, the civil war between right and left that followed in the late 1940s, and the military dictatorship of 1967-74. This complacent view was destroyed by the dramatic breakthrough of Golden Dawn in the elections of 2012. What were the economic and political conditions that allowed this development?

PC: To understand what happened in 2012, you have to recognise that the fascist threat existed long before that. The Nazis were there from the 1990s in Greece as a very small group on the margin of politics that organised physical attacks. However, with the start of the economic crisis in 2007-8, we saw the Greek government and also the European Union scapegoating migrants and refugees, and implementing the European Pact for Asylum and Migration. This opened the space for far-right populist parties and the neo-Nazis of Golden Dawn to try to push the political scene to the right. In this period, before the rise of Golden Dawn, we had an Islamophobic, far-right populist party LAOS (Λαϊκός Ορθόδοξος Συναγερμός, "Popular Orthodox Rally") entering parliament.[1] In fact, when Keerfa was launched in 2009 it was because of the rise of LAOS. LAOS tried to build committees of "citizens" against refugees and migrants. Golden Dawn was also there, involving itself in attacks on refugees and migrants.

---

1   LAOS took 3.8 percent of the vote in the 2007 general election, gaining 10 MPs. Two years later it increased this to 5.6 percent and 15 MPs.

Table 1: Golden Dawn general election results

Year	Votes	Percentage	MPs	Position
1996	4,537	0.1	0	14th
2009	19,636	0.3	0	10th
May 2012	440,966	7.0	21	6th
June 2012	426,025	6.9	18	5th
Jan 2015	388,387	6.3	17	3rd
Sept 2015	379,581	7.0	18	3rd
2019	165,709	2.9	0	7th

In 2010, we saw the introduction of austerity in Greece with the so-called Memorandum imposed by the European Union and the International Monetary Fund. The working class responded to these attacks with a series of general strikes. At the same time there was the start of a process of political crisis. In 2011, the neoliberal conservative party, New Democracy, and the social democratic party, PASOK, formed a coalition government, which LAOS also joined, to push through the Memorandum.

This was the moment when the scale of social polarisation and the use of racism by the government really opened a space for Golden Dawn. With LAOS compromised by its participation in the austerity government, the Nazis seized the chance to try to present themselves as the real opposition.

Golden Dawn sought to further radicalise existing racism by forming attack squads in parts of Athens. Of course, without the support of the police it would have been impossible for them to control even the first area in which they tried to build a base, the Athens neighbourhood of Agios Panteleimonas. Here, they were able to construct a first joint committee with LAOS members, trying to attract support from the local population to kick out foreigners.

But these developments took place in a general political situation that was shifting to the left. There was an escalation of workers' resistance with hundreds of thousands, perhaps millions, striking and demonstrating. We saw the collapse of the traditional parties, both New Democracy and PASOK. In 2009, these two parties together won nearly 80 percent of the vote; in the elections of 2012, they won just 42 percent.

The left-wing Syriza party benefited from this. It won under 5 percent of the vote in 2009, but this jumped to almost 27 percent in June 2012. So what was taking place was a shift to the left, not to the right. However, there was also deep polarisation, and this meant that Golden Dawn was also able to enter parliament. The deepening economic crisis, the collapse of the traditional ruling parties and the government's utilisation of racism opened the doors for the Nazis.

In 2012 a massive police operation was launched under the guise of checks on people's immigration status. The state called this "Operation Xenios Zeus"; this was something of a euphemism as "Xenios" means hospitality and welcoming strangers, not attacking them with thousands of police. Over 100,000 people were strip searched and 6,000 ended up in an infamous detention centre. This whole process paved the way for a wave of pogroms and racist attacks, as well as the murders of Shahzad Luqman in January 2013 and Pavlos Fyssas in September 2013.

The electoral success of Golden Dawn was an escalation of the fascist threat in Greece. Having won parliamentary representation, Golden Dawn began to receive money from the state, and they used this to build across Greece, opening more than 50 local offices in different cities. They used these as bases to organise their attacks and campaigns of hatred against refugees.

Golden Dawn demanded that no children of refugees could attend municipal kindergarten; they demanded that local mayors give them the names of these children so that they could expel them from the kindergartens. They also tried to build a campaign around the slogan "Blood Only for Greeks"; groups of Nazis went into hospitals and made blood donations, then demanded that these only go to Greek patients. Of course, they were kicked out of those hospitals.

They also launched a campaign to hand out free food "only for Greeks", focusing on the centre of Athens, and launched physical attacks, burning mosques and smashing up migrant-owned shops.

MT: If we look around Europe, many of the fascist parties that have made breakthroughs—the Front National (now Rassemblement National) in France and the Freedom Party in Austria, for example—are predominantly electoral organisations and try to appear respectable. Their efforts to build a paramilitary wing have been much more limited. So one of the dangers presented by Golden Dawn was that they were a paramilitary Nazi organisation that made a major electoral breakthrough—as Hitler and the Nazis did in the 1930s. And as you have brought out, Golden Dawn's electoral success doesn't mean they dropped their paramilitary orientation—instead, they sought to use gains at the ballot box to reinforce and deepen it. Unchecked, this could have meant Golden Dawn becoming a beacon internationally, encouraging a hardening up of other fascist currents and showing that you can use votes to build up street thugs and street thugs to build up votes. Can you say more about Golden Dawn's strategy? How did it present itself? What was the message it promoted to try to attract support?

PC: They mainly presented themselves as Greek nationalists opposed to the transformation of the country into a debt colony for German bankers. They also used a lot of antisemitic rhetoric, attacking the left as agents of George Soros and NGOs, who they blamed for an "invasion" of Greece by migrants. This racism was combined with attacks on the "Islamisation" of Greece—their slogan was "Athens is becoming Kabul". They attacked the political forces they held to have betrayed Greece by opening the borders to refugees and Muslims, and they attacked the left, claiming that strikes were destroying the economy and so on.

So the main way they tried to build their forces was through racism and Islamophobia. The use of paramilitary squads was targeted mainly at migrants and refugees but also, of course, the left. Their local offices were bases for these paramilitary forces. Take the example of Nikaia, in the Piraeus area.[2] This is where the Golden Dawn squad that murdered Pavlos Fyssas came from. It had assembled with 20 motorbikes at the local Golden Dawn offices before heading off to kill him.

They used these local offices to build up their paramilitary forces—and did so right in front of the police's eyes. The relationship between Golden Dawn and the police was a scandal. The police continually covered for their actions. It was impossible for a migrant to go a police station and say, "I want to sue the person who stabbed me." The police would simply throw them out. They even attacked migrants' lawyers outside police stations. Police were present at many Golden Dawn attacks but did nothing to stop them. Police were there during the murder of Pavlos Fyssas, and he was killed right in front of their eyes. So they were protecting Golden Dawn.

Also, there were relationships between the New Democracy government and Golden Dawn.[3] The secretary of New Democracy's parliamentary group had discussions with Ilias Kasidiaris, Golden Dawn's spokesperson at the time. New Democracy wanted the support of Golden Dawn for its legislative proposals in parliament. So when New Democracy claims today that it is part of the anti-fascists' victory, it is a joke. After the murder of Pavlos Fyssas and the final crackdown on the Nazis, the Minister of Public Order said he was

---

2 Piraeus is a major port on the edge of Athens.
3 Following the 2012 elections, New Democracy formed a government led by Antonis Samaras.

sending 32 cases regarding Golden Dawn to the prosecutor. Each case involved a violent attack by Golden Dawn, but they had sat on these for years and not sent them for prosecution. One part of the Greek ruling class in a period of crisis opened the space for Golden Dawn. They gave them money, they gave them the space to attack the trade unions, especially in the shipyard area where Communist party trade unionists were attacked.

MT: Shipyard bosses were involved in giving direct support and money to them?

PC: Yes, and so were some of the publishers. You saw stories in the media about how philanthropic Golden Dawn were. There was a famous photo in the media of an elderly woman taking money from a cashpoint while being escorted by a member of Golden Dawn who claimed that he was protecting her from migrants who wanted to steal her pension. In fact, the woman was the mother of the Golden Dawn member and it was all staged.

MT: Which sections of Greek society did Golden Dawn draw its votes and support from in 2012 and after?

PC: Politically, the vote for Golden Dawn came from traditional right voters. Golden Dawn inherited the votes of LAOS, whose support collapsed after they participated in government. So this was a large part of Golden Dawn's vote. Another part of Golden Dawn's vote came from New Democracy. I would say that they took only a small percentage of support from PASOK. On a social level, of course, parts of the petty bourgeoisie were destroyed, such as small shop owners in the central Athens, and some of these turned to Golden Dawn. And part of the state machinery voted for them—the military, the police and the police's special forces all voted in separate centres, and so we know that Golden Dawn got 55 or 60 percent of their votes.

MT: So this was a radicalisation of part of the right-wing electorate?

PC: Yes, but Golden Dawn was also getting votes in working-class neighbour-hoods in Athens and Piraeus, and this was dangerous. Not higher than the average, but still this was a significant political challenge for the left.

MT: So Golden Dawn threatened to get a foothold in working-class communities?

PC: They were trying to break out of central Athens and into places like Nikaia and Perama. This was the rise of the fascist threat to trade unions, I would say. Their strategy was to establish themselves as a political party, preserving the paramilitary branch, and to present themselves as the protectors of Greeks against migrants. In 2012-13 they tried to build a stronger Nazi party. They were already the third biggest party after New Democracy and Syriza. Before the murder of Pavlos Fyssas, they thought they could rise to 20 percent in elections, and leap over the rest of the right. The resistance was crucial in stopping this from happening. Workers' resistance to austerity was not enough. We also needed a specifically anti-fascist struggle.

MT: There has been an attempt to portray Golden Dawn's defeat as a vindication of the mainstream centre against the "extremists". This narrative hides the complicity of New Democracy and the state, but it also erases the key role of the mass anti-fascist movement that targeted the Nazis and ultimately broke them. Could you talk about the dynamic of that movement, and about the role of Keerfa and its strategy of building a united front that targeted the fascists?

PC: This claim that anti-fascism is part of the DNA of liberal democracy is ridiculous. In reality it was the Greek courts that gave Golden Dawn the right to participate in elections. Golden Dawn was not some unknown group. In 2005, for example, the party had to suspend its activities in order to avoid prosecution after they shot at demonstrators from the balcony of their offices. During a trial in 1998 of Golden Dawn members who had physically attacked Socialist Workers Party (SEK) members two years' earlier, a student activist was assualted and put into a coma for two months. Those responsible for that attack were sentenced to prison for many years, and there was a decision by Greek courts to condemn Golden Dawn as a gang. Amazingly, the leader of this attack escaped being captured by the police and eluded prison for years. So the political system knew very well that Golden Dawn was a Nazi gang. So how was it possible to give them a legal permit to participate in elections?

The role of the police in protecting Golden Dawn's actions was crucial. Without this, the anti-fascist movement would have smashed them from 2007. It was impossible for them to stand before the anti-fascists; we would outnumber and defeat them. But the police always defended them. There were many anti-fascists who were attacked by the police and brought before the courts.

When Golden Dawn entered parliament in 2012, we faced tough arguments: "Why do you say they shouldn't have a platform on Greek TV? They are a political party. Why shouldn't they have seats in the parliament or in the municipalities?" We opposed these arguments, but the neoliberal system did not. It took a political fight to isolate the fascists, and this started with naming Golden Dawn as Nazis. It was crucial that the SEK started building an anti-fascist movement against Golden Dawn long before its big breakthrough. We didn't wait until they were making huge gains; we started 20 years before that in the 1990s.

I remember in 1992 when there was a big nationalist campaign over Macedonia, with the Greek state insisting "Macedonia is Greek"—and only

Greek.[4] There is a Macedonian minority in Greece and we supported them, as well as the Turkish minority, against nationalist attacks. There was even prosecution of five of our members for the publication of a book, *The Macedonian Question, the Balkans and the Working Class*. The Nazis attacked our party, then called Socialist Revolution Organisation (OSE), particularly because we supported the right of Macedonians to call themselves Macedonians. Throughout all this period, we organised against the fascists.

In 1998 SEK organised a campaign called "Stop Haider". We saw the rise of Jörg Haider and the Freedom Party in Austria as a threat that could boost the fascists here in Greece. There were few fascists but we knew, given the atmosphere of racism, that they could grow. So we had a tradition of organising against the fascists stretching back for many years before theiy made a big step forward.

Why? Firstly, our analysis of fascism meant identifying the fascist threat not when they get to the point of entering parliament or controlling whole areas, but when they launched the first attacks against trade unionists, the left, migrants, refugees and so on. We built with this approach.

Secondly, we looked to the tradition of Leon Trotsky, who wrote about the need for a united front to beat Hitler's Nazis. This tradition has great lessons for revolutionaries today. Keerfa was this kind of united front. It united activists from trade unions and left-wing parties such as Syriza and from migrant, Muslim and LGBT+ communities. This approach was crucial to outnumbering the Nazis. Between 2007 and 2012, much of the left underestimated the fascist threat. SEK was even criticised by some on the left who said we were advertising the Nazis.

MT: So this approach was contested on the left?

Yes. Some were very critical when we began to organise anti-fascist actions such as a counter-demonstration to the Nazis' first racist protest in Agios Pantelemonias. We were alone on the left, with just some of the anarchists supporting. But the Pakistani community was always there with us from the first moment. Without the Pakistani community we couldn't have made it in a lot of areas. But the most important force was the organised working class—teachers, hospital workers, doctors, the public sector workers' union and so on. Building in the trade unions took a lot of effort because we combined the fight against fascism with the fight against racism and Islamophobia.

We built on the successes of the anti-capitalist movement in Greece from the period of the great protests in Genoa in 2001 and the anti-war movement

---

4   Following the break-up of Yugoslavia in 1991-2, the Greek state opposed the right of one of the newly independent successor states to call itself Macedonia. For years it was referred to as the Former Yugoslav Republic of Macedonia, but today it is called North Macedonia.

in 2003. We organised resistance to the wars in Afghanistan and Iraq, and we fought Islamophobia. Anti-racism was part and parcel of the huge anti-war movement. I would say that we brought all these political achievements from the past into the anti-fascist movement. That is why it was possible for SEK, an organisation of the revolutionary left, to build a united front like Keerfa, which was able to attract trade unions, migrant communities and others in order to outnumber the Nazis.

MT: After the breakthrough of Golden Dawn in 2012, the challenge facing Keerfa was to root out Golden Dawn from each of the localities that it tried to build in. So a movement that could drive down into every area across Greece was needed. Did Keerfa expand as a united front in this period? Did new forces begin to gravitate around Keerfa?

PC: It was amazing that when we started Keerfa in 2009, very quickly we had local groups in more than 70 areas. Many were in the area around Athens, but it was a national network from the very beginning. That was very important. This national network was able to cooperate with other anti-fascist coalitions and local groups that developed in parallel in that period. Until 2012 and 2013, the left underestimated the danger, but after the murder of Pavlos Fyssas, they joined the movement. On this part of the left, there was panic that it was not possible to defeat the Nazis, so the confidence that Keerfa had in its strategy was very important. Keerfa was the heart of that movement, but also its mind. We understood how to make the big political decisions that were necessary. It was necessary after Golden Dawn's electoral successes not to panic but to build locally and to fight back with counter-demonstrations. This worked. Golden Dawn couldn't have an open demonstration to attract people, and it was impossible for them to build their electoral campaigns in 2012. We prevented the electoral campaign of Golden Dawn everywhere. It was amazing. Even when they had entered parliament, it was impossible for them to hold open meetings.

MT: So you were able to push them out of the public space, despite their claims that being in parliament meant that they were respectable?

PC: Yes. We also demanded that the municipal authorities that are responsible for giving political parties spaces for events during elections—halls, squares, election kiosks and so on—refuse these to Golden Dawn. We won some decisions to deny these spaces to Golden Dawn, leading it to cancel its annual "festival of youth" in Athens.

What happened with the trade unions was also very important. When the Nazis tried to stop the children of refugees going to the schools, the teachers were there to register them. In the hospitals, it was the doctors in the health workers' union that kicked the Nazis out. Battle by battle, the power of the working class was there in the war against the Nazis.

We demanded that Golden Dawn be stopped from appearing on ERT, the state-run broadcaster. We ran a big campaign on this issue and got the support of the journalists' union. The manager of ERT claimed that this issue was not his responsibility but that of a committee that monitors the media for hate speech. They kept passing the responsibility between one another. The solution came from the trade union. They simply said, "every time you put the Nazis on a programme, we will strike." Finally, the Nazis took the union to court—and lost. So we won a court decision that meant the Nazis would not appear on TV.

The anti-racist campaign that took place in parallel with all this was also very important. There were huge mobilisations against racism. When the bosses of a strawberry farm in Western Greece shot 30 Bangladeshi workers in 2013 for demanding their back wages, it stirred a huge mobilisation. We organised a strike, which was the first strike and mass mobilisation of these workers. It ended the terror in the area. The Communist Party and the trade unions hadn't been able to operate in this area. We broke all that.

We made both the anti-fascist and anti-racist struggles central. Three things were crucial. The first was the united front tactic, which I have already talked about.

The second was the central role of the organised working class. This was more than just left-wing militants putting on helmets and physically confronting the fascists on their own. We said no to this tactic. We said we needed mass workers' action—and we got it. There was a general strike when Pavlos Fyssas was murdered and this gave us the ability to organise a mass anti-fascist demonstration of 60,000, even without the agreement of the leaderships of the big trade unions. They said they were going to organise a concert. We said, "OK, hold the concert. Have the music in Syntagma Square. But we will march to the headquarters of Golden Dawn." And we marched with 60,000. This forced the government to start the crack down against the neo-Nazis three days after the general strike.

We had a strike on the first day of the trial of Golden Dawn in 2015. We occupied the public spaces in the court—no supporters of Golden Dawn could get in. We had 3,000 demonstrators outside the prison at 8am in the morning in a remote area of Athens. And on 7 October 2020, the day the court finally announced the decision in the trial, hundreds of thousands gathered at 11am in the morning after a call for a general strike from the public workers' union and many others. So mobilising the trade unions to break the Nazis worked 100 percent.

The third crucial part of the anti-fascist struggle was to prosecute the Nazis every time they attacked the left, trade unionists and migrants. The trial of Golden Dawn was built on three big cases—the murder of Pavlos Fyssas, the attack on the trade unionists of the Communist Party and the attack on Egyptian fishermen. The case argued that Golden Dawn was a criminal organisation and that its members were involved in over a hundred other violent attacks.

Keerfa proposed that there should be a civil action by the anti-fascist movement as part of the trial. This is not natural in Greek trials; usually the state would be the prosecutor, but we demanded and won a civil action in this trial. Keerfa had four lawyers in the trial representing the Egyptian fishermen.

It was very important to prosecute the Nazis. There was a big argument about this, with some saying, "come on! What are you doing Keerfa? Going to the courts, the state—this will open the space for the state to attack the left". But that was wrong. The state was already attacking the left and the trade unions, and the state was already protecting the Nazis. So we had to be there to expose all these links between the Nazis, the police and the state.

Even the leader of Golden Dawn had to admit this during a conference, I think around 2017, when Donald Trump's election had given a boost to the far right around Europe. He was asked a question—why isn't Golden Dawn rising when the far right all around Europe is growing? And their leader said there were two reasons. First, the trial meant that they had to show that they were a legal party and couldn't use their paramilitary forces. Second, the anti-fascist movement meant that every time they tried to act in public, they were stopped. We won the trial decision because of the mass campaign and because we mobilised broad forces, including local mayors, politicians from Syriza and even some from the social democrats.

The role of SEK was very important. Compare the record of Syriza in government—how they treated Golden Dawn was an institutional failure. Zoe Konstantopoulou, who became president of the Greek parliament in 2015 following Syriza's victory, argued that the decisions of the Greek parliament were not legal because Golden Dawn MPs were in prison. That was really shameful. You could see Golden Dawn MPs standing with left-wing MPs on symbolic national days at state events. We were right to be very critical of this approach from Syriza.

The campaign around the trial gave us the opportunity to speak to a mass audience and to put pressure on the voters of Golden Dawn. We said, "What you are doing is voting for a criminal. You are voting for a murderer. This is not a party that you can use to show your anger against the system." All these tactics worked—the anti-fascist movement, the anti-racist movement, the workers' resistance and the activity around the trial. This is how we came in the 2019 election to see Golden Dawn kicked out of parliament. That defeat opened the way for the court to find them guilty and to send them to prison. It would have been harder if they had still been in parliament. After that, we saw the splits in Golden Dawn. They lost the strength to maintain a collective strategy to defend themselves and, importantly, they no longer had money. They originally had more than 60 lawyers, who were paid by the Greek parliament. But the success of the campaign meant that the Greek parliament decided to stop giving them money.

MT: Do you have any final thoughts on the international significance of the defeat of Golden Dawn? What are the key lessons for socialists elsewhere facing a fight against fascist and far-right forces?

PC: There is something to add to what I have said already. One of the reasons that it was possible for us to win this fight was the power of the left in Greece. The left is huge in Greece. Without that environment it wouldn't have been possible. It is very important how you relate to the rest of the left, even if they are getting into government. It is very important how you approach working-class people on the left. For me, it's all about the united front and the action of the organised working class. You can win by showing that the Nazis are not a normal political party but a paramilitary gang. And you have to pursue them—even into the courts.

Finally, in this period of great crisis, this is not the end. Even with the biggest victory, we cannot be complacent that this is the conclusion of the story. This is what we are arguing now. We have moved to the next stage for the anti-fascist movement. Another far-right populist party, Greek Solution, has managed to enter parliament. This is a split from LAOS, led by Kyriakos Velopoulos, and is nationalistic, Islamophobic and so on. And there are still active groups of Nazis in the Greek islands, where the government is closing the borders. These Nazis are murdering refugees and attacking the left and the refugee solidarity movement.

So we are not at the end of the story. We have to keep building the anti-racist movement. Otherwise a space will open again for the Nazis. The New Democracy government is using the rhetoric of Hungarian prime minister Victor Orban. It talks about the replacement of the Greek population by migrants, claiming that Muslims are "invading" and that the refugees are spies of Turkey's president, Recep Erdoğan. Greece and Turkey are in competition over control of gas resources in the Mediterranean and this is driving vitriolic, nationalist and racist rhetoric. So it's very important that we continue to build the anti-racist movement.

But it's also important to build the socialist alternative against the fascists, because the roots of fascism are in the system. When the system is afraid, it becomes very open to the Nazis. We have to continue to build decisively on the big success that we had on 7 October 2020.

Palestinian youth: a silver lining and a ray of hope
Ilan Pappé

The news from Palestine, as has been the case for a long while now, is bad and depressing on many levels. The announcement of the "deal of the century" and subsequent gestures from the United States towards Israel, capped off two decades in this century which were disastrous to Palestine and the Palestinians—some would say as bad if not worse than the traumatic year of 1948. These US gestures included legitimising the occupation of East Jerusalem and the Jewish settlements in the West Bank, as well as declaring as legal the prospective future annexation of parts of the West Bank to Israel.

The century began with the brutal suppression of the Second Intifada and continued with a policy of incremental genocide against the Gaza Strip since 2006. These were complemented by racist legislation against the Palestinians inside Israel that culminated in the Nation State Law in the summer of 2018, which many rightly refer to as the Israeli Apartheid Law. In those twenty years, ethnic cleansing operations were carried out daily against the Palestinians in the so-called Area C of the West Bank, particularly in the Jordan Valley and the South Hebron region. Meanwhile, a slower but no less destructive process has continued the "Judaisation" of the Greater Jerusalem area and the bisection of the West Bank through both the apartheid wall and territorial wedges created by Jewish settlements that cut the West Bank into two.

All in all, it seems that there is an attempt to depoliticise the Palestine question by delegitimising the Palestinian narrative of the past. There is a total denial of the Nakba and the Israeli responsibility for it as well as a denial of basic Palestinian human and political rights in the present.

The ability of the Palestinians to deal with these calamities and the offensive against their very existence was hampered by two major factors. The first is the disunity in the national movement, and the second the unwillingness of the political elites in the world, particularly in the West, to meaningfully interfere on their behalf. On the contrary, these elites, be they in the government, the press or in the academy, provide immunity for the criminal Israeli polices on the ground.

Yet not all was bleak. Outside of Palestine, the Boycott, Divestment and Sanctions (BDS) movement gained momentum since 2005, reflecting a significant change in the civil society's attitude to Palestine all over the world. A less discernible but no less important phenomenon is the focus of this article—the activity of Palestinian youth, wherever they are. Their activity through Palestine societies at university campuses around the world, culminating each year in the Israel Apartheid Week, has revitalised the global solidarity movement. However, they bring to the fore more than just youthful enthusiasm. These young people also constantly introduce fresh and new ideas, which are—at least for me—a reason not to lose hope and a sign that the Palestinian struggle is far from over. A focused examination of the activities and ideas might help us to assess more clearly the current state of the struggle for freedom in Palestine and its future options.

Palestinian society is one of the youngest in the world. It is not easy to get statistics for every Palestinian community on the globe; nevertheless, in those for which we do have statistics, it seems that around 57 percent of the population is under the age of 24 and 80 percent under 30.[1] It is probable that other Palestinian communities have a roughly similar age structure.

These young people are the ones who would lead the Palestinian cause in the future. This article attempts to map some of the activity and interrelations of these new forces as well as to assess the ideological trends, aspirations, and mood among this group of Palestinians. This might tell us if these youthful impulses, energising the liberation movement as a whole, will be able lead all of us out of the present dismal period, which is one the worst in Palestine's history.

Like the rest of Palestinian society, the youth live in diverse geopolitical spaces. Of course, there are naturally specific agendas and aspirations determined by the locality of any such group—but there are also common objectives and hopes that affect the Palestinian national movement and the liberation struggle.

---

1   For informations about the demographics of the occupied territories, see the Palestinian Statistic Bureau website—www.pcbs.gov.ps/site/lang__en/881/default.aspx#Population

The occupied teritories

Let us start first with the more unique situations and agendas of some of the groups. The first are the young people living in the occupied West Bank and in the besieged Gaza Strip.

Part of the concerns and fears of this group of youth—as indicated both by recent research and my own intuitive impression after spending long periods of time there—are not different from the overall population in the occupied territories.[2] Paramount among this list of concerns is the ongoing trials and tribulations of living under Israeli direct or indirect occupation, which include harassment by the army, settlers and border police. Particularly concerning is the fear of continued closures, curfews and imprisonment without trial.

More unique among young people is the resentment caused by their further marginalisation within the political sphere and a disturbing sense of exploitation in the social one. The Palestinian National Council is relegating Palestinian youth to an insignificant presence—just three members out of 450 council members come from student unions.[3]

There is evidence that the Israeli occupation forces are targeting youth, and in particular children. Most of the Palestinians killed recently by the occupying army are young people. This is a generation born into the geography of disaster created by Israel, with calamitous effects on its mental and physical wellbeing. They were moulded by resisting this reality, shaping their political orientation.

There is also a prevalent suspicion that bureaucracy, nepotism and corruption block the way for young people into the limited professional opportunities offered under occupation. Unsurprisingly, the level of despair among certain sections of the younger generation is higher in the occupied territories than anywhere else in historical Palestine or aboard. Yet, as I shall note, there are youth movements struggling everywhere against the occupation in their own region and also jointly for a different Palestine.

Similarly to the young Palestinians in the refugee camps of Syria, and some in the refugee camps of Lebanon, the existential fear for one's own life and that of one's family plays a dominant role, often overshadowing visions for the future. Nevertheless, one cannot generalise too much. There are, as I will show, incredible initiatives that combine the existential daily struggles of young Palestinians with a more strategic outlook: envisioning a better and different future.

Other concerns are shared by Palestinian youth wherever they are. One such worry is the continued division between Fatah and Hamas, which troubles many

2   Babatudne, 2009.
3   Seif, 2020.

younger Palestinians. There is no great admiration anymore for either, but there is a recognition of their historical role and their current significance for continuing, or disrupting, the struggle for freedom. On the other hand, there is nothing in attitudes towards the Palestinian Authority (PA) that indicates any admiration at all. This was shown by a recent survey from BADIL, a Palestinian non-governmental organisation (NGO); there is a consensus among young people that the PA is a corrupt body and an impediment to mass mobilisation.[4] However, the BADIL survey also showed there is a realisation that, at the moment, the PA cannot be dissolved from below. As the Arab World for Research and Development research centre has noted, there is recognition that the PA "feeds millions of Palestinians".[5] There is a fear that the dissolution of the PA would lead to full occupation, and this has deterred young people from supporting this as a strategy. In 2021, although there is not yet a full survey, it seems that no one is sure whether such a possibility is the worst-case scenario.

Whether in the occupied territories, within Israel or in the rest of the world, there is a frustration with the Palestinian political elite's underestimation of young people's potential. Young activists constantly remind us that the founders of the Palestinian national movement were themselves young people when they started their activity.

The legacies of the First Intifada

For the Palestinian youth in the occupied territories, the formative event that illuminates their options for the future is the First Intifada of 1987. In that uprising young people came into public awareness because of the central role they played. The youth were part of the Unified National Leadership of the Uprising and this participation contributed immensely to their sense of importance and relevance.

Youth in the West Bank and the Gaza Strip conducted what seemed to many in the West to be the sort of peaceful and unarmed resistance they could support, successfully challenging the Israeli depiction of the Palestinian struggle as an act of terrorism. In the eyes of the Palestinians around the world, the youth led the way in a democratic, egalitarian and massive popular resistance. This was a mode of political action that had emerged before, during the Mandatory period, but had then been replaced by guerrilla warfare between 1948 and 1982. The memory of the participation of young people in the intifada still empowers young people, especially students, because it represents a time when they could enthuse a huge public behind them—not just inspiring action on the ground but also acting as a political compass for the future. Among many of these young people there is a

---

4   BADIL Resource Center for Palestinian Residency and Refugee Rights, 2012a.
5   The survey is quoted in Mustakbalna, 2017.

now growing recognition that the achievements of the First Intifada were wasted by the Oslo "peace process", which began in 1993. Nonetheless they feel that the uprising left an enduring legacy of empowerment.

Indeed, the legacies of the First Intifada are widespread. It showed the power of grassroots' actions in the neighbourhoods and the camps, driven by direct democratic decision-making while eliminating what one might call "ideological dramas". These features explain why, despite the imbalance of power between an unarmed society and the strongest army in the region, the uprising lingered on for almost three years.[6]

The "no-nonsense" initiative

These young voices disappeared in many ways during the next, and more militarised, intifada. In many ways, the Second Intifada was a turning point in youth activity, inside and outside historical Palestine. The uprising brought to the fore the paralysing split between the Fatah and Hamas, and this in turn gave rise to youth activism that sought to distance itself from this poisonous split. Young Palestinians in the occupied West Bank called this a move towards "a no-nonsense initiative", and in many ways this initiative continues today, searching for an alternative route into the future. This energy was channelled into civil society, either in the form of NGOs or youth associations, which gathered under the umbrella of an organisation called the Independent Youth Movement.[7]

This initiative grew into a popular movement of resistance that has made a powerful intervention since 2003 amid landmark events such the struggle against the apartheid wall, the Israeli assaults on the Gaza Strip and the Arab Spring. It culminated with a courageous and popular resistance movement, the Great March of Return, at the fences of the Gaza Strip in 2018. More recently, it morphed into localised youth movements. Many of these have their own websites and Facebook pages and are involved in opposing the Israeli attempt to ethnically cleanse large parts of Area C of the West Bank. One such group, for instance, is active in Masafer Yatta (the hilly area south of Hebron). In this region for years now, the army and the settlers have been harassing the local population. In some cases, this has led to the forced eviction of farmers. The youth have resettled these evicted villages so that farmers can return, and they provide escorts for children and farmers who face daily attacks by Israeli settlers on the way to their schools and fields.[8]

This popular movement of protest and resistance is not only directed toward the occupation but also against the mismanagement of power, resources and state

---

6   Hilterman, 1991, p20.
7   https://palestinianyouthmovement.com
8   For one such facebook page, see www.facebook.com/media.yas

funds. The movement guards against signs and gestures of normalisation that can perpetuate the occupation and lend it legitimacy. This is not a new phenomenon; already in the First Intifada, the youth were combating the fatigue felt by some members of the older generation who seemed to have become resigned to the occupation and accepted it as an accomplished fact that cannot be changed.

Therefore, it is unsurprising that many young people would like to re-enact the First Intifada. Indeed, the dismal reality that motivated the intifada in the first place was reinstated after Oslo, and in many ways it is a far worse version of it. The economic situation today is certainly worse, rooted in the Israeli policy of roadblocks, strip searches, deportation, house demolition, separation of families and detention without trial. This is just a partial list of the repertoire of abuses that the occupation inflicts on Palestinians.

It is clear that, just as before, Israel continues to act with particular brutality against non-violent Palestinian individuals and movements. Therefore a new wave of such protest would be met by an even more callous and inhuman response. Some still endorse resorting once more to armed resistance, as was attempted by Fatah and Hamas during the Second Intifada; but this mode of action also generates a cruel Israeli response. In the case of the Gaza Strip, this response verges on the implementation of genocidal policies.

There is no one, single vision of Palestinian youth. Much depends on where one is located. Nevertheless, there are common features and different stresses on the same points. The youth in the occupied West Bank and the sieged Gaza Strip are motivated by concerns about the ongoing political rift between Fatah and Hamas. The focus is still on the end of the occupation but, unlike the older generation, this is much more associated with a full liberation of Palestine. The youth believe that if their views and thoughts were considered, it could end the divisive ideological discord between the main political blocs. They are confident that this unity would play a crucial role in ending the Israeli occupation and gaining freedom for Palestine as a whole. Despite being marginalised (and at times even suppressed) by their leaders, they continue to demand a foothold in politics from above, as well as from below. They are adamant about their right to take part in the process of political decision-making that would determine the future of their homeland.

The "48 Arabs": the Palestinian minority in Israel

The Second Intifada played a different role in the political life of Palestinian youth inside Israel, intensifying youth activism within civil society. Books such as Dan Rabinowitz's and Khawla Abu-Baker's *Coffins on Our Shoulders: The Experience of the Palestinian Citizens of Israel* hailed the young activists as the proud generation, even to the extent of belittling and misunderstanding the sacrifices and successes of the older generation of Palestinians in Israel between 1948 and 2000.[9] This went hand in hand with the expansion of NGOs and civil society as a whole, propelled by enthusiastic youth activity. Here too, the established political forces in the community—the Arab parties in the Israeli Knesset—were respected by the youth, but also criticised for lack of unity. This has somewhat changed in recent years with the establishment of the Joint List, which comprises all the Palestinian political parties in Israel. Quite a few younger politicians made their way into the list, including its head, Ayman Odeh.

More relevant to this article, however, is the growing youth activity geared towards a one-state solution, looking strategically to the BDS campaign and strongly advocating the Palestinian right of return. This kind of activity tries to counter Israeli policies that are meant to de-indigenise the Palestinians inside Israel and portray them as strangers in their homeland.

A very important part of the struggle, and one which influences the local youth's aspirations and visions for the future, are cultural projects that defend the historical memory of the Nakba. These projects include reconstructions of the villages destroyed in the Nakba, showing both how they looked before 1948 and imagining how they might look after the return of the refugees. These programmes have even led to a small group of young people establishing an actual physical presence on one of the destroyed sites.[10]

These young activists keep the Nakba memory alive. For them and so many other Palestinians, what they are living through is "al-Nakba al-Mustamera", the ongoing Nakba. This concept echoes the crucial point made by the late anthropologist Patrick Wolfe about settler colonialism: it is not an event but a structure. Israeli policies towards the Palestinians in the past and in the present are informed by the settler-colonial ideology of Zionism, and the incompletion of the ethnic cleansing of 1948 has shaped Israeli polices towards the Palestinians ever since. Young Palestinians now focus on confronting these polices by demanding rectification of Israel's past crimes as well the cessation of its current agenda of oppression across historical Palestine.[11]

The commemoration of the Nakba by Palestinian youth is now an annual act; every year, thousands join a march of return to one of the many villages destroyed in 1948. It is attended by all the Palestinian politicians and has become a focus of cultural, as well as political, struggle against the 2011 Israeli Nakba law, which prevents public funding of anybody who commemorates the 1948 events as a Nakba. This annual march was initiated by internal Palestinian refugees in

---

9   Rabinowitz and Abu Baker, 2005.

10 See Pappe, 2018.

11 Wolfe, 2006.

the wake of the failure of the 1991 Madrid Conference to broach the question of refugees. In 1995, the Association for the Defence of the Rights of the Internally Displaced in Israel was founded to organise an annual march of return to the site of a different village on 15 May, placing the issue on the Israeli public agenda.

In the world in which they live—between Israeli citizenship and Palestinian nationality—the indigenous dimension of this annual commemoration helps to define their role both in Israel and in the Palestinian polity. A more accurate definition of who they are is helped by the Zionist, in particular Liberal Zionist, objection to their cultural projects of commemoration. One of the gurus of Liberal Zionism, professor Shlomo Avineri, criticised the commemoration as an act of delegitimisation against the State of Israel, seeing it as expressing a hidden wish to solidify a stronger national movement for Palestinian citizens as a foundation for nation-building all over historical Palestine.[12] Avineri's criticisms reveal just how narrow the differences are between all the Zionist political streams in Israel when it comes to the legitimate rights of the Palestinians. The 1948 ethnic cleansing is equally denied by the Israeli "left" and "right". If this denial continues and is not replaced by an acknowledgement of Israel's responsibility for the crime against humanity that it committed in 1948 and has compounded ever since, there is no basis for any meaningful reconciliation in the future.

An important institution in this respect is Mada al-Carmel, founded by author and philosopher Azmi Bishara. This is the only outfit that has provided young Palestinian intellectuals with a space for free discussion about their own history and present conditions: a discussion that is impossible within the Israeli academic establishment. There is a huge human and intellectual capital within the Palestinian community in Israel. Once this community plays a leading role in Palestinian politics in general—a role that both Israel and the Palestine Liberation Organisation have denied—this potential would enhance the movement for freedom and justice.

There are not many proper surveys of the younger generation's attitudes towards a future solution. Nevertheless, evidence suggests a constant shift from support for the two-state solution to an endorsement of a one-state solution. New initiatives evolving around this idea have emerged recently. The most notable among them is the One Democratic State Campaign.[13] This campaign will eventually become a popular movement when the last believers in the two-state solution admit defeat and jettison the idea. Such ideological vacuums never stay vacant, as Karl Marx taught us.

12 Avineri, 2014.
13 See https://onestatecampaign.org/en

Finally, this particular group of young Palestinians place the importance of the human rights agenda next to that of the national agenda. Hence a Palestinian state or full Palestinian sovereignty are, in their eyes, as important as civil, economic and social equality. This is why politicians such as Jeremy Corbyn and Bernie Sanders are highly regarded by them. Some Palestinian members of the Knesset reflect these ideals; however, they are also almost religiously devoted to the two-state solution, unlike their grassroots members and the younger elements of civil society.

This vision, with a strong stress on the right of return, also resonates with young Palestinians in the refugee camps outside Israel and the occupied territories—some of whom have been made refugees once more in Europe since 2012—and among those in the more veteran exile communities.

The refugee and exile communities

The Zionist leadership envisaged that the refugees would either die out or forget the Nakba. This vision did not materialise. On the contrary, despite all Israeli efforts to divide and erase Palestinian society, its people have not abandoned their rights. Instead, they continue steadfastly to confront Israel's policies of expulsion.

A second survey by BADIL clearly indicates that the third and fourth generation of Palestinian refugees did not "forget" their attachment to Palestine. The survey was carried out in the seven areas where the majority of Palestinians reside: Israel, the West Bank, the Gaza Strip, East Jerusalem, Jordan, Syria and Lebanon. It was conducted among Palestinian young people aged between 15 and 19 years. The survey's findings demonstrate that the vast majority of the respondents sees themselves as Palestinians. As the survey states, "The significance of this majority can only be understood by bearing in mind that these communities were born in forced exile and have never set foot in Palestine—denied by Israel." The research results depict patterns of unified Palestinian identity despite Israel's attempts to irreparably damage their social fabric through geopolitical fragmentation.

Furthermore, the survey demonstrates that Palestinian youth in separated geographies hold similar viewpoints about their identity and the future. Being a Palestinian is not just a matter of an identity card, but rather a commitment to a struggle for the full liberation of Palestine.[14] This survey, conducted in 2012, is reaffirmed by recent research on the question. The desire for a solution based on the combination of the right of return with the establishment of a democratic state all over historic Palestine is shown even more clearly when one examines the views of the youth among Palestinian exile communities.

Around the world, this youth is organised in Palestine societies on campus and in movements that encompass all walks of life. Their activity is particularly

---

14 BADIL Resource Center for Palestinian Residency and Refugee Rights, 2012b.

impressive in the US, where they tirelessly organise events in universities, clubs, churches and mosques, among other places. They have little access to mainstream media platforms—but then, the youth are not particularly fervent consumers of this media, and they do not trust it either.

One meta-organisation for this activity is the Palestine Youth Movement (PYM), which particularly represents young Palestinians in the US. PYM defines itself as "a transnational, independent, grassroots movement of young Palestinians in Palestine and in exile worldwide".[15] It refuses to have a clear ideological colouring of the left and right, differentiating it from the 1970s political currents within the Palestinian liberation movement, when each one had its international ideological allies. PYM states:

> Irrespective of our different political, cultural and social backgrounds, we strive to revive a tradition of pluralistic commitment toward our cause to ensure a better future, characterised by freedom and justice on a social and political level for ourselves and subsequent generations.

This resonates with the agenda of quite a few young people who joined the protests around the world since 2008, from the participants in the Arab Spring to the Gilets Jaunes ("yellow vests") demonstrators in France. It is a position that echoes socialist and leftist ideas. Yet, as I have noted before, the traditional left and those like me who fully identify with it need to redefine the essence of a socialist standpoint. It must be universal, not Eurocentric, and it should integrate the good old values with the new perspectives and aspirations of the younger generation. For example, one important issue—which deserves a full article by itself—is the attitude towards Islam as a civilisation, and not just religion, in the Middle East, and how this might be part of a worldview that can be relevant and powerful in reproducing a revolutionary alliance on the ground. Another issue is the fear of fully endorsing the solution of a single, democratic state among established left-wing political organisations such as the Labour party, the TUC and the progressive flank of the Democratic Party.

PYM represents a new alliance of identification that has recently been woven between the Palestinians and analogous struggles around the world, as well with the struggle that characterised the Arab Spring. As its website puts it, PYM activism is "deeply rooted in the Arab regional context, which must be freed of neocolonialism in order for the complete liberation of Palestine to become a tangible reality."

Like their counterparts among other Palestinian groups, PYM is motivated by a strong belief that the youth can reactivate the national movement as a whole

---

15 https://palestinianyouthmovement.com

and move the fight for liberation forward. PYM feels that its advantage is the articulation of a clear endgame: a common vision of a liberated and democratic Palestine. It is familiar with social movement theory and praxis, working professionally to empower young people and prepare them to expand the struggle in the US. Schooling, workshops, conferences, demonstrations and campaigns are its bread and butter through which it ensures a constant presence in the public mind and in public spaces. Time will tell how successful it is, but it does seem that it has paved the way for a wide support among US youth for the Palestinian cause.

The electronic intifada

Both the youth in various areas of historical Palestine and those abroad are avid users of the internet, and this is where ideas are being discussed and articulated into a programme of action and a vision for the future. The PYM has an impressive web presence, and this is also true of many Palestinian youth movements. I have already mentioned some of these: the youth in Hebron, the civil society organisations inside Israel and the various youth committees in the refugee camps. A clear discourse about the future is revealed when one looks closely at the information traffic in and between these various sites. They refer to Palestine as "historical Palestine" and see the country as a whole as occupied and colonised; they see the potential for its liberation by popular resistance with help from outside by campaigns such as BDS. This is a new mode of resistance so brilliantly captured by one of the main loci of this activity, the Electronic Intifada website.

This internet presence transcends the physical barriers that, in the past, made the fragmentation of the Palestinian people the main obstacle for united action and vision. However, we should also take into account that there are young Palestinians under occupation and in refugee communities who do not have easy access to the internet; their world is less shaped by this cyber-discourse and still informed strongly by the daily realities of their existential struggle. Since the outbreak of the Second Intifada and the drop of the average income of Palestinian households living in the 1967 Palestinian territories, there has been a sharp increase in the number of Palestinian internet users, especially young people, through connectivity in schools, universities and cafes. In universities, online methods of instruction have had to develop because students frequently cannot reach their campuses due to conditions of siege.

This reality, however, is constantly changing. Even before the Covid-19 pandemic, and much more so under its influence, there has been a surge in internet usage. Mainly this is in the education system in the occupied territories and inside Israel. The internet has became the main tool of connection between teachers and students, and has thus turned into a means for intense politicisation and cyber-resistance. Similarly, the spread of smartphones is continuously connecting more and more young Palestinians to the internet.

The Palestinians are now the largest group of users of the internet in the Arab world. It is estimated that more than a quarter of the Palestinians under occupation have constant access to the internet. The Palestinian web is predominantly characterised by a unified youth political discourse about the struggle and its aims. As Makram Khoury-Machool, from the European Centre for the Study of Extremism, noted back in 2007, this is part of a "national peaceful political resistance and is one of the most central elements of everyday life".[16]

Conclusion

Taken together, the common thread of the orientation that is proposed by Palestinian youth activity everywhere points to a clear vision of the future without yet finalising the way forward for implementing it.

The vision is one democratic state in Palestine from the River Jordan to the Mediterranean, dismantling the Zionist institutions, allowing the refugees to return and developing a democracy based on economic and political equality. This would also mean a clear procedure for rectifying past evils through redistribution of land and other means of production between the Jewish settler community and indigenous Palestinians. There are still loose threads to be pulled and woven into this tapestry of a future Palestine, but they are beyond the framework of this article. The most important of them, which deserves further discussion in the future, is the whole notion of a secular state and the question of how the youth loyal to political Islam can be part of this new movement. Constructive ideas, such as that of a civic state rather than secular one, have very recently been proposed. One will have to wait to see how these dialogues develop, but their successful progression will have wider implications for the activity of the left in the West and the Arab World.

The means are the mixture of global solidarity, including support for the BDS movement, an expanding network of identification with the struggles of indigenous and oppressed groups around the globe, and a united democratic leadership on the ground that will properly represent the younger generation.

Within this vision, there is still a recognition of the shorter-term targets of such a movement, determined by the particular circumstances of each Palestinian group. Three different modes of action represent a potential way to push forward the popular resistance in each locality. In the West Bank, the focus of Palestinian youth is very localised and confronts specific Israeli policies of ethnic cleansing and oppression. In the Gaza Strip, it is focused on the siege and the right of return

---

16 See Khoury-Machool, 2007.

as two sides of the same coin of Palestinian dispossession. Inside Israel, it is cultural resistance that navigates efficiently between the government's politics of apartheid and denial on the one hand, and the agenda of the established Palestinian parties on the other. All three modes of youth action are less influenced by existing ideological affiliations, are trying to avoid replicating the damaging disunity of national politics, and are committed to non-violent and popular resistance.

Outside of Palestine, there is naturally more stress on visions and long-term strategies. The youth outside Palestine clearly articulates a bold discourse, depicting Zionism as a racist ideology that prevents reconciliation. They face endless and baseless accusations of antisemitism because of this stance, but they have dealt with these quite successfully (and certainly much better than the Labour Party and established left in the Britain).

Although many of the movement's important websites are located in the US, there is clear resentment towards any future Pax Americana. One observer at a youth summit in Ramallah sponsored by USAID reported an example of this. The Independent Youth Movement, which is active in the occupied territories, demonstrated vehemently in a meeting with US officials, writing "USAID, Go to Hell" on a placard. There is a belief that US funds come with selfish interests that will always ultimately demand the return of favours, and thus must be declined.[17]

In the past, and particularly in the 1970s, anti-Americanism characterised struggles against colonialism and imperialism. Nowadays, this is replaced by identification with the struggle of oppressed ethnic and indigenous groups around the world. Nevertheless, the movement still has a strong socialist colouring, because neoliberalism is identified as a crucial part of the coalition of forces that obstructs Palestinian liberation. Neoliberalism is increasingly reognised as another form of settler colonialism, and workers as yet another oppressed group, victimised by the same coalition of forces that are at work in Palestine.

There is also a growing sense that the production of knowledge is an essential tool in the struggle. This is why the campuses are such important sites of this activism, both in terms of students' organisations on the ground and the new orientations in the curriculums and research orientations of faculties. There are now eight centres for Palestine studies around the world, hosting more than 100 postgraduate students a year and working on Palestine as their main topic of inquiry. Many of them revolve around topics that are relevant for the future of Palestine: the struggle against the denial of the Nakba; analysis of antisemitism and Islamophobia in the context of the struggle for justice in Palestine; the relevance of neoliberalism and settler colonialism; the various features of a possible one-state solution; and the practical implementation of Palestinian refugees' right of return.

---

17   Unsleuber, 2011.

Despite this incredible production of knowledge and the energised activism on the ground, there is more clarity about the vision of the future than about how to get there. This where the left can play a crucial role, in Palestine and outside it. However, this requires that the traditional left revitalise itself and find a way to have an impact on the overall strategy, without which this newly found vitality could be wasted, as was the case after the 2008 crash and during the Arab Spring.

Much of this will have to do with the organisation and structures of a social movement. It seems that there was disdain towards organisational matters from both those who participated in the global movements since 2008 against inhuman neoliberal economic policies and in the struggle against corruption and oppression in the Arab Spring. One can understand the source of this kind of resentment. For so many, organisations have been experienced as tools of corruption, based on a unmerited hierarchy and producing stagnation rather than progress. However, it is hard to see any alternative to student groups, workers' unions and other political and social organisations if one wants to turn visions into revolutionary realities. Time will tell whether this energy and motivation can be integrated into either existing outfits or new ones. Yet what is clear is that young Palestinians are here and they are active. If they find the way to organise and coordinate their action, they will affect considerably the struggle for freedom and justice in Palestine.

References

Avineri, Schlomo, 2014, "The Nakba According to Haaretz", *Haaretz* (8 May).

Babatudne, Saka Ganiu, 2009, "The Role of the Palestinian Youth in the Israel-Palestine Conflict" (MA Thesis), Cyprus International University.

BADIL Resource Center for Palestinian Residency and Refugee Rights, 2012a, "One People United: A Deterritorialised Palestinian Identity".

BADIL Resource Center for Palestinian Residency and Refugee Rights, 2012b, "Survey of Palestinian Refugees and Internally Displaced Persons, 2010-2012".

Hilterman, Joost, 1991, *Behind the Intifada: Labor and Women's Movements in the Occupied Territories* (Princeton University Press).

Khoury-Machool, Makram, 2007, "Palestinian Youth and Political Activism: The Emerging Internet Culture and New Modes of Resistance", *Policy Futures in Education*, volume 5, issue 1.

Mustakbalna, 2017, "Palestinian Youth Challenges and Aspirations: A Study on Youth, Peace and Security Based on UN Resolution 2250", https://bit.ly/3mYKiV5

Pappé, Ilan, 2018, "Indigeneity as Cultural Resistance: Notes of the Palestinian Struggle within 21st Century Israel", *South Atlantic Quarterly*, volume 117, issue 1.

Rabinowitz, Dani, and Khawla Abu Baker, 2005, *Coffins on Our Shoulders: The Experience of the Palestinian Citizens of Israel* (University of California Press).

Seif, Samir, 2020, "Youth in the Palestinian National Movement: Painful Truths", *Palestine-Israel Journal*, volume 6, issue 4.

Unsleber, Steffi, 2011, "Destroying Belief in the Resistance? The USAID Funded Palestinian Youth Summit", Palestine Monitor (September 14).

Wolfe, Patrick, 2006, "Settler Colonialism and the Elimination of the Native", *Journal of Genocide Research*, volume 8, issue 4.

Genderquake: socialist women and the Paris Commune
Judy Cox

On 11 April 1871, three weeks into the life of the Paris Commune, a poster appeared on the walls of France's capital:

> Citizenesses, we know that the present social order bears within itself the seeds of poverty and of the death of all liberty and justice... At this hour, when danger is imminent and the enemy is at the gates of Paris, the entire population must unite to defend the Commune, which stands for the annihilation of all privilege and all inequality.[1]

All women who were prepared to die for the Commune were urged to attend a meeting at 8pm at the Salle Larched, Grand Café des Nations, 74 Rue de Temple. Laundresses, seamstresses, bookbinders and milliners attended and there they established a new organisation, the Union of Women. This Union was a part of the socialist First International, which had been established by Karl Marx and other socialists and trade unionists in London in 1864 with the aim of uniting workers across national borders. Within a few days, the Union became one of the most important organisations of the Paris Commune. Socialist women played an indispensable role in organising the working women of Paris to become Communards.

---

1   Thank you to Joseph Choonara, Richard Donnelly, Donny Gluckstein and Rob Hoveman for comments and suggestions.

The Commune lasted only 72 days but in that short time it challenged hierarchies of gender which had been deeply entrenched for centuries.[2] The role played by women in the Paris Commune attracted the attention of both contemporaries and historians. Images of unruly women populated contemporary accounts of the Commune.[3] Historical studies of the Commune have tended to accept and even amplify a series of negative stereotypes that characterised working women as excitable, irrational and habitually violent. They are seen as outside any enduring feminist or socialist tradition. The histories that treat women more objectively tend to restrict discussions of their activities to specific chapters, reinforcing the idea that men had historical agency but women were marginal to events.[4] Imagine reading a history of the Commune with a chapter titled, "Men in the Commune". The female Communards have been the exclusive focus of only three book-length studies, one published in 1964, one in 1996 and one in 2004.[5] This article does not aim to retell the stories of the female Communards, fascinating though they are. It aims to explore the impact of socialist women on the Commune and on the wider socialist tradition.

The foremothers of the Commune

Most studies of the Commune begin on 18 March with the failed attempt of Adolphe Thiers, head of the French government, to disarm the Parisian National Guard.[6] France had suffered a military defeat in a war with Prussia, following the long and bitter siege of Paris. The French government had agreed to surrender, but the population of Paris and the National Guard resisted. When government troops were sent to take the cannons of Paris, thousands of women, men and children rose up to defend them, built barricades and drove the French army out of the city. The emphasis on this revolutionary moment creates the impression that the Commune was a purely spontaneous event. The Commune was indeed born out of this spontaneous rebellion, but it was shaped and driven forward by individuals and organisations steeped in experience of the labour and socialist movements.[7] The role of socialist women in preparing the way for the Commune has been almost completely overlooked by historians, yet the Commune depended on the women who were at the centre of Paris's working-class networks. Male and female members of the International established themselves by leading strikes in the 1860s. Eugène Varlin and Nathalie Lemel led a large strike of bookbinders in 1864.

---

2   Eichner, 2004, p17.
3   Gullickson, 1996, p218.
4   Gullickson, 1996, p10.
5   Thomas, 1964; Gullickson, 1996; Eichner, 2004.
6   Ross, 2015, p41.
7   Gluckstein, 2011, pp59-60.

Lemel defied convention to become a member of the strike committee and she fought tirelessly for equal pay for women. Both Varlin and Lemel became leading Communards.

Two opposing traditions relating to women co-existed uneasily inside the French socialist movement. One went back to the utopian socialism of the 1830s, when Flora Tristan became the first reformer to argue that women could only win equality through the emancipation of the working class.[8] This tradition was developed in the 1848 Revolution by the great socialist leaders Jeanne Deroin and Pauline Roland, who organised women to fight for their rights to work and to vote.

A very different tradition was represented by the misogynistic anarchist-socialist writer Pierre-Joseph Proudhon. Proudhon argued that women were physically weak, incapable of abstract thought and naturally immoral, fit only for marriage or prostitution.[9] In his last work, *Pornocracy: Women in Modern Times*, Proudhon argued that husbands had the right to kill wives who were adulterous, immoral, drunk, thieving, wasteful or obstinately insubordinate.[10] Jules Michelet further popularised these misogynistic views in his accessible novels *Love* (1858) and *Women* (1859). Michelet blamed women for the failure of the revolutions of 1789 and 1848 and considered them to be prisoners of their biology, which left them unreliable, capricious and unsuited to work outside the home.[11] Proudhon and Michelet were very influential in the French section of the International. At the French section's inaugural meeting in 1866, delegates passed a motion that stated: "From a physical, moral and social viewpoint, women's work outside the home should be energetically condemned as a cause of the degeneration of the race and as one of the agents of demoralisation used by the capitalist class".[12] There were opposing voices, including those of future Communards Varlin and Benoît Malon, but the French section of the International remained deeply Proudhonist.

Female campaigners fought back against the sexist ideas of Proudhon and Michelet. One combatant was André Léo. Léo had lived in Switzerland with her husband, a utopian socialist who had been inspired by the ideas of Henri de Saint-Simon and was forced into exile after 1848. Léo was widowed and to survive she published several novels exploring the oppression of women and affirming women's abilities. In 1866 she hosted the inaugural meeting of a new feminist group at her house. The group included Paule Mink, Louise Michel, Eliska Vincent, Noémi Reclus and her husband Élie Reclus, all future

---

8   Moon, 1978, p19.
9   McMillan, 2000, p123.
10   McMillan, 2000, p124.
11   McMillan, 2000, p124.
12   McMillan, 2000, p115.

Communards.[13] The group established improving girls' education as their campaigning priority.

Mink and Michel were two of the leading women of the Commune. They both stood in the revolutionary socialist tradition of Deroin and Roland.[14] Mink was the daughter of an exiled Polish nobleman. When her marriage broke down, she worked as a seamstress and language teacher. She also edited a radical newspaper and built a reputation as an orator in Paris's radical circles. At a public meeting in 1868, Mink challenged Proudhon: "By ceasing to make woman a worker, you deprive her of her liberty and, thereby, of her responsibility so that she no longer will be a free and intelligent creature but will merely be a reflection, a small part of her husband".[15] Michel was the daughter of an unmarried servant. She trained as a teacher but refused to teach in state schools because it would have meant swearing an oath of loyalty to the French Empire. Michel came to Paris to further both her education and the revolution. She was one of the most courageous, determined and audacious women in the revolutionary tradition.

Some male members of the International supported the women against Proudhonism. In 1866, Malon wrote to Léo as a member of the International, assuring her that he was not, "forgetting about the emancipation of women and we receive new support each day. We have convinced almost the entire association of the idea; only the pontiffs of Proudhon remain unconvinced".[16] The first edition of the paper issued by the Batignolles-Ternes section of the Parisian International included a programme, signed by Léo and 16 others, which declared: "It is time to have women participate in democracy instead of making them its enemy by senseless exclusion".[17] The following year Varlin argued:

> Those who wish to refuse women the right to work want to keep them permanently dependent on men. No-one has the right to refuse them the only means of being truly free. Whether done by man or women, there should be equal pay for equal work.[18]

Léo, Mink and Varlin consistently agitated for the International to support both civil rights for women and women's right to work.

Throughout the 1860s women joined the political clubs that attracted large audiences in Paris's poorer districts, at least some of which discussed how to

---

13 McMillan, 2000, p130.
14 McMillan, 2000, p128.
15 McMillan, 2000, p119.
16 Schulkind, 1985, p142.
17 Schulkind, 1985, p142.
18 Schulkind, 1985, p144.

campaign against women's low wages.[19] The political clubs also incubated the desire, "to establish a commune based on cooperation of all energies and intelligences instead of government composed of traitors and incompetents".[20] Early in 1869 demands for a commune could be heard in many clubs, and proceedings often closed with the cry, "Viva la Commune". When the Commune became a reality two years later, the clubs continued to provide a space for debate and organisation and became a living link between the Central Committee and the people. The clubs debated what actions the Commune should take and made their views and priorities known to the Central Committee. Through the clubs, women could organise direct action against profiteers and urge support for reforms they wanted. Many Parisian women were in relationships with members of the National Guard, but few went through a marriage ceremony. Only married women could claim a wives' allowance from the Commune, a discriminatory policy that caused much anger. The demand for allowances for the unmarried partners of national guardsmen originated in the clubs and was later granted by the Commune.[21]

Some clubs were mixed, some were segregated and both provided a platform for female leaders to emerge. An English reporter from the *Daily News* described one club where "respectably dressed women with their grown up daughters, little shopkeepers' wives with their young families" mixed with "those repulsive females of almost all degrees of age who form the typical furies of excited Paris mobs".[22] Reporters were horrified to hear women advocating not only an end to marriage but also for equality between the sexes.[23] Michel presided over the Club of the Revolution, which voted to arrest any priests who were in league with the "monarchist dogs" and to set up corporations of women and men to undertake necessary public works.[24] At the Club of the Free Thinkers, Nathalie Lemel and Lodoyska Kawecka, who dressed in trousers and wore two revolvers hanging from her sash, argued for divorce and the liberation of women. At the Club of the Proletarians a laundress, known only as Madame Andre, was the secretary. One regular speaker was a Citizeness Thiourt, who demanded that cannons be placed in the well-to-do squares of Paris and that women be given the right to bear arms.[25] Léo, Michel and Lemel toured the clubs arguing that capitalist exploitation must be abolished.[26]

---

19 Ross, 2015, p51.

20 Ross, 2015, p43.

21 Thomas, 1964, p37.

22 Gullickson, 1996, p113.

23 Gullickson, 1996, p113.

24 Thomas, 1964, p85.

25 Thomas, 1964, pp83-5.

26 Thomas, 1964, p88.

Before the storm: women under siege

The year 1870 began with a huge political revolt in Paris. Emperor Louis Bonaparte's cousin, Pierre, murdered a Republican journalist, Victor Noir. The murder sparked outrage and many women joined the 100,000 who marched through Paris in protest. A wave of repression was unleashed against members of the International. In the summer, the emperor declared war on Prussia but within weeks French forces had been defeated. On 4 September 1870 news of the defeat reached Paris. Thousands surged onto the streets, the Second Empire was overthrown and a Government of National Defence was established. The new government, however, refused to represent the interests of those who had installed them in office. The government's attempts to surrender to the Prussian army sparked weeks of unrest led by Parisian workers and the National Guard, whose members were drawn from the working class.

On 18 September 1870 many women were in the streets demanding the right to take up arms in defence of the French city of Strasbourg, which was besieged by Prussian troops. Louise Michel and André Léo led a delegation of women, students and school pupils to the Hotel de Ville, where they were locked up for a few hours.[27] On 19 September Prussian troops laid siege to Paris. Around 100,000 rich citizens fled and 200,000 refugees from neighbouring towns entered the city. "Vigilance committees" were set up. Michel refused to recognise the segregated nature of the vigilance committees and joined the men's committee. She later described how "no one was very much bothered by the sex of those who were doing their duty. That silly problem was over and done with".[28] Necessity led to an erosion of gender discrimination.

Food supplies to the city were blocked and women protested against long queues and catastrophic food shortages. Women needed new ways to organise and socialist women were at the heart of creating them. Nathalie Lemel ran a cooperative restaurant called La Marmite.[29] She was active in several of the many mutual aid groups which the police kept under surveillance because they had the potential to turn into resistance groups.[30] La Marmite was based on solidarity between those working in supply, catering and production, bound together with a hefty dose of socialist propaganda.[31] Victorine Brochon, another member of the International, ran a cooperative bakery in La Chapelle which donated a

---

27 Thomas, 1964, p38.
28 Thomas, 1964, p36.
29 Thomas, 1964, p32.
30 Thomas, 1964, p6.
31 Thomas, 1964, p7.

proportion of its funds to new cooperatives.[32] Many more socialist women were at the centre of efforts to feed the people during the siege, efforts which placed them at the centre of mutual aid networks and political organisation.

An attempted insurrection in Paris on 22 January 1871 demanded that the government be replaced by a Commune. Large numbers of women and national guardsmen massed on the streets of Paris. However, the failure of the insurrection led to a backlash and then on 28 January the French government officially surrendered to Germany.[33] A general election held on 8 February was a massive defeat for the left with landowners, aristocrats and army officers forming the majority of those elected. The French section of the First International had 50,000 members in the spring of 1870 but after the February elections, leading members felt they were on the brink of collapse as support drained away.[34] However, some glimpses of the insurgency to come were nevertheless visible. On 26 February, a rumour that German troops were planning to enter Paris in order to take the city's cannon brought a huge crowd of national guardsmen, women and children out to defend the cannon they had paid for with their subscriptions.[35] Through all the turbulent events of 1870 and the first months of 1871, women were leading the crowds, urging defiance and creating the basis of the organisations which would create a worker's government.

The Universal Republic

The French government decamped to the safety of Versailles, on Paris's western fringes. On 18 March, Thiers, who had surrendered to Germany as the government's "chief executive", sent troops to disarm the Parisian National Guard. It was milkmaids who raised the alarm. The women of Paris swarmed among the government troops as they attempted to remove the cannon. Prosper Olivier Lissagaray, a socialist and a historian of the Commune, noted that "it was the women who were first to act".[36] Women formed a human barricade between the government's soldiers and the National Guard. A government supporter, General Louis d'Aurelle de Paladines, described the significance of the women's actions:

> The women and children came and mixed with the troops. We were greatly mistaken in permitting these people to approach our soldiers, for they mingled

---

32 Thomas, 1964, p6.
33 Germany had been formed just ten days earlier when, off the back of his military victories against the French, Prussia's King Wilhelm I was proclaimed headed of a unified German Empire at a ceremony in the Palace of Versailles.
34 Ross, 2015, p54.
35 Thomas, 1964, p42.
36 Lissagaray, 1976, p65.

among them and the women and children told them: "You will not fire upon the people." This is how the soldiers of the 88th, as far as I can see, and of another line regiment found themselves surrounded and did not have the power to resist those ovations that were given to them.[37]

When the officer in charge, General Claude Lecomte, ordered the troops to fire on the crowd, they refused. Lecomte was taken prisoner and later shot.

Before March 1871, the Commune existed only as a political aspiration, a rallying cry and possible different future—but with the government gone and the army and police driven out, a real, living Commune based on the "anonymous power of Monsieur Tout-le-monde ('Mr Everyone')" was established.[38] A great sense of freedom brought a mass movement of men, women and children exploding onto the streets. One witness described the atmosphere:

> There was, first of all, a grandiose festival, a festival that the people of Paris, the essence and symbol of the French people, and of humanity in general, created for itself and for the spring. Spring festival in the city, festival of the disinherited and the proletarians, revolutionary festival and festival of the revolution.[39]

The revolution transformed all interactions: "The social life of the city was recalibrated according to principles of cooperation and association".[40] All this energy and commitment was rapidly channelled towards running the vital services of the city.

Paris's state institutions had disintegrated or been destroyed by the government at Versailles. "All the respiratory and digestive apparatus of this city of 1,600,000 collapsed".[41] The crisis was so deep that the cemeteries had ceased to bury the dead and some 300,000 were out of work.[42] The General Council of the National Guard stepped up to take over running the state until elections were held. All foreigners were admitted to citizenship, all state functionaries either eliminated or paid a workers' wage and subject to immediate recall. Priests and nuns were despatched to private life. Manual workers and those from subordinate positions took over the jobs of the highly-paid bureaucrats and began to organise public services such as the post office.

The people of Paris transformed their physical environment, destroying the symbols of the old regime. On 10 April the guillotine was dragged to the Place

---

37 Thomas, 1964, p45.
38 Ross, 2015, p57.
39 Gluckstein, 2011, p7.
40 Ross, 2015, p25.
41 Lissagaray, 1976, p85.
42 Lissagaray, 1976, p85.

Voltaire and publicly burned by a crowd led by women. On 16 May the Vendôme Column, which glorified Napoleon's imperialist conquests, was torn down and the square was renamed the Place Internationale. Communards tore down the symbols of the old order, but they also demanded positive change. The Commune had a policy of creating "communal luxury", a phrase coined by Eugène Pottier, who wrote the "Internationale" in order to commemorate the Commune.[43] "Communal luxury" was a programme for public beauty in which art would be integrated into public life rather than treated as a private commodity enjoyed by the wealthy.[44] The radical painter Gustave Courbet worked for the Commune's Arts Commission. He described the enormous efforts people went to in order to reorder their society:

> I have breakfast and preside over meetings for 12 hours each day. My head has begun to spin, but despite this mental torment, which I am not used to, I am enchanted. Paris is a true paradise! No police, no nonsense, no exaction of any kind, no arguments! Everything in Paris rolls along like clockwork. All the government bodies are organised federally and run themselves".[45]

As art and politics became intertwined, female artists found their voice. Singer Rosalie Bordas, known as La Bordas, was born in Monteux in 1840 and learnt to sing in the Red Café, which was run by her parents. She moved to Paris and sang for the Paris Concert and in 1870, during the siege, she sang "La Marseillaise" and waved a tricolour on stage. She was committed to the Commune, performing revolutionary songs while wrapped in a red flag in order to raise funds for the wounded.[46]

The Commune demonstrated that working class people were capable of organising society more efficiently and fairly than the privileged politicians and bureaucrats that they had replaced. However, many of the Commune's supporters had a wider ambition: to lay the basis of a socialist society. Elise Reclus, who had been a member of André Léo's feminist circle, wrote:

> The Commune set up for the future a new society in which there are no masters by birth title or wealth, and no slaves by origin, caste or salary. Everywhere the word "Commune" was understood in its largest sense as referring to a new humanity, made up of free and equal companions, oblivious to the existence of

---

43 For more on Pottier and the Internationale, see Gluckstein, 2008.
44 Ross, 2015, pp 39-67.
45 Gluckstein, 2011, p9.
46 Thomas, 1964, p110.

old boundaries, helping each other in peace from one end of the world to the other.[47]

They believed that the Commune could inspire an international movement towards egalitarianism and freedom.

Building a new society

Arthur Arnould published a book called *State and Revolution* in 1878, 40 years before Lenin's work of the same name. In it, Arnould explained the Commune's unique ambitions:

> The Paris Commune was something *more* and something *other* than an uprising. It was the advent of a principle, the affirmation of a politics. In a word, it was not only one more revolution. It was a new revolution, carrying in the folds of its flag a wholly original and characteristic programme.[48]

To implement this programme required the mass involvement of the previously marginalised people of Paris. On 26 March, around 200,000 male Parisians elected a General Council to organise the Commune. When the results were declared, a third of those elected were members of the First International. The results were greeted with a "dazzling spectacle of hope for change, tens of thousands on the streets, the 'Marseillaise' playing, red flags waving, seas of banners and bayonets glinting in the sun".[49]

Women were not allowed to vote in these elections and their exclusion has prompted some historians to question whether women were really included in this "Universal Republic". Historian James McMillan argues that "it cannot be claimed that women's rights were at the top of the Commune's priorities".[50] There are a number of reasons for this perception of the Commune. When the government troops were driven out of Paris, the Federation of the National Guard filled the vacuum of power. Based on military service, it was an entirely male organisation. The National Guard ceded power to the formal institution of the Commune that was the town council of Paris, albeit one which was rapidly adapting to the revolution taking place in the streets. The inheritances of the past shaped the formal structures of the Commune, even while the mass movement was establishing new priorities and aspirations. One such inheritance was the voting system used under the Second Empire that excluded women and reflected the entrenched nature of sexism in French society.

---

47 Ross, 2015, p24.
48 Ross, 2015, p58.
49 Gluckstein, 2011, p42.
50 McMillan, 2000, p133.

A further reason for the negative interpretation of the role of women in the Commune lies within feminist histories that equate feminism with a "vocabulary of rights" that limits definitions of feminism to the pursuit of equal civil rights for women.[51] The female Communards rejected the idea of civil rights and instead demanded the right to work and to organise collectively. They did not present themselves in terms of civil rights and so have been overlooked in feminist histories of France.

The exclusion of women from the formal institution of the Commune might have been challenged if the Parisian Revolution had survived for more than a few weeks. There was constant debate about the role women should play in the Commune. André Léo complained that women who wanted to support the Commune were at times rebuffed by male militants who did not want women to act as nurses and supply the front lines.[52] The Marxist wing of the First International was the only political organisation in France which supported the female franchise. At least four socialist members of the Commune—Eugène Varlin, Benoît Malon, Édouard Vaillant and the Hungarian Leó Frankel—took initiatives that promoted women's equality in their areas of responsibility. One historian of the Commune, Gay Gullickson, argues that since no women were members of the Commune's leading bodies—the Central Committee, the Communal Council and the National Guard—the Commune could not represent their interests.

However, Gullickson's argument overlooks the ways in which the Commune did respond to female activism. Indeed, it was the first French regime to appoint women to positions of responsibility, where they lead welfare programmes, made vital appeals for support to provincial cities and transformed education.[53] Evictions were banned, and allowances for unmarried partners of national guardsmen and their children were introduced. Many contemporaries saw this as the Commune's most revolutionary measure.[54] Communard Arthur Arnould wrote:

> This decree, which raises woman to the level of man, which puts her, in the eyes of morals and the law, on a footing of civic equality with man, placed itself upon the plane of living morality, and delivered a mortal blow to the religio-monarchical institution of marriage as we see it functioning in modern society.[55]

Arnould was being a little optimistic in his assessment, but it was a move of great significance for working-class women. Other important reforms included

---

51 Jones and Verges, 1991, p492.
52 McMillan, 2000, p133.
53 Schulkind, 1985, p135.
54 Thomas, 1964, p 54.
55 Thomas, 1964, p54.

banning the sale of the many thousands of items left in pawn shops. The Commune also organised public assistance schemes, distributing tokens to the poor and setting up public canteens. In April, the Commune announced it was requisitioning the houses left empty by the rich for the use of poor families.[56]

A second problem with Gullickson's argument is that she approaches the Commune from the top down rather than the bottom up. The militant women's organisations in the Commune and leading women activists such as Louise Michel did not see the vote as central to their vision of collective liberation. They tended to be dismissive of the right to vote and focused instead on the right to work and to bear arms, which they saw as more fundamental and immediate. They found ways to shape the Commune through organising in their communities and workplaces, their unions, committees and clubs.

In its 72 days, the Commune did not completely uproot centuries of women's oppression. It did, however, both promote women to positions of authority and enable women to have real power over their lives. When assessing the Commune's record, it should be remembered that nowhere internationally, with the exception of one area of Australia, did even property-owning women have the right to vote in major elections in 1871. No women served in the French government until three women were appointed by the Popular Front coalition of 1936. These women were appointed rather than elected because they could not stand for office or vote in an election until 1945. Viewed from an international and historical perspective, the Commune stands out as a form of government that encouraged the active support of women.

In return, women made huge sacrifices to support the Commune. They had none of the time, freedom and energy bestowed by running water and toilets in their homes, by gas, electricity and public transport. They had to manage their periods, pregnancies and childbirth without basic hygiene, pain relief and medical support. They had little or no education, no health service and no pensions.[57] In normal times they were seen as inert and resigned and in thrall to the Catholic Church. Yet during the Commune those women began to act as if they felt they would be listened to, as if they could make a difference. And make a difference they did.

On 1 April the government declared war on Paris. On 11 April the Union of Women for the Defence of Paris was established. It aimed to mobilise women to defend the Commune, treat the wounded and carry out important work. Its committees met daily in most districts of Paris and it became "the Commune's

---

56 Holmes, 2014, p103.
57 Schulkind, 1985, p130.

largest and most effective organisation".[58] The Union aimed to organise the defence of Paris's revolution and to instigate long-term changes in women's labour to eradicate the masters and exploiters. It issued an address calling on the Commune to abolish all forms of gender inequality and describing sex discrimination as a means employed by the ruling class to maintain their power. This was the first time a significant French women's organisation explained their inferior status in terms of class.[59]

The achievements of the Union were huge. It provided staff for orphanages and care for old people, recruited nurses and canteen workers, provided speakers for public meetings. The Union asked for space in local halls so it could meet and staff a desk providing information, aid and expenses for printing leaflets and posters—all of which the Commune provided. Nightly meetings of the Union were attended by between 3,000 and 4,000 women.[60]

The driving force behind the Union was an outstanding revolutionary socialist leader, Elisabeth Dimitrieff. Dimitrieff had escaped from her native Russia for less repressive Geneva, where she was one of the signatories of the founding document of the Russian section of the International. The document sought to synthesise Marx's economic theories with the beliefs of the influential writer Nikolai Chernyshevsky in the emancipatory potential of the traditional peasant commune. In Geneva, Dimitrieff met future Communards and supporters of women's rights, Eugène Varlin and Benoît Malon. Dimitrieff also edited a journal, *The People's Cause*. Its founding statement declared:

> As the foundation of economic justice, we advance two fundamental theses:
> The land belongs to those who work it with their own hands: to the agricultural communes.
> Capital and all the tools of labour belong to the workers: to the workers' associations.[61]

These ideas resurfaced in the Commune. Dimitrieff spent three months in London, discussing her journal with the Marx family. She requested to be sent to Paris and there she established the Union of Women. Dimitrieff's politics shaped everything she did. She sought out working-class women, recruiting laundresses and seamstresses to the Union.

The Union of Women was not the only organisation created by socialist women to support and influence the Commune. Beatrix Excoffon and Anna

---

58 Ross, 2015, p72.
59 Schulkind, 1985, p139.
60 McClellan, 1979, p152.
61 Ross, 2015, p69.

Jaclard were members of the Women's Vigilance Committee. Then there was Anna Korvin-Krukovsky, born in Russia to an aristocratic family. In the 1860s, the great Russian writer Fyodor Dostoyevsky had proposed to her but she rejected him. Anna and her sister, the mathematician Sophie Korvin-Krukovsky, escaped from Russia and managed get to France and Germany respectively. Anna met Victor Jacland at a revolutionary meeting, and in 1869 the two were forced into exile in Switzerland. They returned to Paris when the Second Empire fell in 1870, and he was elected to the Central Committee of the National Guard. Anna helped to establish the Montmartre Vigilance Committee, which ran workshops, recruited ambulance nurses, sent women speakers to clubs and hunted down draft dodgers.[62] It was another organisation which enabled women to express their own aspirations and organise to achieve them.

How women shaped the Commune

To explore how women shaped the Commune, I will look at four key areas: women's work, women's education, women's attempts to spread the revolution and women's attitude to their new state.

Women's work

The Commune gave women work. Lissagaray saw 1,500 women sewing sandbags for the barricades, while another 3,000 worked on making cartridges.[63] Benoît Malon and Leó Frankel were both members of the International and were also in charge of the Commission for Labour. They believed this commission was the most important mechanism for implementing lasting social change.[64] Frankel explained:

> The people created its political organism as a mean of realising the very aim of the revolution, that is the emancipation of labour, the abolition of monopolies, privileges, bureaucracy, speculative, capitalist and industrial feudalism.[65]

The Commission for Labour was shaped by and absolutely depended upon the Union of Women.[66] On 16 April the Communal Council decreed that workshops whose owners fled to Versailles would be passed to the "cooperative association of workers who were employed there".[67] Dimitrieff believed that taking over the workshops was a way to transform labour by introducing equal pay, shorter

---

62 Thomas, 1964, p78.
63 Lissagaray, 1976, p239.
64 Thomas, 1964, p 68.
65 Gluckstein, 2011, p17.
66 Gluckstein, 2011, p39.
67 Gluckstein, 2011, p19.

working hours and ending the competition between women and men. Frankel and Malon drew up a plan for women's labour and put Dimitrieff in charge. She envisaged the workshops as free associations of labourers working for their collective profit:

> In taking work away from the bondage of capitalistic exploitation, the formation of these organisations would eventually allow the workers to run their own business.[68]

The working class was not yet powerful enough to organise production collectively through workers' councils. Nevertheless, Dimitrieff, Frankel and Malon tried to separate labour from exploitation by workshop owners and instead direct it according to the needs of both consumers and producers.

Education for emancipation

André Léo, Paule Mink, Louise Michel and Noémi and Élie Reclus had developed their ideas about female education in the 1860s. The Commune afforded them the opportunity to put their ideas into practice. The Commune's Education Committee included these veterans of the 1860s women's organisation as well as Jaclard and Dimitrieff. The Education Committee was no moderate means by which women could extend their traditional domestic role into the public sphere. It was a tool for empowering women and enabling them to participate in the Commune while simultaneously subverting gender stereotypes.[69] Despite the desperately limited means at its disposal, the Commune prioritised introducing education for girls. The radical newspaper *Le Père Duchêne* explained why:

> If only you realised, citizens, how much the revolution depends on women, you would have your eyes opened on girls' education. You would not leave them, as has been done until now, in ignorance![70]

For many female Communards, education for girls was both a question of equality and of reforming human nature for a future socialist society.

Education became both free and secular. This meant turfing out nuns and priests and recruiting more teachers, with female teachers being awarded equal pay. The commission drew up plans to establish day nurseries. Parental and community engagement was another priority. Twice a week the Society for a New Education, which was composed of three women and three men, brought teachers

---

68 Thomas, 1964, p70.
69 Eichner, 2004, p98.
70 Gluckstein, 2011, p27.

and parents together to discuss the curriculum and the methods used in schools.[71] The committee took a radical approach to education: "Any official direction which is imposed on the judgement of pupils is fatal and must be condemned... It tends to destroy individuality".[72] Women did not just sit on committees. Mink opened a girls' school in the chapel of Saint-Pierre de Montmartre. Marcelle Tinayre, who was the first female school inspector in France, took charge of the secularisation process in the 12th Arrondissement area of Paris.

Spreading the revolution

The Communards understood that the Paris Commune could not survive if it remained isolated from the rest of the country. After initial uprisings in other major towns were crushed, practical and political support from the small farmers around Paris was vital to feeding the city. Women were at the forefront of reaching out to the peasantry. Léo was largely responsible for writing a manifesto for rural workers, "To the Workers of the Countryside", although Malon also contributed to it. Some 100,000 copies were printed. "What Paris wants is the land for the peasants, the tools for the workers and work by and for everyone", Léo argued.[73] What does it matter, she continued, if the oppressor is called a landowner or a manufacturer? The pamphlet pointed out that "if Paris falls, the yoke of poverty will remain on your neck and pass onto your children".[74] Léo proposed ways that the capital could reach out to the rest of the country and Mink toured the provinces raising support.[75] Léo and Mink were entirely right to direct their efforts towards winning support outside Paris. Marx argued that it was the Commune's isolation from the countryside that proved to be fatal. No press reports reached the small villages. Their inhabitants had no chance to see that the Commune represented their "living interests" and "real wants" without communication from the Communards.[76]

Dimitrieff also urged the General Council to increase its efforts to break out of isolation, but she set her sights on other European nations rather than the countryside. She understood that the military forces were regrouping at Versailles, but believed that if the Commune could deepen its efforts at reform, it would also deepen its international support: "If the Commune is victorious, our political organisation will be transformed into a social one, and we will create

71 Thomas, 1964, p96.
72 Gluckstein, 2011, p27.
73 Ross, 2015, p218.
74 Thomas, 1964, p103.
75 Thomas, 1964, p104.
76 Ross, 2015, p215.

new sections of the International".[77] Dimitrieff wrote optimistically to Marx, outlining how revolt might spread across Europe:

> In general, the internationalist propagandising I am doing here, in order to show that all countries, including Germany, find themselves on the eve of the social revolution, is a very pleasing proposition to women.[78]

According to Dimitrieff, women were particularly tuned in to the idea that the revolution must spread to countries such as Germany. Her strategy did not have the opportunity to become a reality.

Finishing the revolution

The Commune replaced the army and the police with the National Guard. Many radicals, including many women, wanted to use this revolutionary wing of the workers' state to overthrow the government at Versailles. However, Dimitrieff was one of the very few Marxists in the leadership of the Commune. Thus, discussions on whether to march on Versailles took place between Proudhonists who, as anarchists, did not believe in political action and Jacobins who were from a middle-class political tradition. The Blanquists were the main group to argue for the march on Versailles but they were too small to win wide support. On 2 April, Versailles launched an attack on a Parisian suburb. Women helped build new barricades and decided to lead an action of their own and launched an appeal in several newspapers:

> Let's go to Versailles. Let's tell Versailles what the revolution of Paris is. Let's tell Versailles that Paris has made the Commune because we want to stay free. Let's tell Versailles that Paris has made ready to defend herself because people tried to take her by surprise and disarm her. Let's tell Versailles that the Assembly is not the law, Paris is.[79]

Beatrix Excoffon, known in her district as "The Republican", described the gathering on the following day:

> I told my mother I was leaving, I kissed my children and off I went. At the Place de la Concorde, at half past one, I joined the procession. There were between 700 and 800 women. Some talked about explaining to Versailles what Paris wanted; others talked about how things were a hundred years ago, when the women of

---

77 McClellan, 1979, p152.
78 Singer-Lecocq, 2011, p130.
79 Thomas, 1964, p48.

Paris had already gone to Versailles to carry off the baker and the baker's wife and the baker's little boy.[80]

"The baker and the baker's wife and the baker's little boy" is a reference to the women's march on Versailles that took place in 1789. At that time, a hungry mob of women and men had laid siege to the Palace of Versailles and captured King Louis XVI and his family. Many female Communards invoked this militant revolutionary tradition of women's activism rooted in the Great French Revolution. However, unlike in 1789, the women's marches of 1871 were turned back by the National Guard, who feared the women would be shot by government troops.

Louise Michel was one of the most ardent supporters of a military attack on the government. She even volunteered to go to Versailles to assassinate Adolphe Thiers herself. She fought so bravely that the 61st Battalion gave her a Remington rifle and on receiving it she declared: "Now we are fighting. This is a battle. There is a rise, where I run ahead crying 'To Versailles! To Versailles!'"[81] Michel instinctively knew that if the government at Versailles was not crushed, it would be unceasing in its efforts to overthrow the Commune.

After the defeat of the Commune, Paule Mink argued that the moderate minority in the Central Council lacked the courage to deliver a fatal blow against the government. In the face of the brutal suppression of the Commune, Mink drew the conclusion that centralised, organised revolution was the right strategy to achieve socialism. Lenin explored the experience of the Commune in his *State and Revolution* (1917) and raised the same criticism as Mink. He wrote that revolutions must:

> Suppress the bourgeoisie and crush their resistance. This was particularly necessary for the Commune; and one of the reasons for its defeat was that it did not do this with sufficient determination. The organ of suppression, however, is here the majority of the population, and not a minority, as was always the case under slavery, serfdom and wage slavery.[82]

Michel, Mink and Lenin all made similar observations. The Commune had created a new kind of state, based on the engagement of the majority, but failed to direct its power against the old order, which would never stop seeking the means to destroy any hope of a different society.

---

80 Thomas, 1964, p49.
81 Thomas, 1964, p126.
82 Lenin, 1917.

Women on the barricades

On 21 May, troops sent from Versailles entered Paris and the entire population was summoned to the barricades. All contemporary accounts of the last days of the Commune pay tribute to the courage of women as they built barricades, nursed the wounded, supplied the National Guard with food and drink and fought alongside men. There was no great separation between nursing and fighting. Louise Michel described how women answered a call to volunteer to treat the wounded and often took up their rifles.[83] André Léo noticed that officers were hostile to the nurses but the rank and file troops welcomed them.[84] The Union of Women met on the same day that the government troops entered Paris. Nathalie Lemel, red flag in hand, led the women out to the barricade at Batignolles. Elisabeth Dimitrieff urged all devoted and patriotic women to organise the defence of the wounded. Anna Jaclard and André Léo issued an appeal from their vigilance committee to the women of Monmartre, asking them to support a summons from the Commune: "The women of Montmartre, inspired by the revolutionary spirit, wish to attest by their actions to their devotion to the revolution".[85] The women acted as ambulance nurses under fire and many were captured, raped and shot dead by the government troops.

Fighting was a revolutionary act, which is why, as Edith Thomas pointed out, the same women who attended the political clubs were also those who climbed the barricades. The French government used brutal force to crush the Commune, with some 20,000 men, women and children executed during what became known as "Bloody Week". Women were involved in all the military engagements during Bloody Week and many were listed among the wounded and the dead. One name on the list was that of Blanche Lefebvre, a laundress at the Sainte-Marie des Batignolles washhouse. She was a member of the Club of the Social Revolution, which had been set up on 3 May in the local church. Lefebvre was also a member of the Central Committee of the Union of Women.[86] She was one of 120 women who held the barricade at the Place Blanche for several hours until they ran out of ammunition and were overrun. Those taken at the barricade were shot on the spot. Lefebvre was one of them. She was aged just 24.

---

83 Thomas, 1964, p113.
84 Thomas, 1964, p118.
85 Thomas, 1964, p114.
86 Ray, 2012.

The myth of the pétroleuse

It took the government troops seven long days of shelling, hand to hand combat and mass executions to retake Paris. Their revenge on women was particularly harsh. Women were systematically humiliated, stripped, raped and murdered by government troops.[87] Malon attributed the troops' ferocity to lessons learned by the French army in its colonial subjugation of North Africa.[88] Communards were shot where they were captured, but all working-class women were under suspicion. The women of the Commune were considered to have "unsexed themselves". *The Times* reported that the women forgot, "their sex and their gentleness to commit assassination, to poison soldiers, to burn and to slay".[89] Opponents called female Communards evil, amazons, furies, jackals. *The Pall Mall Gazette* described the female Communards as, "hideous viragoes—furies intoxicated with the fumes of wine and blood".[90] Wealthy society women lined up to abuse women prisoners and beat them with their parasols as they were dragged past on their way to prison.[91] The myth of the "pétroleuse", women who burnt down buildings, began to circulate, justifying repression by dehumanising its victims. Despite the myth, out of the 1,051 women who were arrested during the Bloody Week, only five were convicted of arson.[92] Historians researching archives at the French Ministry of War have found, amidst the records of arrests, trials and pleas for clemency, evidence of the "dramatically varied way that women participated in the revolutionary struggle of 1871".[93] These women were not protected by their sex: the state punished them precisely because they were women who refused to submit to oppression.

Dimitrieff escaped from Paris and sent a telegram from Geneva informing the International of her safe arrival.[94] According to Lissagaray, Dimtrieff ran a hotel on the shores of Lake Geneva where she nursed refugees from the Commune.[95] She then continued her agitation in Russia, turning towards political terrorism, perhaps as a result of her frustration at the defeat of the Commune. Malon, Léo and Mink also escaped to Geneva.[96] Victor Jaclard was arrested and transferred to prison camp at Versailles but managed to escape and he and Anna also fled to

---

87 Gullickson, 1996, p181.
88 Ross, 2015, p213.
89 Gullickson, 1996, p178.
90 McMillan, 2000, 135.
91 Thomas, 1964, p136.
92 McMillan, 2000, p135.
93 Jones and Verges, 1991, p495.
94 McClellan, 1979, p153.
95 Abidor, 2010.
96 Eichner, 2004, p157.

Geneva. Thousands of others were not so lucky. Beatrix Excoffon was sentenced to transportation, although this was commuted to ten years in prison. Many thousands of other working women were summarily executed without a trial or imprisoned simply for expressing support for the Commune, for example, by allowing their shops to become meeting places.

Their stories illustrate the hopes that the Commune aroused among its supporters and how they experienced change in every aspect of their lives. A laundress named Marie Wolff was one of those prosecuted. On 27 May, four escaped prisoners who were supporters of the Versailles government were arrested. Wolff, who was an ambulance nurse, took part in their execution. Before the Commune, Wolff had served time in prison for theft and burglary. During the Commune she carried a red banner and a belt with weapons stuck in it. On 25 April 1872, Wolff was sentenced to death for her role in the execution of the prisoners. Her sentence was commuted to hard labour for life.[97]

Marguerite Tinayre was a teacher and supporter of the International. Her husband, who was unpolitical, was shot as he searched for her. She was sentenced to transportation but escaped to Geneva and then Budapest with her five children. Tinayre was excluded from an amnesty of 1879 because she continued with her "socialistic and internationalist intrigues".[98] She was eventually allowed back to Paris.

The revenge of the ruling class was brutal, but it did not crush the revolutionary spirit of the female Communards. Eliska Vincent, veteran of Léo's 1866 feminist group, was almost executed for her role in the Commune, but went on to lead a women's suffrage organisation and edited a paper, *Equality*.[99] Michel dared the court to sentence her to death. They declined and sentenced her to penal transportation. She met Lemel in the penal colony of New Caledonia in the South Pacific Ocean. Michel returned to Paris after a total amnesty was declared in 1880. She was arrested on a demonstration of unemployed workers in 1883 and sentenced to six years of solitary confinement. She was arrested again in 1890 but escaped to England, where she taught refugee children. Michel returned to France and died of pneumonia in January 1905. More than 100,000 attended her funeral. When the Commune fell, Mink was touring the provinces to win support for the Commune. She managed to escape to Geneva with her daughter. She never stopped organising for socialist revolution. When she was buried on May Day 1901, thousands of mourners joined the funeral procession through the streets of Paris, calling "Vive la Commune" and "Vive la Internationale". Over 600 police, 500 soldiers and 100

97 Thomas, 1964, p165.
98 Thomas, 1964, p179.
99 McMillan, 2000, p195.

cavalry were required to patrol the streets.[100] Her funeral underlined the continuing importance of the Commune in the socialist tradition.

Conclusion: agitating and squawking

One historian of the Commune describes it as an "incubator for embryonic feminist socialisms".[101] It would be more accurate to say that women's role in the Commune encouraged experienced socialist women to reach out to other working women. Mink wrote in the Geneva-based newspaper of the International, *Equality*, addressing women:

> It is in the name of women that I speak, in the name of women to whom the International has given the rights and duties equal to those of men... Only socialism will be able to emancipate women materially and morally, as it will be able to emancipate all those who suffer![102]

Socialist men who supported women's emancipation were also keen to draw the lessons of the Commune. In 1871, just weeks after the defeat, Malon argued that "one important fact demonstrated by the revolution in Paris is the entry of women into political life... Women and the proletariat can only hope to achieve their respective liberation by uniting".[103] At the same time, Leó Frankel wrote:

> All the objections produced against equality of men and women are the same sort as those which are produced against the emancipation of the Negro race. Firstly, people are blindfolded and they are told that they have been blind since birth. By claiming that half of the human race is incompetent, man prides himself on appearing to be the protector of women. Revolting hypocrisy! Just let the barriers of privilege be lowered and we shall see.[104]

In 1879, the national workers' congress in Marseille marked a decisive shift in attitude of organised French workers and a "majority rallied behind the notion of complete civil and political equality".[105] The motion was ardently defended at the congress by Hubertine Auclert, a working-class socialist. She was acclaimed by the Congress, elected as chair of both the session and the commission, and the Congress adopted a resolution proclaiming the "absolute equality of the sexes".[106]

---

100 Eichner, 2004, pp179-80.
101 Eichner, 2004, p18.
102 Eichner, 2004, p182.
103 Schulkind, 1985, p160.
104 Schulkind, 1985, p137.
105 McMillan, 2000, p116.
106 Schuklind, 1985, p160.

The Paris Commune impacted powerfully on the Marx family. Marx initially opposed the Parisian uprising as premature. Yet once it was underway, he and the whole family threw themselves into supporting it. Marx was vilified as the "red doctor" and sinister insurrectionist who had instigated the Commune. Two of the Marx daughters, Eleanor and Jenny, were lucky to escape after visiting France in April 1871. Defeat brought refugees flooding into London and many found their way to the Marx family home. Jenny and the third sister Laura married Communards and Eleanor was engaged for a while to Lissagaray, whose invaluable history of the Commune she translated. The Commune also shaped the international socialist movement and was commemorated by the British working-class movement for decades with anniversary celebrations, speeches and events.

Marx described the Communards' greatest achievement as the new ways of organising they created, the Commune's "actual working existence".[107] The experience of 1871 prompted Marx to distance himself from the idea that revolutionary perspectives must be based on capitalist "progress". Rather, he saw non-capitalist forms of communal property ownership as creating potential allies for the working class. History progresses not through self-contained stages but rather through the interactions of town and country, worker and peasant. Despite its disastrous ending, the Commune was a new point of departure of world-historic importance. As Lissagaray wrote, the Commune was "the first attempt by the proletariat to govern itself".[108] The only alteration Marx ever made to *The Communist Manifesto* was in 1872 when he added the line: "The working class cannot simply lay hold of the ready-made state machinery and wield it for their own purpose." For Marx, the Commune showed how the oppressive state could be broken and replaced with a democratic state run by the majority.

On the brink of the October Revolution of 1917, Vladimir Lenin drew on the experience of the Commune. He described how the abolition of the standing army and all officials being elected and subject to recall "signifies a gigantic replacement of certain institutions by other institutions of a fundamentally different type: democracy, introduced as fully and consistently as is at all conceivable, is transformed from bourgeois into proletarian democracy".[109] When he defended the Bolsheviks from accusations that the party was too small to govern Russia, he argued that:

> We have a "magic way" to enlarge our state apparatus tenfold at once, at one stroke—a way which no capitalist state ever possessed or could possess. This

---

107 Ross, 2015, p35.
108 Lissagaray, 1976, p3.
109 Lenin, 1917.

magic way is to draw the working people, to draw the poor, into the daily work of state administration.[110]

The Communards were the first to demonstrate this latent magic within the working class.

The Marxist analysis of the state is constantly under pressure from those who argue that the idea of "smashing the state" is outmoded and that many state-run services, such as health, education and welfare, must be preserved and extended rather than smashed up. The Communards did not "smash" the post office, the cemeteries or the schools; they took them over and ran them for the benefit of the majority. As Lenin put it, the revolution must "cut the wires" that tie the useful aspects of the state from the capitalist interests that distort and limit them and from repressive institutions such as the police and army.

Rosa Luxemburg turned to the Commune in the last article she wrote, published in January 1919. She described how the Commune had ended in terrible defeat, like so many heroic working-class struggles. Then she asked:

> Where would we be today without those terrible defeats, from which we draw historical experience, understanding, power and idealism? We stand on the foundation of those defeats; and we cannot do without any of them, because each one contributes to our strength and understanding.[111]

The Commune was a working-class revolution that was necessarily also a "great gender event" because it depended on women's active involvement, creativity and courage.[112] It was the visible involvement of women that made the Commune so appalling to its opponents. One wrote:

> Those females who dedicated themselves to the Commune—and there were many—had but a single ambition: to raise themselves above the level of man. They were all there, agitating and squawking, the gentleman's seamstresses, the gentleman's shirt makers, the teachers of boys, the maids of all work. During the final days all these bellicose viragos held out longer than the men did behind the barricades.[113]

Across the English Channel, a *Times* reporter joined in the abuse, sneering: "If the French nation were composed only of the French women, what a terrible nation it would be".[114] If the unruly women of Paris had been in charge of the

110 Lenin, 1918.
111 Luxemburg, 1919.
112 Holmes, 2014, p105.
113 Lissagaray, 1976, p419.
114 Holmes, 2014, p106.

whole country, it is conceivable that the revolution could have spread across Europe. Perhaps then, this brief but inspiring example of workers' power could have won more time and so provided us with many more examples of how working-class people can organise together to create a socialist society.

Bibliography

Abidor, Mitchell, 2010, *Communards: The Story of the Commune of 1871 as Told By Those Who Fought For It* (Marxist Internet Archive).

Eichner, Caroline J, 2004, *Surmounting the Barricades: Women in the Paris Commune* (Indianna University Press).

Gluckstein, Donny, 2008, "Decyphering the Internationale: The Eugène Pottier Code", *International Socialism 120* (autumn), https://isj.org.uk/decyphering-the-internationale-the-eugene-pottier-code

Gluckstein, Donny, 2011, *The Paris Commune* (Haymarket Books).

Gullickson, Gay L, 1996, *Unruly Women of Paris: Images of the Commune* (Cornell University Press).

Holmes, Rachel, 2014, *Eleanor Marx: A Life* (Bloomsbury).

Jones, Kathleen, and Francois Verges, 1991, "'Aux citoyennes!': Women, Politics and the Paris Commune of 1871", *History of European Ideas*, volume 13, issue 6.

Jones, Kathleen, and Francois Verges, 1991, "Women of the Paris Commune", *Women's Studies International Forum*, volume 14, number 5.

Lenin, Vladimir, 1917, *State and Revolution*, in *Collected Works*, volume 25 (Progress), www.marxists.org/archive/lenin/works/1917/staterev

Lenin, Vladimir, 1918, "Can the Bolsheviks Retain State Power?", in *Collected Works*, volume 26, www.marxists.org/archive/lenin/works/1917/oct/01.htm

Lissagaray, Prosper Olivier, 1976, *History of the Paris Commune* (New Park).

Luxemburg, Rosa, 1919 "Order Prevails in Berlin", *Die Rote Fahne* (14 January 1919), https://bit.ly/3pJ5y2X

McClellan, Woodford, 1979, *Revolutionary Exiles: The Russians in the First International and the Paris Commune* (Routledge).

McMillan, James F, 2000, *France and Women 1789-1914: Gender, Society and Politics* (Routledge).

Moon, Joan, 1978, "Feminism and Socialism: The Utopian Synthesis of Flora Tristan", in Marilyn J Boxer and Jean H Qutaert (eds), *Socialist Women: European Socialist Feminism in the Nineteenth and Early Twentieth Century* (Elsevier).

Ray, Claudine, 2012, "Louse et les autres, le combat des femmes dans la Commune", Les Amies et Amis de la Commune de Paris 1871 (24 March), www.commune1871.org/la-commune-de-paris/histoire-de-la-commune/dossier-thematique/les-femmes-de-la-commune/564-louise-et-les-autres-le-combat-des-femmes-dans-la-commune

Ross, Kristin, 2015, *Communal Luxury: The Political Imaginary of the Paris Commune* (Verso).

Schulkind, Eugene, 1985, "Socialist Women in the 1871 Paris Commune", *Past & Present*, volume 106, issue 1.

Singer-Lecocq, Yvonne, 2011, *Rouge Elisabeth* (Pascal Galodé).

Syson, Lydia, 2015, "Citoyennes: Women of the Paris Commune", Lydia Syson website, https://bit.ly/3pItK5r

Thomas, Edith, 1964, *The Women Incendiaries* (Secker & Warburg).

FROM BOBBY TO BABYLON

Blacks and the British Police

Darcus Howe was born in Trinidad in 1943. He came to England in 1962. For over 50 years he was a political activist and journalist. His writing ranged over sport, through literary criticism to political commentary.

From Bobby to Babylon, originally published in 1988, brings together a series of articles and interviews providing the background and context to the urban rebellions which exploded across Britain in the wake of the Brixton riots of 1981.

From Bobby to Babylon Blacks and the British Police | Darcus Howe

£8

Available from:
www.bookmarksbookshop.co.uk
publications@bookmarks.uk.com
+44 (0)20 7637 1848

the socialist bookshop
bookmarks

Belarus: revolt in the shadow of Stalinism
Tomáš Tengely-Evans

When Aleksander Lukashenko rigged the Belarusian presidential election in August 2020, he expected things to follow a well-practiced pattern.[1] After previous elections during his 26 year rule, the Eastern European country's liberal nationalist opposition would cry fraud at the results. Some ordinary people would take to the streets or protest in other ways. A round of arrests and police intimidation would quell the resistance until the next presidential election came along in five years time. This time round Lukashenko claimed 80 percent of the vote, with just over 10 percent going to his liberal challenger, Svetlana Tichanovskaya. Tichanovskaya had played down talk of revolution during the election campaign, and she showed no sign of wanting to lead an opposition to oust Lukashenko in the aftermath of the fraudulent result. She fled to neighbouring Lithuania and, when people did take to the streets, made an appeal for people to "be reasonable and respect the law" and "not to resist the police, not to go to the square".[2]

This all changed, decisively, on the two nights of state-orchestrated violence that followed the official results on 9 August. Revulsion at police beatings,

---

1   Manenkov and Litvinova, 2020. Thanks to Joseph Choonara, Richard Donnelly and Martin Upchurch for comments on an earlier draft of this article.
2   Roth, 2020

detention and torture spurred mass protests and, crucially, a wave of workers' action at dozens of state-owned companies in August.

The fallout from the rigged election has led to the most prolonged and bitter stand-off between Lukashenko and an opposition movement in the history of his regime. Since 16 August, tens of thousands of people have turned Minsk into a sea of red and white, the colours of the opposition's flag, in a weekly Sunday demonstration. Thousands more have taken to the streets of towns and cities across the country, including industrial centres and rural areas that were previously supportive of the Lukashenko regime. Numbering between 100,000 and 300,000 in Minsk, these demonstrations were truly phenomenal—a huge social fact in a country of around 9.5 million. In October Lukashenko turned up for "talks" with opposition leaders being held at a KGB prison, signalling both the impact of the movement on him and his unwillingness to consider genuine negotiations.[3]

A sense of determination—and hope—ran through Belarusian society in the aftermath of the result. In an interview in August, a supporter of the independent trade unions who had been on the streets of Minsk described an "excited" atmosphere during the protests and strikes with people "shouting for freedom and rights". During one protest "around the city people were just singing songs, and the philharmonic theatre had organised some concerts on the streets". "We have not been free for 26 years and the feeling now is, 'it's time,'" the worker continued, "we will win this battle and we will crush Lukashenko".[4]

However, the revolt reached a critical stage in October when a "people's ultimatum" failed to break the stalemate between Lukashenko and the opposition. Tichanovskaya threatened that "all enterprises will begin a strike, all roads will be blocked and state-owned stores will no longer have any sales" unless the president stepped down by Sunday 25 October.[5] On the final day before this ultimatum expired, around 100,000 people took to the streets of Minsk once again and faced down increasing police violence. Some videos on social media showed police pre-emptively raiding flats and arresting people.[6] The following day, Monday, thousands of people protested. Students came to the forefront of the struggle with walkouts and protests at universities in Minsk. Significantly, workers did protest at some companies, including the Minsk Tractor Factory, the Belaruskali fertiliser mines and the Grodno Azot chemicals complex, which were at the heart of the strikes in August.[7] However, workers' resistance failed to take off at dozens of state-owned

---

3   Belarus's national intelligence agency has retained the name of the Soviet Union secret police force, the Committee for State Security (KGB).

4   Tengely-Evans, 2020a.

5   Tengely-Evans, 2020b.

6   See https://twitter.com/HannaLiubakova/status/1320430864388542464

7   Walker, 2020.

companies in the same way as in August. Where workers did take action, reports suggest it was patchy, unsustained and did not significantly impact production.[8]

The Belarusian movement hung in the balance as this journal went to press. Nevertheless, it has already thrown up important debates for a world witnessing a global wave of revolt. What makes ordinary people rise up? What is the power of the working class in these explosions? Can workers win their own social demands? These questions are central to the rebellion in Belarus, but they are also important for all of those fighting to change the world.

Yet the revolt in Belarus also has a very specific importance for socialists. Upheavals in countries that were once part of the officially "socialist" Soviet Union and Eastern Bloc inevitably raise a fundamental question: "what is socialism?" In 1989 revolutions tore down those Stalinist regimes, which stood exposed as brutal state capitalist dictatorships rather than workers' states. However, the legacy of Stalinism casts a long shadow in Eastern Europe and over sections of the Western left, which have taken an ambiguous and sometimes hostile attitude towards the movement in Belarus. The left's old illusions in the Stalinist system, as socialist or at least more progressive than Western capitalism, are easy to cling onto with Belarus. After the collapse of the Soviet Union, the Lukashenko regime retained much of the old Communist imagery and a high degree of state ownership and control of the economy.[9] Although no one would claim Russia under Vladimir Putin is socialist, many still see its influence in the region as a bulwark against the United States and NATO. This leads some to argue that the overthrow of Lukashenko would be a victory for US imperialism and inevitably lead to free market shock therapy.

During the Cold War, much of the Western left fell in line behind Stalinist Russia. In contrast, the International Socialists (IS), forerunner's of the Socialist Workers Party, stood under the slogan "Neither Washington nor Moscow, but International Socialism". IS argued for a socialism from below based on workers' self-emancipation rather than increased state control. It unequivocally stood with workers' and students' struggles in the Eastern Bloc and advocated revolution on both sides of the iron curtain. Today, those politics are still vital to understanding the Belarusian revolt and supporting its workers' movement.

The streets and the workplaces

Fury erupted on the day of the presidential election, 9 August, after an exit poll gave Lukashenko an overwhelming victory. Thousands of people took to the streets of Minsk and other cities in spontaneous protests encouraged by opposition news channels on the Telegram app. Riot police from the Special Purpose

---

8   Tengely-Evans, 2020c.
9   Carter, 2020.

Police Detachment (OMON), backed up by paramilitary units from the KGB, unleashed a wave of repression. In the days that followed, state forces used tear gas, stun grenades and water cannon, stormed blocks of flats and hunted down protesters. They murdered three people, put 200 in hospital and detained up to 7,000 across the country.[10] At one protest in Brest, a city in western Belarus, an ambulance arrived and people carried the badly injured towards it, only for riot police to jump out from it and beat up protesters.[11] The following morning queues lined up outside prisons, with people demanding to know what had happened to friends and relatives while others milled around the streets. Rather than deterring people, the state's violent reaction brought in new layers of people who would not have previously opposed the regime or been involved in politics at all.

Three opposition Telegram channels—Nexta Live, Belamova and MK Belarus—had put out a call for a general strike from noon on Tuesday 11 August. There were plenty of reasons to be sceptical as to whether a "general strike" would involve workers' collective action. Often in movements against authoritarianism and corruption, a "strike" involves businesses closing for the day in support of protests or workers joining in as individuals. For instance, during the Euromaidan protests in neighbouring Ukraine in 2014, opposition figures made calls for a "general strike" but organised labour played no role.[12] In Slovakia's movement in 2018, which brought down a social-democratic prime minister after a mafia corruption scandal and the murder of journalist Ján Kuciak, some protesters described themselves as "strikers". Again though, this did not involve organised workers.

In Belarus the workers' movement has been severely repressed under the Lukashenko regime. The last strike had been on the Minsk metro network in 1995. There is the Federation of Trade Unions of Belarus (FPB), which was the successor of the state-run unions from Stalinist Russia. However, this is not a real trade union—a workers' organisation that fights for better conditions—but rather an appendage to the regime. Indeed, FPB president Mikhail Orda was Lukashenko's campaign chief during the presidential election. The independent unions, organised through the Belarusian Congress of Democratic Trade Unions (BKDP), came out of the strikes that precipitated the fall of Stalinism in Belarus in 1991. Although the BKDP is legal, trade unionists face "considerable harassment and intimidation" and regular spells in and out of jail.[13]

---

10 Glushakov, 2020.
11 Nexta Live Telegram channel, 11 August 2020—https://web.telegram.org/#/im?p=@nexta_live
12 Glasse, 2014. For a general analysis of the Euromaidan uprising in Ukraine, see Ferguson, 2014.
13 International Centre for Trade Union Rights, 2018.

Despite these weaknesses, the call for a general strike in Belarus turned out to be different to those made in countries such as Ukraine.[14] On the Tuesday after the election, 11 August, workers at the VI Kozlov electrical engineering factory in Minsk put their demands to management. These included to "immediately end violence against unarmed civilians", the "release of people detained during the peaceful demonstrations" and to "turn on the internet". Some passers-by gathered to support the Kozlov workers.[15] Two sections at the Grodno Azot petrochemicals complex, which is one of the regime's largest firms, also struck. Workers at the Minsk Margarine Works food company walked out, with passing cars beeping their horns in support. Staff at the Institute of Chemistry of New Materials at the National Academy of Sciences, a sort of state-run think-tank, also protested as part of the general strike call. Trolleybus drivers on one of Minsk's fleets refused to work after they found out a driver had been injured during protests. There were also reports that workers downed tools after an "uneasy" atmosphere at the RUE Belenergosetprojekt scientific research facility in the capital. Outside Minsk, Belshina tyre factory workers in the industrial city of Babrusyk walked out to demand free elections. A statement from one worker read: "We, the workers of Belshina, are in solidarity with the people of Belarus. We have declared a strike." The Zabinka sugar refinery in Brest gathered and demanded a meeting with the chairman of the district executive committee, a local appointee of the regime.[16]

Many of the workers' actions did not resemble a traditional strike—a vote for action, a walkout and a picket line outside the factory.[17] Often workers would gather in the morning or at lunchtime, then put demands to management that centred around free elections, police violence and the release of prisoners. There are crucial differences between workers holding a mass meeting and then returning to work, and a strike that aims to shut down production. However, we should not be dismissive of action that falls short of a full walkout. The workers' action was important in forcing the regime to back off from widespread police violence against protesters. Moreover, when workers fight back, they begin to change their ideas about both society and themselves as they taste their potential power. Slogans at the Belaruskali mine included, "We're Not Serfs—We're Workers!"[18] In one small sign of the regime's loss of legitimacy, a group of workers at the Minsk tractor factory

---

14 For a round up of the workers' action on the first day, see Tengely-Evans, 2020d.

15 Nexta Live Telegram channel, 11 August 2020.

16 Nexta Live Telegram channel, 11 August 2020.

17 Edwards, 2020.

18 Kassabov, 2020.

took a stand during the first day of workers' action. Initially, the group was tiny. Out of a workforce of some 14,000, around 70 engineers and technicians from several departments walked out and rallied outside the main building. Yet when the Deputy Director for Ideological Affairs, a regime stooge at the company, came out at lunchtime and tried to frighten them back into work, they refused to listen. "No one believes ideologues anymore," blasted the opposition Telegram channel Nexta Live.[19] The strike at the factory would grow, with some strike leaders saying 4,000 workers took part at its height.[20]

On the Sunday 16 August, unprecedented crowds numbering between 100,000 and 300,000 took to the streets of Minsk. The following morning the city was already a throng of protesters and striking workers. In an attempt to assert his authority, Lukashenko prepared for a "meeting with the people" outside the MZKT heavy goods vehicle factory. He tried to strike a defiant tone, telling workers, "We held elections, and as long as you don't kill me, there won't be any other elections." Workers chanted, "Go away!" A visibly shaken Lukashenko persevered but concluded by saying, "Thank you. I said everything. You may now chant, 'Resign'."[21] His authority melted away in scenes reminiscent of the downfall of Romanian dictator Nicolae Ceaușescu in 1989.[22] Throughout that day workers' action spread through Minsk and other industrial centres across Belarus.[23] In the capital workers marched from one company to another to show solidarity, including the Kozlov plant, the MZKT factory, the MAZ car plant and the MTZ tractor works. Media workers at the state's STV and ONT news channels and BT radio station stopped work, and a huge rally took place outside the ONT building on Communist Street. Around 130 workers at the Belenergosetprojekt scientific research company downed tools and went to the rally. Outside the capital, there were stoppages at the Belaruskali potash mines and the Navapolatsk refinery, while workers marched through the BelAz industrial vehicle company's departments to get people behind the protests. Elsewhere, video from the BMZ steel works in Zlobin, south eastern Belarus, showed workers rallying outside the factory.[24]

---

19 Nexta Live Telegram channel, 11 August 2020.

20 Walker and Roth, 2020.

21 Kalinovskaya, 2020.

22 During the 1989 revolutions in Eastern European, Romania's Stalinist ruler Ceaușescu called a huge rally in support of the regime on 21 December. As he started speaking from the balcony of his palace in Bucharest, dissent spread through the crowd. He was whisked away in a helicopter. By 25 December he lay in a pool of blood. See Nicolae Ceaușescu's last speech with English subtitles—www.youtube.com/watch?v=wWIbCtz_Xwk

23 For a round-up of the strikes between 11 and 17 August, see Tengely-Evans, 2020e.

24 Nexta Live Telegram channel, 17 August 2020.

Emboldened by the protests and strike wave, Tichanovasksya assumed the leadership of the movement. She quickly issued a fresh statement that reneged on her earlier exhortations for people to avoid a confrontation with Lukashenko:

> I am ready to take on the responsibility and serve in this period as a national leader so that the country calms down, returns to a normal rhythm, so that we free all political prisoners in the shortest possible period and prepare for new presidential elections.[25]

She and other opposition leaders began to look to the strikes as a powerful weapon. They encouraged strikers to set up local and national committees and to join the Coordinating Council of Belarus (CCB), the body they set up to manage the transition to democratic rule.

However, the political punch of the strikes and fears about their economic impact drove the Lukashenko regime to move against nascent forms of worker organisation.[26] This was apparent at the Belaruskali potash mines, where strikes had disrupted production at one of the regime's most profitable exporters. Authorities arrested Siarhei Charkasau, co-chair of the strike committee at the Belaruskali mines and vice president of BKDP-affiliated Belarus Independent Union, as well as workers Raman Liavonchyk and Pavel Razumovskiy. In Minsk, authorities arrested MTZ strike committee chair Sergey Dylevsky—who has now been forced to flee the country—and MTAZ strike committee member Anatoly Lavrinovich. They also detained Liza Merliak, the international secretary of the independent trade union that has been part of organising stoppages at the Grodno Azot chemicals complex. Although anger remained on the shop floor, the campaign of arrests and intimidation had successfully stalled the strike wave. In some enterprises workers turned to "go slows", with action varying from working as slowly as possible to sabotage.

The Belarusian revolt has seen impressive self-organisation and women have taken to the fore. At the top, three women have headed the opposition movement. When Lukashenko disqualified Sergei Tichanovsky from standing in the presidential election, Tichanovskaya stepped in. Maria Kalesnikova and Veronika Tsepkala, from two other disqualified electoral campaigns, united behind her. Lukashenko dismissed Tichanovskaya's bid in July, saying, "Society is not mature enough to vote for a woman." The burden of the presidency, he continued, would cause her to "collapse, poor thing".[27] He was in for a rude shock as the movement took off.

---

25 Walker and Roth, 2020.

26 For example of economic impact, see Charter 77, 2020.

27 Makhovsky, 2020.

Tens of thousands of women have taken to the streets in the Sunday protests and a series of Women's Marches, facing down the police. A lot of mainstream coverage of women's role in the movement has simply played to gender stereotypes and reinforced patronising sexist views. Al Jazeera, for example, talked about Tichanovskaya's "transformation from a frightened housewife". Their coverage largely misses how struggles can become festivals of the oppressed, as ideas about the way society should be run are challenged. One woman protester told Reuters:

> This movement of women has been such a shock and a surprise, and all of us women are now asking where everyone has been all this time. Now this is not just about politics. If is about family life, it is about relationships with husbands. We have a very patriarchal society, but when the revolution is over that will have to change.[28]

Belarus and global revolt

Belarus has to be seen in the context of a global wave of revolt that was taking place before the Covid-19 pandemic.[29] Each country that has experienced an uprising is unique. Yet there are also common drivers such as urbanisation and the growth of the working class, the impact of three decades of neoliberalism, high unemployment and anger against unrepresentative elites. Although the onset of the coronavirus pandemic dampened this international wave of protest, the ruling classes' handling of the pandemic, including in Belarus, has fuelled people's anger. The *Financial Times* remarked:

> Long live the Belarusian revolution! But what is happening there is just part of a global protest trend, only briefly interrupted by Covid-19. The past year has seen almost unprecedentedly large protests from Hong Kong to Lebanon to Minneapolis. We are reliving 1968, but bigger: an almost invariably peaceful street is replacing parliament as the main arena of opposition. The trend encompasses rich countries and poor ones, democracies and dictatorships.[30]

In the former Stalinist bloc the failures flowing from the transition from state capitalism to free market capitalism have spurred unrest. To understand the revolt in this context, we need to do three things. Firstly, we need to look at Lukashenko's rise to power after the collapse of the Stalinist bloc; secondly, examine Belarusian capitalist development after 1991; and, thirdly, analyse the development of a new opposition after 2017.

---

28 Goldsmith, 2020.

29 For a general analysis of these international revolts, see Choonara, 2019.

30 Kuper, 2020.

The Soviet Union—state capitalism, stagnation and collapse

Lukashenko came to power in the chaos that followed the collapse of the Soviet Union and its satellite states in the Eastern Bloc in 1989-91. The Soviet Union claimed to be a "socialist state". Its constitution said that "all power belongs to the working people" and was exercised through their democratic organisations, the workers' councils of soviets that had taken power during the Russian Revolution of 1917.[31] In reality, the Soviet Union and Eastern Bloc were state capitalist societies where workers had no control.[32]

The Russian Revolution was a genuine socialist revolution in which the working class, in alliance with the peasantry, had taken power and briefly ran society. However, by the 1920s, the revolution was transforming itself into a counter-revolution. To survive in backward Russia, the new workers' state needed revolution to spread to advanced capitalist states in Europe. Unfortunately, workers' revolution, most crucially in Germany, failed to break through. Russia was engulfed by a brutal civil war as 14 imperialist armies invaded to support the Whites, who fought for a return of the old order. Although the Red Army won the civil war, the working class was decimated. As workers who had made the revolution died on the front line and production collapsed to below pre-war levels, the soviets—the basis of workers' power and socialism—were hollowed out.[33]

However, the Bolshevik party, which had given leadership to the revolution, remained in charge of a sprawling bureaucracy.[34] Initially, it balanced between different class forces in Russia, as it tried to defend the gains of the revolution and stave off societal collapse. However, by the late 1920s the bureaucracy—with Stalin at its helm—developed into a new ruling class with its own set of class interests. This ruling class, the state bureaucracy, behaved in similar ways to bosses in capitalist countries. Under capitalism, bosses exploit workers to get their hands on profit, but this process is not driven forward by greed but rather by competition. Competition is a coercive force on individual capitalists that forces them to reinvest profits into the latest technology and the most efficient methods of production to get ahead of their rivals. This leads to a system, as Marx put it, of "accumulation for accumulation's sake, production for production's sake".[35]

The interaction of capitals through competition enforces what Marx called the operation of the "law of value". This affects the organisation of production,

31 Fundamental Law of the Union of Soviet Socialist Republics, 1936.
32 Cliff, 1974.
33 For a thorough explanation, see Harman, 1967.
34 For a discussion on the problems, see Lenin, 1922.
35 Marx, 1976, p742.

the division of labour, the allocation of resources and so on. If the Soviet Union is viewed in isolation, the law of value could not apply to its economy, since the division of labour and investment were directed by the state's Five Year Plans.[36] Yet when viewed in relation to the global imperialist system, the law of value did in fact act upon the Soviet economy, because the Soviet Union was locked into international military and economic competition with capitalist states.[37] Stalin argued in 1931: "We are fifty or a hundred years behind the advanced countries. We must make up this gap in ten years. Either we do it or we will go under".[38]

As state capitalist societies, the Soviet Union and the Eastern Bloc were marked by capitalist crisis and class struggle just as much as the West. The Soviet economy saw impressive growth rates after the Second World War. Yet beneath the surface, there were profound economic problems underlined by a lack of dynamism compared to Western capitalism. Internal growth could not overcome international pressure for more capital accumulation. Moreover, the Soviet Union's backward position meant the pressure of the Cold War arms race placed a particularly heavy burden on the economy, subordinating other investment decisions and development. The Soviet Union continually came up against the limits of capital accumulation set by its national economy.

The Soviet economy was supposedly smoothly organised through the Five Year Plans rather than the chaos of the free market, with its waste and inefficiency. In reality though there were fits and starts between and during each plan. Huge industrial projects were "frozen". Investment was suddenly redirected from one sector to another, causing anarchy in production and imbalances between different branches of the economy. This mayhem and waste wasn't rooted in planning or corruption—it flowed from the drive to accumulate. The state would step in to "cool down" the national economy in order to stave off a crisis of overaccumulation, but that simply exacerbated turmoil and inefficiency.

By the 1970s, Soviet state capitalism was in the throes of profound stagnation. The Stalinist regimes faced a dilemma. State capitalist economies such as Poland, East Germany and Hungary had begun to integrate into world capitalism in order to overcome the limits to accumulation set by their national economies. This strategy was an alternative to autarky and further stagnation, but it also made these economies more vulnerable to global shocks and downturns.

The Soviet Union's growing reliance on oil exports meant that a drop in oil prices in the mid-1980s sent shockwaves through its economy. This coincided with US president Ronald Reagan's new arms race. Between 1981 and 1985 there

---

36 Cliff, 1974, pp202-212.
37 For a more detailed explanation of how state capitalism operated, see Tengely-Evans, 2018.
38 Stalin, 1931.

was "practically no economic growth" as "production of 40 percent of all industrial goods actually fell".[39] In recognition of the scale of the crisis, Michael Gorbachev was chosen as the new Communist Party boss. From 1985 he brought in a series of reforms known as Glasnost (openness) and Perestroika (reconstruction). Nonetheless, the crisis was so bad it could no longer be solved by reform. When these measures proved insufficient to nurse the system back to health, it provoked further splits and opened the door to a wave of workers' struggles in the late 1980s.

In Belarus, then part of the former Soviet Union, the Stalinist bureaucracy was particularly conservative and resisted the reforms. However, it was shaken in April 1991 when a powerful movement exploded. This included protests and strikes at around 70 important state-owned enterprises.[40] A combination of splits at the top and pressure from the workers' movement forced Belarus's rulers to declare independence from the Soviet Union in 1991. The Belarusian parliament had already passed the Declaration of State Sovereignty of the Belarusian Soviet Socialist Republic on 27 July 1990, with Stalinist hardliner Lukashenko the only MP to vote against independence. Belarus's parliament, its so-called Supreme Soviet, was made up of the Communist Party and a array of independents after elections in 1990. Under Gorbachev's reforms, candidates who were not Communist Party members had been allowed to stand in elections to the parliaments of the Soviet Union and its constituent republics. The Belarusian Popular Front, a nationalist and conservative group, manage to form a small parliamentary faction.

In August 1991 the conservative section of the Soviet bureaucracy made a last ditch attempt to preserve the state capitalist set up. An alliance of conservative bureaucrats in Moscow, the KGB secret police and Communist Party bosses in Belarus, Azerbaijan, Kazakhstan, Kyrgyzstan, Tajikistan, Turkmenistan and Uzbekistan staged a putsch against Gorbachev. The coup failed after three days and precipitated the dissolution of the "Soviet Union" into 15 republics. The defeat of the putsch caused a huge crisis for the Belarusian bureaucracy. In the aftermath, the pressure became overwhelming; Belarus made its declaration of sovereignty constitutional on 25 August and became formally independent on 10 December.

Belarus—Europe's last dictatorship?

Belarus, with its huge state enterprises and Stalinist-era symbolism, can seem like a pickled society compared to the rest of Europe Europe. Liberals refer to Lukashenko as "Europe's last dictator", suggesting he is simply a hangover from a previous age. This obscures the fact that the Lukashenko regime is very much a

---

39 Crouch, 1997.
40 Charter 77, 2016.

product of what followed the collapse Soviet Union in 1991. Russia and Eastern Europe moved from state capitalism to Western-style capitalism. Tony Cliff, who developed the theory of bureaucratic state capitalism, argued it was a "side step". Although the political setup changed, social relations between capital and labour remained the same. A range of political forces fought to shape the transition. They included figures from the old bureaucracy who sought to maintain control, sometimes rebranding themselves as "democratic" or as nationalists. There were also different sections of the opposition movements, including conservatives, liberals, social democrats and small groups of anti-Stalinist socialists.

The ruling class saw that, though its ruling party had lost power, it could retain its class power. Chris Harman argued in 1991:

> The old people at the top...raved about betrayal and even on occasions fantasised about telling their police to open fire. But key structures below them were already run by people who, at least privately, accepted the new multinational capitalist common sense.[41]

Parliamentary democracy posed little threat to their rule. Communist politicians and bureaucrats became "democratic" politicians and bureaucrats. Sometimes they ended up in new democratic governments through so-called "Round Table Talks" with the opposition. The managers of state-owned firms became the owners of private companies.

The new governments, whether democratic or authoritarian, accepted the logic of global capitalism. However, the way the transition played out and how the ruling class sought to maintain its power differed from state to state. Russia and most of the states in Central Europe and the Baltic adopted free market "shock therapy" to varying degrees. This involved rapid liberalisation of trade and the economy, combined with a programme of mass privatisation.[42] Neoliberal poster children such as Poland saw new private firms grow in importance.

In contrast, states within the former Soviet Union itself relied far more on the state sector or newly privatised industry after 1991. In the Czech Republic, Hungary and Lithuania, for instance, new private companies accounted for around 55-65 percent of new value added, compared to just 10-20 percent in Russia and Belarus.[43] Even Russia, which pursued mass privatisation, didn't see a large growth of new

---

41 Harman, 1990.
42 With the advice of Harvard economist Jeffrey Sachs, Poland adopted the Balcerowicz Plan in 1989. Again, with the advice of Sachs, Russia undertook the largest programme of privatisation in history. Finance minister Anatoly Chubais sold off 800 companies a month. By the end of the programme in the 1990s, 77 percent of Russia's large and medium-sized companies and 82 percent of small companies were private.
43 World Bank, 2002, p39.

private sector firms compared to Central Europe and the Baltic. Its "voucher privatisation" allowed a small number of "oligarchs" to buy up shares, concentrating wealth and ownership in their hands. They were often drawn from the old bureaucracy and state security apparatus. Although they reaped huge benefits from liberalisation, they wanted to protect their position from new competitors. The transition across the region lent itself to a "wild west capitalism" that involved widespread corruption and the growth of organised crime. Continuing neoliberal reforms in the 1990s and 2000s accentuated these problems.[44]

Belarus, as well as some central Asian republics, notably Turkmenistan and Uzbekistan, pursued barely any liberalisation or privatisation. The state capitalist infrastructure was kept in place, as was lots of the old Communist imagery, as a way of the ruling class maintaining its power. Figures from the old bureaucracy and the nationalist opposition jockeyed for position in the new reality of the early 1990s. In 1995 Lukashenko stood on an "anti-corruption" ticket and won the presidential election overwhelmingly. He appealed to stability and sovereignty. Through keeping the state capitalist infrastructure intact and staving off mass unemployment, he was able to forge a social contract with large parts of the urban and rural working class. Nelly Bekus, a Belarusian academic at Exeter University, argues:

> Lukashenko...won his popularity with the idea that a nation-state can become a continuation of Soviet development. Unlike many other former Soviet nations that dismissed their socialist past, Lukashenko's ideology asserted the active role played by Belarusians in Soviet modernisation, presented as an important milestone on their way to becoming a modern and developed nation.[45]

Lukashenko—Russia's man?

The Lukashenko model was based on importing Russian oil at subsidised prices, refining it and then re-exporting it. After the collapse of the Soviet Union, Russia's rulers sought to rebuild imperialist power in its "near abroad", and this included fermenting or intervening in a series of ethnic conflicts and civil wars in former Soviet republics in the 1990s. It also meant that Russia was willing to subsidise the Lukashenko regime in order to keep Belarus in its orbit. In 2015 Putin strengthened his control of the "near abroad" by creating the Eurasian Economic Union (EAEU) with Armenia, Belarus, Kazakhstan and Kyrgyzstan. This built on the Eurasian Economic Community, which existed between 2000 and 2014, and was designed to compete with the European Union. Belarus has been part of this process and Lukashenko is the nominal head of the EAEU's

44 Upchurch, 2012
45 Bekus, 2020.

supreme council. However, Lukashenko was never "Russia's man". Although the two countries did sign a Treaty of State Union in 1999, it is not worth the paper it is written on.

Instead, Lukashenko has balanced between rival imperialisms—the US, the EU and Russia—and there have been significant tensions with Russian president Vladimir Putin. Russian oligarchs, in particular, have wanted to loot state assets through privatisation. Prior to the protests, Lukashenko and Putin were involved in a stand-off over closer ties and oil prices.[46] Lukashenko rejected Putin's demands that Belarus subordinate itself further to Russian rule through a closer state union. This stand-off reflected Lukashenko's willingness to tilt to the West. From the early 2000s Lukashenko began to bring in some free market reforms, such as wage restraint and changes to contracts, hoping to attract foreign investment. The increasing liberalisation of Belarusian capitalism accelerated during the global financial crash in 2009. The centrepiece of its new investment strategy was the information technology sector, one of the largest in Eastern Europe. Meanwhile, the old state-owned enterprises have been shedding workers, who have found new work in the retail and service sectors. This group of workers accounts for around 45 percent of Belarusian workers.[47] However, the vast state-owned enterprises are still central to the economy. Their size, and the focal points they provide for whole area, means that workplace and community can fuse. This is a factor that helped spread the movement to the factories.

The process of free market reforms culminated in the "parasite tax" of 2017—a form of workfare dressed up in Stalinist-era rhetoric. More than half a million people, who were formally registered as unemployed, found themselves with a $230 tax bill.[48] This triggered protests and hollowed out some its traditional sectors of support. The demonstrations also gave birth to new opposition figures, and the memory of them has fed into the the current democracy movement.

The parasite tax was important for setting the stage in the current president election. Although Lukashenko was hated by many, the old opposition did not have widespread support. This traditional opposition was dominated by "liberal nationalists". This is not to say Lukashenko is an "anti-nationalist" or simply pro-Russian. Lukashenko and the traditional, liberal nationalist opposition rely on competing visions of Belarusian nationalism. Alongside support for liberal market politics, it distinguishes itself from Lukashenko by appealing to a "Golden Age" in the 17th century. They emphasise, for instance, Belarus' ties to the Polish-Lithuanian Commonwealth and the historic struggles surrounding

46 Lemlich, 2020.
47 Glushakov, 2020.
48 Liasheva, 2017.

the Belarusian language. In the context of Western and Russian imperial rivalry, this form of nationalism bolsters liberal arguments that Belarus should tilt to the West. Lukashenko has also appealed to a nationalism rooted in the Stalinism period. These competing nationalisms appeal to complex views around identity. For example, even though a majority of people declare their nationality to be Belarusian, the majority also say they speak Russian rather than Belarusian.

During this presidential election, instead of focusing on nationalist talking points such as Belarus' historic links to Lithuania and Poland, the new opposition tapped into anger over "bread and butter" issues such as Lukashenko's handling of the pandemic. As Bekus argues:

> In place of the political opposition that challenged Lukashenko over the last two and half decades—which was traditionally preoccupied with the issues of national ideology, language, identity policy and geopolitical re-orientation towards Europe—this year Lukashenko's opponents entered the political scene with ideas that called on Belarusians to reflect on the deteriorating conditions of their lives and appealed to their understanding of political normality.
>
> Sergei Tikhanovsky is founder of a popular YouTube channel, in which he revealed the struggles of ordinary Belarusians and the incompetence of the authorities. His reportage contrasted this with the polished propaganda image of a Belarus full of success stories that is constantly channelled by the official media. His reports made clear that the longer Lukashenko stayed in power, the more distant his picture of Belarus became from people's real life experience.[49]

The opposition candidates were supposed to be Tikhanovsky, banker Viktar Babaryka and Valeri Tsepkalo, a former diplomat and head of Lukashenko's prized IT park. Precisely because they had a wider social base than the old opposition, Lukashenko was forced to move pre-emptively and disqualify them. This failed to stop discontent at the base of society, and the electoral commission had to allow Tichanovskaya and three other candidates onto the ballot paper. Momentum gathered behind Tichanovskaya after the Babaryka and Tsepkalo campaigns united behind her.

These broader trends have been accentuated by the coronavirus pandemic and Lukashenko's right-wing populist denial of the threat that it poses. Many will remember the Belarusian soccer team playing while other states were going into lockdown. Sociologist Volodymyr Artiukh notes:

> Lukashenko was blamed for denying the threat of the virus; state agencies were accused of hiding the real scale of the pandemic and of lacking the capacity to

---

49 Bekus, 2020.

fight it. By contrast, grassroots activism gained respect for helping Belarus' healthcare system to cope. However, it has not been so much the epidemiological situation itself that has fuelled the current popular discontent, but rather its economic and ideological consequences.[50]

The politics of the workers' movement

The Coordinating Council of Belarus (CCB) was set up by Tichanovskaya to manage a transition to democratic rule. This body brings together a whole array of political forces, including liberal opponents of the regime, bosses, some strike leaders and even a former Lukashenko culture minister. This reflects the contradictions within the opposition. Although the opposition partly flowed out of an earlier popular revolt against free market reforms, its programme is based on continuing Lukashenko's economic policies with more vigour. Figures who favour more free market policies are ascendant in the leadership of the CCB. One member, Pavel Daneyko, was a co-founder of the Institute of Privatisation and Management in 1994, which taught the managers of state-owned companies to squeeze more out of workers. Raising social demands could cut against such forces, but such social demands are not central to the workers' movement. There is a political question too—the independence of the working class from other social forces in the opposition. Even though there is a national strike committee, for instance, it is politically subordinate to the overall coordinating body.

Mass movements do not happen in an ideological vacuum, including those involving the organised working class. The shadow of Stalinism means that mass movements in Eastern Europe tend to be caught between defending parts of state capitalism and looking to the market as an alternative to authoritarianism, corruption and economic stagnation. These debates were evident right through the workers upsurge in Belarus. Minsk tractor works strike leader Sergei Dylevsky says that the lack of oligarchs is "far from an achievement." "On the contrary, it means that any sound businessman, be it a millionaire or billionaire, does not want to invest in Belarus and its enterprises," he says, deploying a classic "common sense" argument used by the right.[51] Another worker says he wants "fair privatisation" and the "development of a market economy". "I mean not full privatisation by Russian oligarchs or international companies," he explains. "I do not mean part privatisation by businessmen and workers buying shares, and the state control of 50 percent." One Telegram channel has raised the demand of a "ban on privatisation", but its reach is limited. This is not an argument for writing

---

50 Artiukh, 2020
51 Nechepurenko, 2020.

off the movement against Lukashenko. However, it does mean that there will have to be a battle over what comes next if Lukashenko is forced out.

There were small signs that the contradictions in the opposition could develop. During struggles, economic and political demands can flow into one another. It is important not to take a mechanical view that workers begin with the economic and then build up to the political.[52] During the "go slows", many workers were using heath and safety to slow down production. One message from the Belaruskali strike committee Telegram broadcast list showed how political demands could flow into economic ones. It says complaints include "that there is practically no ventilation in the mine" and "this is most likely due to the saving of electricity and in connection with the latest events in the city". "Thus, the management of the enterprise are trying to shift the economic problems onto the shoulders of employees," it says, linking the political situation to the economic plight of workers. Pointing to attacks on both the political rights and economic situation of workers, it continues, "They took away the our voice, now they are trying to take away our health. Can we tolerate this any further?"[53]

The failure of the "people's ultimatum"
More than three months of mass protests and workers' action have weakened the Lukashenko regime and further hollowed out its social base. Every regime relies on a combination of force and fraud to maintain its rule. For Lukashenko, fraud has failed. He is increasingly relying on force to maintain his rule, rather than mediating organisations such as the old state trade unions. There do not appear to be any serious cracks within the military, police and security apparatus, but he will not be able to rule indefinitely with force alone. This situation means the regime is more brutal, but it is also more brittle and could be shattered by a return to mass workers' action.

Despite the failure of the "people's ultimatum", there were some signs of workers still trying to fight back collectively—and of the potential power they have. On the first day after the ultimatum, photographs sent out by the Belaruskali strike committee broadcast list showed several workshops at VI Kozlov electro engineering works in Minsk at a standstill. One statement says:

Two workshops, the 16th and the 6th, are on strike. Stopping work in them means stopping the entire plant—a workforce of 3,000 people. The electrical engineering company receives its main profits from the sale of transformers. The transformer is designed like this—a tank case, into which a core is placed. No tanks means

---

52 Luxemburg, 1906.
53 From the Belaruskali strike committee's Telegram channel, September 2020.

no transformer. The tanks are produced in the 16th workshop by 40 to 50 highly qualified workers who have joined the strike. A similar number of key workers, 30 to 40, work in the 6th workshop, where the situation is similar.[54]

The message explains that around 30 to 40 percent of workers remained in the workshops while the rest "took sick leave or the day off at their own expense". Workers "who stayed do the minimum possible" in the face of bosses' threats of bringing in parts from Turkey and action against ringleaders. There are signs here of both the weakness of the working class movement and the objective power that it holds. At the time of writing, there do not seem to be many signs of a revival of mass strikes.

Neither West nor East—but Belarusian workers
In the context of the stalemate, both Lukashenko and the opposition are look-ing to outside help. Western states are scrambling to pose as supporters of the fight for democracy in Belarus, but those same states were willing to court the regime when it suited their interests. Britain trained Belarusian troops—including in "urban warfare tactics"—before condemning the regime's crackdown on protesters. Meanwhile, Russia is biding its time, seeking to safeguard its interests in its "near abroad". Putin is backing Lukashenko to stop Belarus tilting explicitly towards the West, but he could be willing to court another figure with more legitimacy. If Lukashenko clings on with Russian help, Putin will demand privatisation and a broader neoliberal restricting of the Belarusian economy in the interests of Russian imperialism.

The left should reject both imperialist sides and back the Belarusian protests, pointing to our common cause against those at the top of society. During the summer of 1968 there were important risings in both the capitalist West and state capitalist East. Chris Harman, writing in *Socialist Worker*, reported:

> In Chicago, police supported by troops with fixed bayonets mercilessly beat up peaceful and unprotected demonstrators. In Prague, Russian tanks patrol the streets. There are important differences between American and Russian society. But both have in common this much: they are controlled by small ruling classes that will use all the resources of modern technology to keep down the workers who may threaten their rule.[55]

This past year, US police have meted out baton blows, bullets and tear gas to put down an uprising against racism and police murder. At the same time in Minsk,

---

54 From the Belaruskali strike committee's Telegram channel, September 2020.
55 Harman, 1968.

military vehicles patrolled the streets and riot police beat up protesters. Supporting the Belarusian movement requires internationalism and solidarity. A real alternative to Lukashenko's authoritarianism is not Western-style capitalism, but workers fighting for democracy, social justice and a society where they really are in charge.

Bibliography

Artiukh, Volodymyr, 2020, "More Contagious Than Coronavirus: Electoral Unrest Under Lukashenko's Tired Rule in Belarus", Open Democracy (4 August), www.opendemocracy.net/en/odr/electoral-unrest-under-lukashenkas-tired-rule-in-belarus

Bekus, Nelly, 2020, "The Crackdown in Belarus", *Tribune* (13 August), https://tribunemag.co.uk/2020/08/the-crackdown-in-belarus

Carter, Kristian, 2020, "Belarus: Nationalised Industries or EU Privatisation", *Morning Star* (3 September), https://morningstaronline.co.uk/article/belarus-nationalised-industries-or-eu-privatisation

Charter 77, 2016, "Minsk Mass Rallies Tore Up Foundations of Soviet Power in April 1991", (7 April), https://charter97.org/en/news/2016/4/7/198572

Charter 77, 2020, "The 'Belaruskali' Strike Committee: The Economic Consequences of the 'Italian Strike' Are Obvious" (16 September), https://charter97.org/en/news/2020/9/16/393386

Choonara, Joseph, 2019, "A New Cycle of Revolt", *International Socialism* 165 (winter), http://isj.org.uk/a-new-cycle-of-revolt

Cliff, Tony, 1974 [1947], *State Capitalism in Russia* (Pluto Press).

Crouch, Dave, 1997, "The Reform That Failed", *Socialist Review* (January), http://pubs.socialistreviewindex.org.uk/sr204/crouch.htm

Edwards, Maxim, 2020, "Belarusian Workers Support Protesters with Growing Strikes", Global Voices (13 August), https://globalvoices.org/2020/08/13/belarusian-workers-support-protesters-with-a-general-strike

Ferguson, Rob, 2014, "Ukraine: Imperialism, War and the Left", *International Socialism* 144 (autumn), https://isj.org.uk/ukraine-imperialism-war-and-the-left

Glasse, Jennifer, 2014, "Protests Herald Unstable Year for Ukraine", Al Jazeera (3 January), www.aljazeera.com/news/2014/1/3/protests-herald-unstable-year-for-ukraine

Glushakov, Yury, 2020, "Belarus Will Never Be the Same", Open Democracy (21 August), https://bit.ly/3mHz0Va

Goldsmith, Belinda, 2020, "'Women in White' from Belarus Protest Globally For Peace and New Vote", Reuters (17 August), https://reut.rs/37xtq1d

Harman, Chris, 1967, "Russia: How the Revolution was Lost", *International Socialism* 30 (first series, autumn), www.marxists.org/archive/harman/1967/xx/revlost.htm

Harman, Chris, 1968, "East and West, Tanks and Cops Defend 'Freedom'", *Socialist Worker* (7 September).

Harman, Chris, 1988, *Class Struggles in Eastern Europe 1945-83* (Bookmarks).

Harman, Chris, 1990, "The Storm Breaks", *International Socialism* 46 (spring), www.marxists.org/archive/harman/1990/xx/stormbreaks.html

International Centre for Trade Union Rights, 2018, "Profile of Belarus", www.ictur.org/Profile_Belarus.html

Kalinovskaya, Tatiana, 2020, "Belarus Workers Chant 'Leave' at Lukashenko as Anger Mounts over Vote, Moscow Times (17 August), https://bit.ly/2VHqeL4

Kassabov, Ognian, 2020, "In Belarus, Labor is Struggling to Find Its Voice", *Jacobin* (30 August), www.jacobinmag.com/2020/08/belarus-election-lukashenko

Kuper, Simon, 2020, "From America to Zimbabwe, the World is Taking to the Streets", *Financial Times* (20 August).

Lemlich, Clare, 2020, "Belarus-Russia Integration Talks Reflect Deepening Imperial Tensions", Marx21 US, https://marx21us.org/2020/01/03/belarus-russia-integration-talks

Lenin, V I, 1922, "Fourth Congress of the Communist International", in *Collected Works*, volume 33 (Progress), www.marxists.org/archive/lenin/works/1922/nov/04b.htm

Liasheva, Alona, 2017, "Belarus's parasites", Jacobin (4 May), https://jacobinmag.com/2017/04/belarus-lukashenko-decree-three-social-dependency-parasites-tax-unemployment

Luxemburg, Rosa, 1906, *The Mass Strike, the Political Party and the Trade Unions*, www.marxists.org/archive/luxemburg/1906/mass-strike

Makhovsky, Andrei, 2020, "Dismissed as 'Poor Things', Three Women Try to Unseat Male President of Belarus", Reuters (22 July), https://reut.rs/2VxMEy9

Manenkov, Kostya, and Daria Litvinova, 2020, "Belarus Poll Workers Describe Fraud in 9 August Election", Associated Press (1 September), https://bit.ly/3mT15sA

Marx, Karl, 1976, *Capital*, volume 1 (Penguin).

Nechepurenko, Ivan, 2020, "Laying Down His Tools, Belarus Worker Takes Up Mantle of Protest Leader", *New York Times* (21 August), www.nytimes.com/2020/08/21/world/europe/belarus-protest-election-Lukashenko.html

Roth, Andrew, 2020, "Belarus Opposition Candidate Implies Threat to Children After Leaving Country", *Guardian* (12 August), www.theguardian.com/world/2020/aug/11/belarus-opposition-candidate-lithuania-protests-svetlana-tikhanouskaya

Stalin, Joseph, 1931, "The Tasks of Business Executives", in *Works*, volume 13 (Foreign Languages Publishing House), www.marxists.org/reference/archive/stalin/works/1931/02/04.htm

Tengely-Evans, Tomáš, 2018, "The Prague Spring of 1968: A Glimpse of Socialism?", *International Socialism* 159 (summer), http://isj.org.uk/the-prague-spring

Tengely-Evans, Tomáš, 2020a, "Protests Calls For Freedom in Belarus as Lukashenko Issues Threats", *Socialist Worker* (24 August), https://socialistworker.co.uk/art/50532/Protests+call+for+freedom+in+Belarus+as+Lukashenko+issues+threats

Tengely-Evans, Tomáš, 2020b, "Belarus Revolt Faces New Repression, But Threatens General Strike", *Socialist Worker* (15 October), https://socialistworker.co.uk/art/50781/Belarus+revolt+faces+new+repression%2C+but+threatens+general+strike

Tengely-Evans, Tomáš, 2020c, "Belarusian Workers and Students Defy Repression to Face Down Lukashenko", *Socialist Worker* (28 October), https://socialistworker.co.uk/art/50842/Belarusian+workers+and+students+defy+repression+to+face+down+Lukashenko

Tengely-Evans, Tomáš, 2020d, "Workers Strikes and Protests Increase Pressure on Regime in Belarus", *Socialist Worker* (12 August), https://bit.ly/3kCarY2

Tengely-Evans, Tomáš, 2020e, "Strikes and Protests Spread as Belarusian Regime Clings to Power", *Socialist Worker* (17 August), https://bit.ly/33L5xlK

Upchurch, Martin, 2012, "Persistent Economic Divergence and Institutional Dysfunction in Post-communist Economies: An Alternative Synthesis", *Competition and Change*, volume 16, number 2.

Walker, Shaun, 2020, "Workers and Students Launch Anti-Lukashenko Strike", *Guardian* (26 October), https://bit.ly/36zBy1R

Walker, Shaun, and Andrew Roth, 2020, "'Resign!': Alexander Lukashenko heckled by factory workers in Minsk", *Guardian* (17 August), https://bit.ly/3lT7WRA

World Bank, 2002, "Transition, The First Ten Years: Analysis and Lessons for Eastern Europe and the Former Soviet Union", https://openknowledge.worldbank.org/handle/10986/14042

Cedric Robinson, racial capitalism and the return of black radicalism
Ken Olende

The terms "black radicalism" and "racial capitalism" have become buzzwords in the revitalised international discussion about race that has arisen in parallel with the Black Lives Matter movement since 2013. Indeed, the idea that capitalism is inherently linked to racism is a common sense among many left-wing activists. Nevertheless, how exactly to understand that link is no set-tled matter. In a recent seminar on racial capitalism, former *Race & Class* editor Arun Kundnani said of the concept, "We are still in the process of deciding what we mean by it".[1] The term has been taken on a range of meanings. These extend from the idea that capitalist firms actively downplay the racial disadvantage faced by black people, as a recent article on the Vox website suggested, to the sophisticated argument about the interaction between racism and capital in Gargi Bhattacharyya's *Rethinking Racial Capitalism* (2018).[2]

However, the core concept was developed in the 1980s by the radical black scholar Cedric Robinson, and it is his version that this article will centre around.

---

1 Kundnani made the comment at the online "What is Racial Capitalism?" seminar, organised by the Havens Wright Center for Social Justice on 15 October 2020.
2 Illing, 2019. The vogue for the idea of racial capitalism has also fuelled recent discussions in US journals *Monthly Review* and *Boston Review*. See *Boston Review*'s "Race Capitalism Justice" issue (winter 2017) and *Monthly Review*'s "Racial Capitalism" issue (July-August 2020).

Kundnani has correctly pointed to the reasons behind the concept's popularity on the left, which "lies in its apparent bridging of the economic and the cultural, of the class struggle and the struggle against white supremacy, allowing us to understand police and plantation violence as linked to capital accumulation".[3]

Robinson developed the concept over a number of years. For him, "racial capitalism" meant that capitalism has been inseparably linked to ideas of race and racism throughout its history. Capitalism built up its wealth from the transatlantic slave trade and colonial exploitation. For Robinson, there is no such thing as non-racist capitalism. Because of this, he argues that a "black radicalism" is necessary; racially oppressed peoples, particularly those of African descent, have been exploited by the capitalist system since its foundation, and they are also key to liberation from it. He states that "racial regimes are constructed social systems in which race is proposed as a justification for the relations of power".[4]

This article will examine how Robinson's concept of racial capitalism developed, particularly in his central work, *Black Marxism* (1983). It will also look at his shifting and contradictory relationship with Marxist ideas. Robinson emerged from the black movement of the 1960s in the United States and was concerned with how capitalism, imperialism, class and race intersect. He looked to many activists and intellectuals from the black radical tradition who had been drawn to Marxism. Although he was highly critical of what he saw as the failures of Marxist theory around race, class and liberation, he has still inspired many who work within the revolutionary Marxist tradition. The activist and theorist Angela Davis, for instance, said that Robinson "challenged us to think about the role of black radical theorists and activists in shaping social and cultural histories".[5]

Nevertheless, this article will critique Robinson's ideas about Marxism in relation to three specific and important questions: whether racism pre-dated capitalism; whether the working class is a "universal" class, able to lead all oppressed people to freedom; and how a dialectical understanding of history relates to determinism. Where possible, I will look to black writers in the Marxist tradition to emphasise a vital recognition that emerges from a reading Robinson's works: just how closely black theorists have been involved in developing Marxist theory.

Indeed, some of Robinson's criticisms of Marxism can act as a corrective to reductionist attitudes in some strains of the left that relegate battles against oppression to matters that can be resolved simply through the class struggle. In some cases, these fights can even be seen as a distraction. The black Marxist Hubert Harrison described one example of such attitudes. When working as an

---

3   Kundnani, 2020.
4   Robinson, 2012, pxii.
5   Johnson and Lubin, 2017, p241.

organiser in 1912 for the American Socialist Party, which was then a significant organisation, he was outraged that it permitted racially segregated branches. He wrote, "Southernism or socialism—which? Is it to be the white half of the working class against the black half, or all of the working class together?"[6] The party maintained segregation and lost Harrison. A more contemporary example is in modern-day France, where much of the left has gone along with an establishment Islamophobia that hides behind "secularism" and the supposedly progressive values of the French Republic. In the case of both the US in the 1910s and France in the 21st century, the practical result is to drive a part of the working class away from socialist politics.

Ideas that link racism directly to capitalism can also provide a platform from which to critique currents in black politics that see reforming the system as a solution and downplay the importance of class. In *Futures of Black Radicalism* (2017), US professor Darryl C Thomas, reflecting on Robinson's ideas, argues that:

> One of the consequences of neoliberal, globalised US capitalism for many African Americans is a growing difference in life chances between poor and affluent blacks... a divide that is beginning to be reflected in black politics and black public opinion.[7]

In recent decades the anti-racist movement internationally has tended to break up into more specific interest groups in a way that reduces the possibility of solidarity. Perhaps the clearest example of this is American Descendants of Slavery, an organisation founded in 2016 that focuses on reparations for slavery but rejects solidarity with other racially oppressed groups such as migrants from Africa and the Caribbean.[8] This kind of division is something that Robinson himself always rejected. For instance, writing on the fatal shooting of a black man, Michael Brown, in Ferguson, Missouri, in August 2014, Robinson drew connections between the false justifications and lies issued by US police and those issued by the Israeli army during its assaults on Gaza.[9] His insistence on always looking to make such links is a key strength of his work.

Who was Cedric Robinson?

Robinson was born in 1940 in the black, working-class district of Oakland, California, which would later become the launchpad for the Black Panther Party. He was raised by his extended family during a great wave of black migration to the cities. In 1959—without the support of his school—he arrived at the

---

6   Perry, 2009, p183.
7   Thomas, 2017, p5.
8   See https://ados101.com/about-ados
9   Robinson, 2019a, p354.

University of California, Berkeley, to study social anthropology. Unaware of the racist assumptions made about black people:

> He simply showed up...and stood in the registration line... Perhaps because he followed an international student, was dark skinned, and projected a sense of entitlement at a university with so few black students, the registrar assumed he was an African national and asked if his government planned to pay his fees.[10]

He got in, working to pay his way, and became a student activist. In 1961 when the US organised the failed Bay of Pigs invasion of revolutionary Cuba, Robinson organised a protest. He also invited Malcolm X to speak on campus. Later, he completed a doctorate at Stanford University in California, although much of the work was undertaken while visiting the University of Sussex in South East England. These writings became his first book, *The Terms of Order* (1980), which argued against the hierarchical political structure that Robinson identified with the core of Western thought. In its place, he proposed a specifically "black radicalism".[11] He went on to become director of the Center for Black Studies Research at the University of California, Santa Barbara. Thomas describes the agenda that Robinson set while in this role:

> He established workshops every weekend...to examine issues related to Marxism, anarchism, radical black politics, political theory, gender and feminism... Guest lecturers included C L R James, Robert Williams, James Boggs and Grace Boggs.[12]

Robinson wrote *Black Marxism*, his key text, while living in Cambridge, England. He worked with the Institute of Race Relations and activist intellectuals such as Ambalavaner Sivanandan, Paul Gilroy and C L R James, who were all central in developing anti-racist strategy and theory in Britain. The trip affected his political development. Race had become a central issue in British politics. An anti-racist movement developed that focused on "political blackness": the oppression of non-white people who had faced colonisation, whether they were of African descent or Asian. Sivanandan, who was Sri Lankan, stressed particularly the links between culture, identity and resistance, saying, "We do not need a cultural identity for its own sake but to make use of positive aspects of our culture to forge correct alliances and fight the correct battles".[13]

Black Marxism explores the relationship between racism, anti-racism and Marxism. The book is ambitious and wide-ranging; at its best, it is a celebration

---

10   Kelley, 2016.
11   For more details, see Kelley, 2016.
12   Thomas, 2005, pp2-3.
13   Sivanandan, 1990, p76.

of people gaining agency over their own lives. It has sections on the development of capitalism, the working class and nationalism, but the strongest part looks in depth at the emergence of a black radical tradition over the past 500 years. It talks of people and ideas transported from Africa, and it examines maroon populations across the Americas—slaves who had escaped and mixed with local peoples. Robinson convincingly describes the significance of these communities and the ideological danger they posed to the institution of slavery:

> All capitalists believed the brutality of the slave system to be a practical necessity. Maroon settlements like those of Jamaica, Cuba and North America had to be destroyed, or failing that, quarantined. They could not be allowed to contaminate a labour upon which so much depended.[14]

Many of *Black Marxism*'s themes are expanded in *An Anthropology of Marxism* (2001). This is a fascinating history of socialist thought and its interaction with dissident European Christianity, even though it is ultimately flawed by its reductionist view of Marxism. His *Black Movements in America* (1997) is also a valuable history and includes a detailed analysis of how class has affected the development of African American resistance. Robinson died in 2016, as a new anti-racist movement was starting to blossom. His major works are now back in print, alongside an illuminating new collection of his essays, *On Racial Capitalism, Black Internationalism and Cultures of Resistance*, which was published in 2019.

Racial capitalism

Robinson argues that capitalism can never be divorced from the racial concepts that grew up with it:

> The development, organisation and expansion of capitalist society pursued essentially racial directions, and so too did social ideology. As a material force, then, it could be expected that racialism would inevitably permeate the social structures emergent from capitalism.[15]

He cites two broadly related reasons for this interrelated development of capitalism and racism. Firstly, capitalism emerged in Europe, where he argues there was already racial division of a kind unseen elsewhere in the world. According to Robinson:

> The bourgeoisie...were drawn from particular ethnic and cultural groups; the European proletariat and the mercenaries of the leading states from others; its

---

14 Robinson, 2000, p140.
15 Robinson, 2000, p9.

peasants from still other cultures; and its slaves from entirely different worlds. The tendency of European civilisation through capitalism was thus not to homogenise but to differentiate—to exaggerate regional, subcultural, and dialectical differences into "racial" ones.[16]

Secondly, in the centuries before industrial capitalism arose, mercantile capitalism was dominant, developing on the back of the transatlantic slave trade, with its racial exploitation and oppression of Africans. This too inseparably bound capitalism and racism together, producing racial capitalism.

Robinson came across the term "racial capitalism" in Britain. It was developed by South African Marxists to understand the apartheid regime.[17] These theorists challenged an orthodoxy among South Africa's opposition African National Congress (ANC) that apartheid was alien to capitalism. Instead, they argued that racism had been vital to the development of South African capitalism. Although this central position is convincing, the specific arguments—that parts of the South African economy remained pre-capitalist, allowing the super-exploitation of the black population—are less so.[18]

Robinson took this theory, which was originally intended to explain the peculiarities of South African apartheid, and generalised it to all capitalism. He argued from this that, "The historical development of world capitalism was influenced in a most fundamental way by the particularistic forces of racism and nationalism".[19] He concluded that a specifically European tendency to racialisation must have pre-dated capitalism, but also that it is inherent to the development of the system. One proposition following from this is that racism is not the oppression of black people by white but rather any systematic oppression on ethnic grounds.

This generalised theory was partly an evolution of ideas developed by the undeservedly little-remembered Oliver Cromwell Cox, a black American thinker. Robinson combines arguments from two periods in Cox's career. The first is from his major work, *Caste, Class and Race* (1948).[20] Robinson neatly summarises this argument: "Capitalism and racism were historical concomitants. As the executors of an expansionist world system, capitalists required racism

---

16 Robinson, 2000, p25.
17 See for instance the Anti-Apartheid Movement pamphlet *Foreign Investment and the Reproduction of Racial Capitalism in South Africa*, which may have been the first to use the term "racial capitalism"—Legassick and Hemson, 1976.
18 Variations on the theory were put forward by Harold Wolpe, Neville Alexander and others. Alex Callinicos critiqued them at some length in his *South Africa Between Reform and Revolution*. See Callinicos, 1988, pp84-88.
19 Robinson, 2000, p9.
20 Cox, 1970.

in order to police and rationalise the exploitation of workers".[21] Cox argued that racism developed out of chattel slavery, rather than the trade in African slaves developing because of racism:

> If white workers were available in sufficient numbers, they would have been substituted. As a matter of fact, part of the early demand for labour in the West Indies and on the mainland was filled by white servants, who were sometimes defined in exactly the same terms as those used to characterise the Africans.[22]

The plantation owners were driven by "a practical exploitative relationship with its socio-attitudinal facilitation—at that time only nascent race prejudice." Racism and its associated structures developed with it and out of it. This closely echoes the description of the origin of chattel slavery of Africans put forward by the Trinidadian historian Eric Williams, who was himself influenced by C L R James:

> The reason was economic, not racial; it had to do not with the colour of the labourer, but the cheapness of the labour. As compared with Native American and white labour, Negro slavery was eminently superior.[23]

As the black US historian W E B Du Bois bluntly put it in 1947, "It was Karl Marx who made the great unanswerable charge to the sources of capitalism in African slavery".[24] Williams and Cox each developed similar arguments built on the method developed by Marx and Friedrich Engels, who had themselves not written specifically about the origins of racism. It is not clear to what extent Williams and Cox were aware of one another's work.[25] Cox did not define himself as a Marxist, but commented that if his book sometimes seems Marxist, "It is not because we have taken the ideas of this justly famous writer as gospel, but because we have not discovered any other that could explain the facts so consistently".[26] At this point in Cox's theoretical development, there was no distinction between the racism developing through capitalism and racial capitalism.

---

21 Robinson, 2019a, p79.

22 Cox, 1970, p332.

23 Williams, 1964, p19-20.

24 Du Bois, 1965, p56.

25 A single footnote in Cox's book refers to Williams, listing him as one of three writers who saw the slave trade from Africa developing because of the productivity of the enslaved African workers—Cox, 1970, p338.

26 Cox, 1970, pxi. He later retreated from the book's more radical aspects, seeing change emerging within existing US society. His last book, *Race Relations*, is very much about how black people can advance within the existing system through a "slow, but irrepressible rise toward social integration and justice"—Cox, 1976, p289.

However, Cox went on to develop a theory of capitalism as a system in his later books, and this was a second source of arguments for Robinson.[27] He examined early mercantile capitalist development, particularly through city-states such as Venice, and came to regard Marx's analysis as crudely determinist due to its emphasis on the role of the proletariat. Cox considerably modified his position on the origins of racism, saying that the Marxist understanding was hampered by:

> The rigid ideas concerning the role of industrial workers in modern revolutionary movements and the earlier Marxian predictions giving precedence to the more advanced capitalist nations in the succession of socialist revolutions.[28]

Cox saw Marxism as only concerning the development of industrial capitalism but not earlier mercantile systems, and thus alleged that racism pre-dated the emergence of capitalism. Robinson built upon this argument to suggest that there is a separate European dynamic of race:

> Racism...has its genesis in the "internal" relations of European peoples. As part of the inventory of Western civilisation it would reverberate within and without, transferring its toll from the past to the present.[29]

He emphasises the "nascent race prejudice" referred to by Cox, seeing its emergence as coinciding with "the reappearance of urban life at the end of the first Christian millennium".[30] He also argued that outside factors, such as Islamic ideas, had no influence on slavery in Europe: "The traditions of European slavery were already quite ancient and quite elaborately rationalised by the time of the appearance of Islam in the 7th century".[31] However, this is an oversimplification. As historian of slavery Robin Blackburn has pointed out:

> The gradual change in attitudes towards slavery in Western Europe was, like the notion of Christendom itself, deeply marked by confrontation with Islam. It was only after the Muslim advance to the heart of Europe that Christian doctrine began cautiously to modify its acceptance of the enslavement of believers.[32]

Slavery became marginal to most European economies in the Middle Ages, and so attitudes towards it changed.[33] It was the emergence of powerful

---

27 In this period, Cox's arguments foreshadow Immanuel Wallerstein's world system theory—see Hier, 2001, pp69-86.
28 Cox, 1964, p218.
29 Robinson, 2000, p9.
30 Robinson, 2000, p67.
31 Robinson, 2000, p95.
32 Blackburn, 1997, p42.
33 Blackburn, 2011, p15.

Islamic states that led to the idea of a separate Christendom, a Christian realm defined in opposition to Islam. The Islamic states banned the enslavement of co-religionists, which was then adopted by Christians.[34] The ban did not survive the rise of the transatlantic slave trade, even though the idea that conversion might lead to freedom was still common among slaves in the 18th century.

The transtlantic trade reduced and removed whatever traditional rights unfree labourers had previously held. Ironically, this occurred alongside the rise of ideas of equality produced by the emergence of capitalism, which reconceived human beings as isolated individuals engaging in a set of contractual agreements with one another. This created an ideological contradiction in the institution of slavery that was papered over with the racist claim that black people were somehow inferior. For the plantation owners in the Americas, slaves could not be their equals in ability. This was a problem that had never troubled older societies, in which slaves could be administrators, soldiers or teachers. Robinson writes:

> For the Negro to come into being all what was now required was an immediate cause, a specific purpose. The trade in African slaves, coming as it did as an extension of capitalism and racial arrogance, supplied both a powerful motive and a readily received object.[35]

The strength of this argument is that it links of racism and the creation of the "Negro" to the spread of slavery. However, it leaves out the way that as capitalism developed in Europe there was a shift in ideas about how different groups of people related to each other. Robinson's invocation of the term "racial arrogance" suggests a division between "European" and "non-European" that does not seem to fit with either his account of internal ethnicisation or his picture of a society so recently overshadowed by more technically advanced Islamic civilisations.

The rise of the mercantile capitalist states suggested to Enlightenment thinkers at least an idea of equality, which was absent in the treatment of slaves and colonised subjects.[36] Inequality was explained by racialisation. Such racialisation played a vital role in the slavery practiced in early capitalism, and incidentally chimes with Marx's analysis. As Robinson says:

> For Marx, slavery had been "the chief moment of primitive accumulation", "an economic category of the highest importance". First, African workers had been transmuted by the perverted canons of mercantile capitalism into property. Then,

---

34 Blackburn, 1997, p44.
35 Robinson, 2000, p100.
36 See Harman, 1999, p242-246.

African labour power as slave labour was integrated into the organic composition of 19th century manufacturing and industrial capitalism. This sustained the emergence of an extra-European world market within which the accumulation of capital was garnered for the further development of industrial production.[37]

What is black radicalism?

Robinson always emphasised that liberation involves self-activity and that black people were at the centre of the fight for their own freedom. *Black Marxism* includes extended sections on two black thinkers who were heavily influenced by Marxist ideas—W E B Du Bois and C L R James. Robinson rightly praises James's *The Black Jacobins*, a chronicle of the victorious Haitian slave uprising in the 1790s, and Du Bois's *Black Reconstruction*, which looks at the role of black people in the US Civil War and its aftermath. Robinson saw the methods of social organisation and resistance arising in these periods as rooted in a historical black consciousness:

> It was not...an understanding of the Europeans that preserved those Africans... Rather, it was the ability to conserve their native consciousness of the world from alien intrusion, the ability to imaginatively recreate a precedent metaphysic... This was the raw material of the black radical tradition...constructed from a shared philosophy developed in the African past and transmitted as culture, from which revolutionary consciousness was realised and the ideology of struggle formed.[38]

Although this is true, it must nevertheless be complemented, for instance, by James's recognition of the influence of the ideas of the French Revolution on the Haitian rebels—his book's eponymous "black Jacobins".

Robinson had already discussed the idea that different notions of struggle and equality dominated in Africa. In *Terms of Order* he had talked of the opposition between the rigid hierarchies of the Western intellectual and cultural tradition—in which he included both the Enlightenment thinkers and Marx—and traditions in certain African "stateless societies" of organisation from below. Such societies show "the capacity of human beings to hold together their social structures without the authority of rulers or the presence of political leaders".[39] This marks an important democratic tradition that has influenced anti-racist and anti-colonial movements.

However, as Robinson discussed in other writings, there are also strong authoritarian traditions in parts of Africa. To take a relatively small area

---

37 Robinson, 2000, p113.
38 Robinson, 2000, p309.
39 Robinson, 2016, p185.

as an example, modern Guinea Bissau was subject to "the old Sudanic empires of Ghana (4th century to 11th century) and Mali (13th century to 17th century)".[40] Conversely, there are also traditions of non-hierarchal social organisation in various other parts of the world; for instance, in *An Anthropology of Marxism*, Robinson examines alternative European traditions, including various medieval religious heresies. This raises, but does not settle, the question of whether there is anything specifically black in the liberatory heart of "black radicalism". Is this radicalism perhaps built instead upon long-standing traditions of resistance shared, for instance, with Native Americans and other racially oppressed groups?

Robinson does not claim to be a materialist thinker, and the definition of black radicalism he gives in *Black Marxism*'s conclusion is idealistic and perhaps even mystical. For that reason, it is also hard to dispute:

> One black collective identity suffuses nationalisms. Harboured in the African diaspora there is a single historical identity that is in opposition to the systemic privations of racial capitalism. Ideologically, it cements pain to purpose, experience to expectation, consciousness to collective action. It deepens with each disappointment at false mediation and reconciliation, and is crystallised into ever-increasing cores by betrayal and repression.[41]

In fact, this interpretation of black radicalism contradicts some of Robinson's strongest pieces of historical narrative. For instance, he argues that some of the strongest maroon communities were a mix of Africans, Native Americans and poor whites: "American maroon communities frequently acquired a multicultural and multiracial character".[42] As Peter Linebaugh and Marcus Rediker argue, it was the unity between these different groups that most terrified the elites in the Americas and the Caribbean. Describing the cooperation between slaves, Irish "redshanks" and other poor whites in 17th century Barbados, they write:

> In 1634 servants had conspired to kill their masters and make themselves free, then to take the first ship that came and go to sea as buccaneers... Cooperation between such redshanks and African slaves was a nightmare for the authorities. The Governor's Council announced in 1655 that "there are several Irish servants and Negroes out in rebellion in ye thicketts and thereabouts." This made a

40 Robinson, 2019a, p310.
41 Robinson, 2000, p317.
42 Robinson, 1997, p13.

mockery of a law passed in 1652, "An Act to Restrain the Wanderings of Servants and Negroes".[43]

Robinson recognises the importance of such events and demonstrates how laws were drawn up to separate the black population from other poor people. For instance, in Virginia:

> In 1662 a law was passed preventing a child from inheriting its father's status if the mother was a "Negro woman"; in 1667, another law prevented baptism from free-ing "slaves by birth"; in 1680 a law was passed "for preventing Negro insurrections"; in 1692, another to aid the "more speedy prosecution of slaves committing capital crimes" established special courts for slave trials.[44]

Explaining how rulers isolated both free and enslaved black people from the white poor through the slave codes, Robinson also shows that this did not stop black people leading many insurrections in Virginia and South Carolina.[45] However, he fails to rework his definition of black radicalism on the basis of these facts.

These tensions in Robinson's approach gesture to debates about how racism is constructed. British sociologist Stuart Hall argued that it is not possible to look at either race or racism as unitary and static. Although both have certain unchanging features, "More significant are the ways in which these general features are modified and transformed by the historical specificity of the contexts and environments in which they become active".[46] Thus, in order to understand shifts in racial formations, cultural identities and racism, it is always necessary to examine wider societal interactions within capitalism. Hall applies this understanding very powerfully in his description of the moral panic about the threat of "mugging" in the late 1960s and early 1970s. Mugging was created as a crime that could be blamed particularly on young black men, making them the focus of a response to economic and social crisis.[47] Something similar can be seen more recently with refugees and the government's use of the anti-immigrant "hostile environment" in the health service, housing and employment.[48] As Gargi Bhattacharyya writes in *Rethinking Racial Capitalism*:

> Racial capitalism is not an account of how capitalism treats different "racial groups". It is an account of how the world made through racism shapes patterns of

---

43 Linebaugh and Rediker, 2000, pp125-126.
44 Robinson, 1997, p3.
45 Robinson, 1997, p9.
46 Hall, 1996, p435.
47 See Hall and others, 2013.
48 See Olende, 2020.

capitalist development. In this, racial capitalism is better understood as a variety of racecraft in the economic realm.[49]

Bhattacharyya uses the term "racecraft" to refer to an understanding of racism developed by the Marxist thinkers Karen Fields and Barbara Fields. Fields and Fields argued that whatever the origins of ideas of race, racism is a systematic form of oppression that shifts to accommodate societal changes.[50] In my view, this interpretation gives a solid basis for developing ideas of racial capitalism. It is also one that chimes with Williams's and James's arguments that develop a Marxist understanding of the evolution of racism within capitalism. Fields and Fields write:

> Racism and class inequality in the US have always been part of the same phenomenon. African Americans began their history in slavery. This was a class system so abnormal by the time of the American Revolution that it required an extraordinary ideological rationale—which has ever since gone by the name *race*—to fit plausibly into supposedly republican institutions.[51]

The possibility of unity between black people and other exploited groups in the US concerned Du Bois, who Robinson writes about at length in *Black Marxism*, throughout his long life. As Robinson shows, Du Bois was both drawn towards and resistant to the politics of the US Communist Party (CPUSA). For some time, he believed that the success of racism meant that the interests of white and black workers were divided to such an extent that in the 1930s they were separate and distinct proletariats. In "Marxism and the Negro Problem" (1933), he wrote stingingly about the white American Federation of Labor trade union leadership:

> They have no excuse of illiteracy or religion to veil their deliberate intention to keep Negroes and Mexicans and other elements of common labour in a lower proletariat, as subservient to their interests as theirs are to those of capital.[52]

However, the experience of CPUSA organising showed Du Bois that this was not the case. As Robin Kelley argues in his study of the CPUSA's activities in Alabama:

> Racial divisions were far more fluid, and Southern working-class consciousness far more complex, than most historians have realised. The African Americans who

---

49 Bhattacharyya, 2018, p103.
50 Fields and Fields, 2012.
51 Fields and Fields, 2012, p266.
52 Du Bois, 1933, p103.

made up the Alabama radical movement experienced and opposed race *and* class oppression as a totality.[53]

Robinson is right to focus on Du Bois's masterpiece, *Black Reconstruction*. This work is a detailed exploration of the periods leading up to and following the US Civil War, uncovering the black radical tradition that operated in this era. Du Bois decisively disproved the establishment tale that black people had idly sat by while whites fought over their status. He showed that black slaves had risen up and that they had common interests with poor Southern whites, but he also described how racial capitalism made "two groups of workers with practically identical interests...hate and fear each other so deeply".[54]

Robinson describes Du Bois's achievement in *Black Reconstruction* as having been that, "undaunted by the fact that he was already on forbidden terrain in the thinking of Hegel, Marx and his own American contemporaries", he "ventured further, uncovering the tradition" of black radicalism.[55] Indeed, Du Bois's magnificent book did expand the bounds of Marxist historiography. However, its discussion of black people is hardly "forbidden terrain" within Marxist thought. Marx himself had frequently pointed to black slavery as a weak link in capitalism and a key site of resistance. Even before Civil War had started, Marx wrote to Engels, highlighting the revolts against slavery in US and comparing their importance to the struggle to end Tsarist serfdom: "The most momentous thing happening in the world today is, on the one hand, the movement among the slaves in America...and the movement among the slaves in Russia, on the other".[56]

Robinson's theoretical disagreements with Marxism

Robinson directly challenges what he sees as Marx's views on several issues that have an important bearing on the question of race, and it is to these that I now turn. I will concentrate Robinson's discussions of the origins of racism, the role of the working class and the question of the dialectic. Although these might seem to represent very different aspects of Robinson's thought, they are nevertheless all connected to his interpretation of the role of determinism in Marxist thought.

Robinson, taking his lead from Cox's later writings, believed that racism had developed before capitalism, and that it was therefore a specifically European phenomenon. Yet, simultaneously, he sees the development of racism as dialectically intertwined with the development of capitalism. Various pre-existing

---

53 Kelley, 1990, pxiii.
54 Du Bois, 1998, p700.
55 Robinson, 2000, pxxxii.
56 Quoted in Anderson, 2010, p85.

prejudices had to be modified and reworked over a couple of hundred years in order to create the horrific racism of the late 18th century. This involved considerable shifts in ways of thinking, which were expressed in, for instance, the laws in the Caribbean and American colonies that divided black from white.[57]

Undoubtedly, Marx's and Engels's analyses of the rapidly changing world system were incomplete and have required extension, correction and updating. Indeed, one reason that Marx never completed *Capital* was his attempt to keep up with developments concering the non-European world—both actual contemporary events in the 19th century and discoveries being made at that time about earlier social systems.[58] It is because Robinson seriously engages with Marxism that his occasional disregard for what Marx wrote is so frustrating. Because Robinson describes what he sees as fundamental problems with Marxism, I will focus very clearly on what Marx and Engels actually wrote.

The origin and role of capitalism
Let us begin with Robinson's engagement with Marx's ideas about the origins of capitalism. Robinson argues that Marx believed:

> Unlike previous ("precapitalist", Marxists would say) modes of production, capitalism could not conceal or justify exploitation through ideology. So the extraordinary comprehension of human society of which we are now capable is both a consequence of an accident of birth and the ineluctable accretion of productive forces over millennia. The premise, however, that alone of all social orders, capitalist society unmasks itself, relegates all social understanding before the capitalist era mired in the ideological muck of their own eras.[59]

Robinson thus argues that, according to Marx, capitalism creates "a coherent ordering of things", demystifying the world and social relations.[60] Such an understanding seems to present capitalism as a clean break with previous forms of social organisation, and implies that the forms of consciousness produced by it are superior to other, earlier ones. Robinson did not believe that capitalism involved such a total change in social relations.

However, there are real problems with Robinson's interpretation of Marx here. Marx did not argue that capitalism completely demystified social relations, but rather that it actually created its own distinct forms of mystification. For

---

57 See, for example, my article on the development of racist ideology in the US for more detail—Olende 2017.

58 See Anderson, 2010, p196-236.

59 Robinson, 2019b, 19.

60 Robinson, 2000, pxxviii.

instance, the exploitation of the working class is disguised by the the contract between worker and capitalist, which seems to be a result of fair negotiation between two people within the framework of legal equality. This mystifies and obscures the true nature of capitalist social relations.

In order to stress that capitalism did not involve such a clean and clear break with the past, Robinson emphasises that a series of capitalisms had actually evolved prior to industrial capitalism. These included, for instance, the mercantile capitalism of Venice. This is an important point for Robinson because he views Marx as having privileged the industrial phase of capitalism as "the singular and unprecedented historical development of modern human society".[61] Robinson's claim that Marx identified capitalism with industrialism is important because racism certainly did pre-date this stage of capitalist development. This allows him to argue:

> The historical development of world capitalism was influenced in a most fundamental way by the particularistic forces of racism and nationalism. This could only be true if the social, psychological, and cultural origins of racism and nationalism both anticipated capitalism in time and formed a piece of those events that contributed directly to its organisation of production and exchange.[62]

However, once again there are big problems with Robinson's account of Marx's ideas here. Although Marx did examine the growth of industrial capital in depth, he certainly did not see this as the only form of capitalism, and he did not dismiss earlier forms either. In *Capital*, for example, he looks at both "usurer's capital and merchant's capital", examining how these were key to the economic and ideological development of the system.[63] Indeed, he also emphasised the differences between various bourgeois social formations, calling it naive "to apply the standard of the 14th century to the relations of production prevailing in the 19th century".

A related argument is Robinson's claim that Marx effectively separates an understanding of slavery from his analysis of capitalism. Much of the disagreement centres on the role of slavery in what *Capital* refers to as the "primitive accumulation of capital". Robinson argues that Marx tossed slavery into the "abyss signified by precapitalist, non-capitalist and primitive accumulation", seeing it as somehow outside of the dynamics of the capitalist system.[64] However, this misunderstands the concept of primitive accumulation and its role in Marx's thought. These misunderstandings are perhaps compounded by some of Marx's literary

61 Robinson, 2019b, p82.
62 Robinson, 2000, p9.
63 Marx, 1976, p914.
64 Robinson, 2000, pxxix.

devices in the chapter of *Capital* entitled "The So-called Primitive Accumulation". This chapter opens with an ironic discussion of Adam Smith's interpretation of how some came to be wealthy, which serves merely to legitimate the division of society into classes. Nevertheless, Marx's actual description of the mechanisms for the primitive accumulation of the foundational capital necessary to set the capitalist system in motion are quite different. These included the colonisation of the Americas, the enslavement of Africans and the confiscation of the communal forms of property that existed in feudal peasant communities. Even though these are not the same as the "classic" form of exploitation in which a capitalist creams off surplus labour from a worker, they were nonetheless still guided by capitalist imperatives of profit-making. Slavery, colonial plunder and other forms of primitive accumulation were thus internal to the logic of capital for Marx.[65]

Marx's understanding that primitive accumulation was very much internal to the dynamics of capitalism are expressed in some of his concrete historical analyses of of colonialism and enslavement. John Bellamy Foster and others have recently written excellently on Marx's view of slavery in the US and its integration with capitalism. They argue:

> In volume 3 of *Capital*, Marx pointed to the vast surplus labour expropriated from slaves, and the fact that the slaves themselves were a form of capital asset, forming the basis of fictitious or speculative capital. Therefore, there seemed to be little doubt, in his estimation, that the plantation economy of the antebellum South was, as far as economic concerns alone were considered, enormously profitable. This included the market for the breeding of slaves.[66]

During the Civil War, Marx was also very clear that the outcome of the conflict would have an important impact on the development of the capitalist system. If the South succeeded in seceding from the United States, he explained, the racialisation of capitalism would be deepened:

> The slave system would infect the whole Union. In the Northern states, where Negro slavery is unworkable in practice, the white working class would be gradually depressed to the level of helotry.[67]

The proletariat as a "universal" class

A second important issue over which Robinson mounts an argument with Marx is the question of the role of the working class in history. Robinson's concerns

---

65 Marx, 1976, p873-875.
66 Foster, Holleman and Clark, 2020, p107.
67 Quoted in Anderson, 2010, p90. The term "helot" can refer to a slave or a serf.

are partially animated by the emergence of new forms of resistance to imperialism in the 20th century. These included guerrilla wars and other forms of anti-colonial struggle that are not directly related to the struggle of the industrial working class. Robinson argues that Marxists' focus on "the proletariat as the revolutionary subject" and "the class struggle between the proletariat and the bourgeoisie" makes Marxism unfit to deal with the 20th century; this is "an era for which it was not prepared".[68]

Of course, these claims sits awkwardly alongside the fact that Marxism's approach to racial issues and the colonial world did in fact make it attractive to black radicals of the 20th century. Grace Campbell, who in 1923 became the first black woman to join the CPUSA, explained, "My interest in Communism was inspired by the national policy of the Russian Bolsheviks and the anti-imperialist orientation of the Soviet state".[69] Yet Robinson's arguments seem to better reflect the ideas of French post-structuralist philosopher Michel Foucault than those of black militants such as Campbell. Foucault, in a passage quoted by Robinson, states, "Marxism exists in 19th century thought like a fish in water. That is, it is unable to breathe anywhere else".[70]

Somewhat duplicitously, such arguments suggest that Marxism was a suitable radical ideology for the 19th century and is simply now outdated. However, those who deploy these claims often tend to believe that Marx was actually wrong back in the 19th century as well. Robinson argues that because of the persistence of slavery and other forms of unfree labour such as "peonage and serfdom" during the development of capitalism, it was never actually the case that "working class consciousness" amounted to the "negation of bourgeois culture".[71] Other social forces, such as those resisting imperialism, might play such a role instead. Because capitalism developed as a system of worldwide exploitation, it was never a "closed system" that existed in an isolated condition in Europe; other, global revolutionary forces must be taken into account.

These arguments are very important because of the role that deterministic and reductive accounts of social development have played in the history of Marxist thought. The reformist tradition associated with the Second International of mass socialist parties that existed prior to the First World War, and the Stalinist tradition that emerged from the ideology of the Soviet bureaucracy after the reversal of the gains of the Russian Revolution, are both characterised by a stageist theory of history. In this view, historical development in each separate

---

68 Robinson, 2000, p43.
69 McDuffie, 2011, p34.
70 Robinson, 2016, p213 and Robinson, 2019b, p88. For the original source, see Foucault, 1994, p261.
71 Robinson, 2000, p4.

country moves through a set of predetermined phases. Within each phase, a specific class is central for historical progression to the next stage. Thus, the capitalist class was an oppositional force in feudal society that ultimately conducted a revolutionary struggle to overthrow the aristocracy and create a new form of society. Similarly, the working class is the force that will ultimately overthrow capitalism and create socialism.

Although such approaches reflect the real stress that Marx put on the power and potential of the working class, they also exclude other strata in society from the revolutionary process. In practice, this led to the disregarding or subordination of anti-imperialist struggles.

A very different understanding of political change was put forward by Leon Trotsky, the Russian Marxist theorist. Trotsky rejected the idea of one pre-determined stage of development following another that characterised the Stalinist distortion version of Marxism.[72] He argued that the accomplishment of socialism was possible among colonised and semi-colonised people through what he referred to as "permanent revolution". Although permanent revolution would have to involve the working class taking a leading role in the revolutionary process, Trotsky also saw that other social forces such as the peasantry and national liberation movements could also play a role. This understanding of revolutionary possibilities and strategy was based on an analysis of uneven and combined development:

> Historical backwardness does not imply a simple reproduction of the development of advanced countries, England or France, with a delay of one, two, or three centuries. It engenders an entirely new "combined" social formation in which the latest conquests of capitalist technique and structure root themselves into relations of feudal or pre-feudal barbarism, transforming and subjecting them and creating peculiar relations of classes.[73]

Critics of Trotsky's view might complain that it still centres on the agency of the proletariat, which is too often identified with white, male, European industrial workers. Yet as Joseph Choonara has argued in this journal, the working class is bigger, more international and more diverse than at any time in history:

> Around 1.8 billion people now engage in wage labour, an increase of 600 million since 2000. Not only is the working class vast, it is also more concentrated in towns and cities than ever before. The urban share of the global population has,

---

72 One example of this is the understanding of South African society during apartheid that was developed by the ANC, which is discussed above.

73 Trotsky, 1938.

since 2000, risen from 47 percent to 56 percent—an extra 1.4 billion people live in urban settings compared to two decades ago... For example, Chile's urban labour force rose from 3.7 million in 1990 to 7.3 million in 2018, Ecuador's from 3.3 million in 2000 to 5.1 million in 2018.[74]

The question of whether the working class is a universal class—capable of leading all other oppressed social strata towards liberation—necessarily involves reckoning with the disparity between its potential and its actuality. This is an issue that is underplayed by deterministic views of history. Marx's argument that the working class is the key to universal liberation in no way implies that it is immune to prejudices such as racism. Unfortunately, Robinson fails to see the tensions between potential and actuality as a productive one. For instance, he notes Marx's well-known claim, "The English working class will never accomplish anything before England has got rid of Ireland".[75] Here, Marx is asserting that the English working class of the 19th century was hamstrung by its allegiance to British imperialism and its animosity towards the conquered Irish people, who formed a large part of the industrial workforce in England. Marx stresses that a central task of any revolutionary movement would be to challenge and undermine racism within the working class, and that it cannot take political power without doing so. However, Robinson sees things differently. He endorses Marx's statement that racism undermined the revolutionary capacity of English workers, but then simply underlines the level of anti-Irish sentiment in 19th century England. This effectively dismisses the revolutionary potential of the working class.

Nevertheless, there are good reasons to view the working class as a universal class with the power to lead all oppressed people to liberation. Hal Draper has summed up Marx's reasons for considering the proletariat fit for this task:

> The working class is atomised when it is unorganised. Class organisation brings class characteristics to the fore and, as a function of organisation, class characteristics increasingly take precedence over merely individual reactions, the greater the scale of mass involvement.[76]

This process means that, even though anti-Irish racism was certainly an important fact in the English working class of the 19th century, the first mass working class movement—the Chartists—had two very prominent Irish leaders, Feargus O'Connor and Bronterre O'Brien.[77] Similarly the Chartists' leader in London, William Cuffay, was a black man and an example of the black

---

74 Choonara, 2019, p23.
75 Robinson, 2000, p41.
76 Draper, 1978, p40.
77 Foot, 2012, p115.

radical tradition in Britain; indeed, his last name is probably an anglicisation of the Twi name Kofi.[78] This phenomena of people from racially oppressed groups coming to the fore during periods of heightened struggle is a constant feature in the history of capitalism. Note, for instance, how the Civil Rights Movement and the Black Power movement revitalised the wider US left. Similarly, many of the leaders of the Russian revolution in 1917 were from the heavily persecuted Jewish population—including Leon Trotsky, Grigori Zinoviev and Karl Radek.

These considerations show that Marxism is a flexible theory. It can account for the importance of European industrial development and the emergence of an industrial working class in the historical trajectory of capitalism. However, it also has the theoretical resources to understand changes in the working class, such as its massive growth in the Global South, and the revolutionary potentials of social strata outside the working class. Of course, Marxism tries to develop an understanding of how Western capitalism came to dominate, but this is hardly a simple case of Eurocentrism. Attempts to understand how European societies came to dominate the rest of the world and shape global economic and social development have a long history. From the 17th century onwards, thinkers in the Ottoman Empire and across the Muslim world thinkers tried to explain how Islamic civilisation became overshadowed by the West:

> The beginnings of Muslim modernist thought resulted from this soul-searching inquiry. The "Fathers of Muslim Modernism"—Jamāl al-Dīn al-Afghānī, Muhammad Abduh in Egypt, and Sir Sayyid Ahmad Khan in India—attempted to provide a response and thus revive and renew their people.[79]

The Meiji Restoration of 1868 and the subsequent technical modernisation of Japan were entirely presaged on a section of the ruling class moving to develop along the lines of Europe to avoid being dominated by Western powers, as happened to China after its defeat in the Opium Wars.[80] The sort of contradictions that can be produced by such questions of uneven economic development were exemplified by James Africanus Horton. Horton was an African from Sierra Leone who took up a leading position in the British navy in the region; the imperial government trained Africans for the practical reason that Europeans tended to die of tropical diseases. In 1868 he published his *West African Countries and Peoples*, arguing that West African colonies

---

78   Chase, 2007, p305. Twi is a language spoken by several million people in central and southern Ghana.

79   Quoted in Margulies, 2018, p108.

80   Harman, 1999, p365.

should be granted dominion status within the British Empire. Horton is a highly contradictory figure; he was furious at the systematic racism of empire, but he saw the adoption of European civilisation as the way forward for Africa. He is now little more than a historical footnote, but his life does show the real choices that existed for people faced with imperialism in the 19th century.

Finally, it should be noted that these issues are also related to the question of whether capitalism needs to constantly renew itself by exploiting non-capitalist social formations. The idea that "primitive accumulation" of capital is actually a permanent and central feature of capitalism has enjoyed a long pedigree within the Marxist tradition. It was developed by Rosa Luxemburg in the early 19th century, but has more recently been discussed by the Marxist geographer David Harvey. Harvey talks of the exploitation of "non-capitalist social formations or some sectors within capitalism that has not yet been proletarianised".[81] This includes such diverse capitalist exploits as the privatisation of publically owned services, the sale of social housing stocks and the confiscation of land from indigenous people. Harvey has argued that, in the modern world, this kind of "accumulation by dispossession" has "moved to the fore as the primary contradiction within the imperialist organisation of capital accumulation".[82] This gels well with Robinson's belief, shared by many post-colonial theorists, that the working class cannot be a universal class because some of the most important areas of exploitation lie outside capitalism. However, Harvey's arguments have been convincingly challenged, for instance, by Chris Harman in this journal.[83]

Hegel, Marx and dialectical philosophy

A third and final important issue over which Robinson attacks Marx is the question of dialectical philosophy. Even many of those who regard themselves as Marxists see the notion of dialectical thinking as either an early aberration or an unnecessary bolt-on to Marx's ideas. However, the understanding of motion and contradiction in the dialectical method, which Marx developed from his engagement with the German philosopher G W F Hegel, is key to understanding the dynamic of the modern world. Although the Marxist theory of ideology was developed more systematically by later thinkers such as Georg Lukács and Antonio Gramsci, it is implicit in Marx's writing. An understanding of change through contradiction is particularly important when considering ideas of race as a specific form of ideology. How can capitalism both make us more alike, drawing the world's population into the two opposing camps of the bourgeoise and the proletariat, but

---

81   Quoted in Harman, 2007, p102.
82   Harman, 2007, p116.
83   Harman, 2007.

simultaneously develop national differences that cause people to see themselves as increasingly dissimilar? The answer is that capitalism is a system that develops through such contradictions; think, for instance, of how capitalism emphasises individual choice and yet makes life across the globe increasingly homogenous. The ideology of racism emerges to justify inequality in a society that exposes the equality of all people. Thus, far from being a hangover from pre-capitalist ideology, it is a phenomenon that developed out of capitalism's internal contradictions.

Hegel's philosophy, from which Marx developed his ideas about dialectics, emerged from the rapid and radical social change triggered by the French Revolution. In his *Phenomenology of Spirit*, for example, Hegel discusses episodes in the French Revolution, such as the Jacobin's Reign of Terror, as expressions of the dialectical development of various contradictory "shapes of consciousness". Importantly, Hegel understood these social changes in an idealistic manner: as products of shifts in the forms of social consciousness that human societies instantiate. Ultimately, he understood these shifts as happening within the all-encompassing consciousness that he refers to as *Geist* (spirit):

> A new product of the spirit is being prepared. Philosophy's chief task is to welcome it and grant it recognition, while others, impotently resisting, cling to the past and the majority unconsciously constitute the masses in which it manifests itself.[84]

Although Marx took up Hegel's idea that history is a product of the tension between contradictions that are instantiated by social forces and forms of consciousness, he also inverted Hegel's idealism. Instead of seeing social structures and processes as a result of the work of *Geist*, Marx argues that various forms of consciousness emerge within the framework of a material organisation of society. This material organisation is itself contradictory, involving tensions, for instance, between the forces of technological development and the existing modes of exploitation, which hold back technical innovation.

Robinson's critique of Marx's relationship Hegel is paradoxical. His first approach is to attack Marx for being too caught up in the thought of Hegel, and thus having succumbed to Eurocentrism. Indeed, Hegel assigned a special importance to Europe, seeing Ancient Greece as the originator of "freedom" and supporting colonialism. Moreover, he was completely dismissive of much of the non-European world. After a short discussion of Africa in his *Philosophy of History*, he writes, "At this point we leave Africa, not to mention it again. For it is no historical part of the world; it has no movement or development".[85] Yet as I have argued above, building upon theories of how Europe came to predominance is not

---

84 Quoted in Sullivan and Gluckstein, 2020, p9.
85 Hegel, 2001, 117.

Eurocentric in itself. Marx's appropriation of Hegel would only be Eurocentric if he had replicated Hegel's conceits about European superiority, which he did not.

Conversely, however, *An Anthropology of Marxism* celebrates Hegel's anger at capitalist development, which he sees as a materialist impulse, and then suggests that Marx had ignored this in order to dismiss Hegel as a "mystical idealist". Thus Robinson argues that Marx actually minimised his debt to Hegel.[86] This is a strange allegation, not just because it flatly contradicts Robinson's earlier attacks, but also because Marx never hid his admiration for Hegel:

> When I was working on the first volume of *Capital*... I openly avowed myself the pupil of that mighty thinker... The mystification from which the dialectic suffers in Hegel's hands by no means prevents him from being the first to present its general forms of motion in a comprehensive and conscious manner.[87]

The truth is that Marx was as much against the reductivism of crude materialism as he was crude idealism. Indeed, Marx's early thought was shaped by its confrontation with both Hegelian idealism *and* determinist materialism. His *Theses on Feuerbach* open with a critique of crude materialism:

> The chief defect of all hitherto existing materialism...is that the thing, reality, sensuousness, is conceived only in the form of the *object of contemplation*, but not as *sensuous human activity, practice*, not subjectively. Hence, in contradistinction to materialism, the *active* side was developed abstractly by idealism—which, of course, does not know real, sensuous activity as such.[88]

Black radicalism today

Any political theory is an interaction with developments in the world and cannot afford to be static. Marx died just as European empires were about to occupy much of Africa. Many of the responses to colonialism by the theorists of the Second International were deeply inadequate; this includes Eduard Bernstein's support for German colonialism and Karl Kautsky's acquiescence in imperialism in the First World War. At the International's 1907 Stuttgart conference, Lenin was outraged that many of the German delegation favoured a "socialist colonial policy".[89] Much of Robinson's critique relates to those who developed Marxism after the deaths of Marx and Engels, and he does note that "mechanistic or vulgar Marxists have understood the political in terms much more shallow and much less ambiguous

---

86 Robinson, 2019b, p81.
87 Marx, 1976, p102.
88 Marx and Engels, 1970, p121. See also Anderson, 1995, pp12-15.
89 Lenin, 1907.

than Marx himself".[90] Nevertheless, he does not always maintain this distinction in his analysis, often blurring the lines between Marx's ideas and those of his later interpretors. Moreover, Robinson tends to approach Marx's ideas in a reductive and one-sided fashion, and to see the later development of concepts that are already found in Marx as somehow fundamental breaks with Marxism.

Du Bois wrote in 1935 that "the emancipation of man is the emancipation of labour and the emancipation of that majority of workers who are yellow, brown and black".[91] The danger is that Robinson introduces an essentialism into his definition of black identity that tends to pull away from his call for anti-capitalist, anti-racist unity. This can lead to the idea that socialists form a "white left", and that there is an inherent dynamic among black people that leads to unity, regardless of class. Nevertheless, Robinson's ideas can also inspire a coming together of different groups in order to fight racism, especially when he talks about the origins of racism in an evolutionary and non-essentialist manner. Often, his writing is subtle, illuminating and powerful. For example, writing about Virginia at the turn of the 18th century, he explains:

> The invention of the idea of a race, along with the idea of ineradicable differences between races, made it possible for people...to believe simultaneously in "liberty" and "freedom" for themselves and in their right to dominate and to oppress others.[92]

The revival of Robinson's idea of black radicalism and current discussions about racial capitalism are important and positive. Nevertheless, it is also important to contest some of his positions, particularly those that might lead new activists to dismiss Marxist analysis as deterministic or Eurocentric. Marxism has an incredibly important position in the history of black thought and anti-racist movements.

Many of the black thinkers Robinson admired, such as James and Du Bois, retained a deep connection to the theoretical tools of Marxism. In 1989, during his last interview, James argued:

> Marxist theory is a scientific, intellectual theory such as the world has never seen before, and properly used...always with the feeling that history brings things new, that you didn't see before, with the basic Marxist guide you can manage.[93]

Of course, recognising the importance of the Marxist tradition does not imply that all analysis that claims to be within that tradition is valid. Yet an

---

90 Robinson, 2016, p3.
91 Du Bois, 1998, p16.
92 Robinson, 2019a, p140.
93 James and Fitzpatrick, 1989.

engagement with Marxist ideas will be much more productive for those organising the anti-racist struggle today than an engagement with the post-modernist views that suffuse, for example, post-colonial theory. Such theories typically overlook the huge expansion of the global working class, arguing that different oppressed social groups are not cut across essentially by class interests and thus have many divergent and contradictory interests.

Returning to talking in terms of class in a Marxist sense does not mean reducing everything to economic determinism. There is a real need to emphasise the power of the working class and the culpability of capitalism in the maintainence and renewal of racism. The struggle against racism might then reach its logical conclusion with the upending of the whole capitalist system.

The 2020 Black Lives Matter movement has shown both the importance of black radicalism and how it can work with other forces, including white people who want to challenge racism. The power of multiracial demonstrations has been shown everywhere from Portland, Oregon—one of the whitest cities in the US—to Bristol in South West England. Theoretical frameworks for understanding and fighting racism can be judged by their success—both in terms of the number of people mobilised and the effects they achieve. As Angela Davis recently said:

> Marxism, from my perspective, has always been both a method and an object of criticism. Consequently, I don't necessarily see the terms "Marxism" and "Black Marxism" as oppositional.[94]

Of course, questions of identity and how it is informed are important, and an understanding of identities as being fluid and in a constant process of creation is very useful. Those West Indians hit by the government's appalling treatment of them during the Windrush scandal had been part of forging a new sense of what it is to be British over the past 70 years. The common sense conception of Britishness that has emerged out of their struggles helped to raise wider questions about the Tories's "hostile environment" policies.

However, the idea that the radicalism needed to challenge structural racism is located only among people of African descent is disarming. The notion that there is something in the African DNA that makes it more radical can lead to dead ends, including looking to black politicans such as Barack Obama. As Keeanga-Yamahtta Taylor has written, "The hopes initially vested in Obama, who has instead acted to silence and quell black rebellion, have bought the question to the fore: can we get free in America?"[95]

---

94 Johnson and Lubin, 2017, p246.
95 Taylor, 2016, p218.

The two central aspects of Robinson's theory belong together. It is not enough to record that capitalism is a racist system; the black radicalism that has constantly resisted it since its beginnings must also be recalled. If Robinson's ideas are used to disavow Marxism, this risks isolating that black radicalism from the great theoretical insights offered by the deepest thinkers in the Marxist tradition: Marx, Engels, Lenin, Du Bois, James, Hubert Harrison, Claudia Jones, Angela Davis, Stuart Hall and others. These voices are lost to black radical thought if the current of radical anti-racism within the Marxist tradition is denied. As Robinson himself said:

> The black radical tradition was an accretion, over generations, of collective intelligence gathered from struggle. In the daily encounters and petty resistances to domination, slaves had acquired a sense of the calculus of oppression as well as its overt organisation and instrumentation. These experiences lent themselves to a means of preparation for more epic resistance movements.[96]

96 Robinson, 2000, pxxx.

References

Anderson, Kevin B, 1995, *Lenin, Hegel and Western Marxism* (University of Illinois Press).

Anderson, Kevin B, 2010, *Marx at the Margins* (Chicago).

Bhattacharyya, Gargi, 2018, *Rethinking Racial Capitalism: Questions of Reproduction and Survival* (Rowman and Littlefield).

Blackburn, Robin, 1997, *The Making of New World Slavery* (Verso).

Blackburn, Robin, 2011, *The American Crucible: Slavery, Emancipation and Human Rights* (Verso).

Callinicos, Alex, 1988, *South Africa Between Reform and Revolution* (Bookmarks).

Chase, Malcolm, 2007, *Chartism: A New History* (Manchester University Press).

Choonara, Joseph, 2019, "A New Cycle of Revolt", *International Socialism 165* (winter), http://isj.org.uk/a-new-cycle-of-revolt

Cox, Oliver Cromwell, 1964, *Capitalism as a System* (Monthly Review Press).

Cox, Oliver Cromwell, 1970 [1948], *Caste, Class and Race* (Monthly Review).

Cox, Oliver Cromwell, 1976, *Race Relations* (Wayne State University Press).

Draper, Hal, 1978, *Karl Marx's Theory of Revolution, Volume 2: The Politics of Social Classes* (Monthly Review).

Du Bois, W E B, 1933, "Marxism and the Negro Problem", *The Crisis*, volume 40, number 5 (May), www.webdubois.org/dbMNP.html

Du Bois, W E B, 1965 [1947], *The World And Africa: An Inquiry into the Part Which Africa Has Played in World History* (International Publishers).

Du Bois, W E B, 1998 [1935], *Black Reconstruction in America 1860-1880* (Free Press).

Fields, Karen E, and Barbara J Fields, 2012, *Racecraft: The Soul of Inequality in American Life* (Verso).

Foot, Paul, 2012 [2005], *The Vote: How It Was Won, How It Was Undermined* (Bookmarks).

Foster, John Bellamy, Hannah Holleman and Brett Clark, 2020, "Marx and Slavery", *Monthly Review*, volume 72, number 3, https://monthlyreview.org/2020/07/01/marx-and-slavery

Foucault, Michel, 1994 [1970], *The Order of Things* (Vintage).

Hall, Stuart, 1996 [1986], "Gramsci's Relevance for the Study of Race and Ethnicity", in David Morley and Kuan-Hsing Chen (eds), *Stuart Hall: Critical Dialogues in Cultural Studies* (Routledge).

Hall, Stuart, Chas Critcher, Tony Jefferson, John Clarke and Brian Roberts, 2013 [1978], *Policing The Crisis: Mugging, the State and Law & Order* (Palgrave Macmillan).

Harman, Chris, 1999, *A People's History of the World* (Bookmarks).

Harman, Chris, 2007, "Theorising Neoliberalism", *International Socialism* 117, https://isj.org.uk/theorising-neoliberalism

Hegel, G W F, 2001 [1837], *The Philosophy of History* (Batoche).

Hier, Sean P, 2001, "The Forgotten Architect: Cox, Wallerstein and World-System Theory", *Race & Class*, volume 42, issue 3.

Illing, Sean, 2019, "How Capitalism Reduced Diversity to a Brand", Vox (19 February), www.vox.com/identities/2019/2/11/18195868/capitalism-race-diversity-exploitation-nancy-leong

James, C L R, and John Fitzpatrick, 1989, "You Never Know When It is Going to Explode", *Living Marxism* (April).

Johnson, Gaye Theresa, and Alex Lubin, 2017, "Angela Davis: An Interview on the Futures of Black Radicalism", in Gaye Theresa Johnson and Alex Lubin (eds), *Futures of Black Radicalism* (Verso), https://bit.ly/30NdSot

Kelley, Robin D G, 1990, *Hammer and Hoe: Alabama Communists During the Great Depression* (University of North Carolina).

Kelley, Robin D G, 2016, "Cedric J Robinson: The Making of a Black Radical Intellectual", *CounterPunch* (17 June 2016), https://bit.ly/343k4cu

Kundnani, Arun, 2020, "What is Racial Capitalism?", Arun Kundnani blog (23 October), www.kundnani.org/what-is-racial-capitalism

Legassick, Martin, and David Hemson, 1976, *Foreign Investment and the Reproduction of Racial Capitalism in South Africa* (Anti-Apartheid Movement), https://bit.ly/37TEBSf

Lenin, V I, 1907, "The International Socialist Congress in Stuttgart", *Proletary* (20 October), www.marxists.org/archive/lenin/works/1907/oct/20.htm

Linebaugh, Peter, and Marcus Rediker, 2000, *The Many-Headed Hydra: Sailors, Slaves, Commoners, and the Hidden History of the Revolutionary Atlantic* (Beacon).

Löwy, Michael, 1989, "'The Poetry of the Past': Marx and the French Revolution", *New Left Review*, I/177.

McDuffie, Erik S, 2011, *Sojourning for Freedom: Black Women, American Communism and the Making of Black Left Feminism* (Duke).

Mahamdallie Hassan, 2015, "Islamophobia: the Othering of Europe's Muslims", *International Socialism* 146, http://isj.org.uk/islamophobia-the-othering-of-europes-muslims

Margulies, Ron, 2018, "Looking Back to Imagine the Future: The Political Impact of Imperialism on the Rest of the World", *International Socialism* 159, https://isj.org.uk/looking-back-to-imagine-the-future

Marx, Karl, 1976 [1867], *Capital*, volume 1 (Penguin).

Marx, Karl and Engels, Friedrich, 1970 [1846], *The German Ideology* (Lawrence and Wishart).

Olende, Ken, 2017, "A Hard Road to Travel: Black People and Racism in the 19th Century United States", *International Socialism* 156, https://isj.org.uk/a-hard-road-to-travel-black-people-and-racism-in-the-19th-century-united-states

Olende, Ken, 2020, "The 'Hostile Environment' for Immigrants: The Windrush Scandal and Resistance", in Emily Luise Hart, Joe Greener and Rich Moth (eds), *Resist the Punitive State* (Pluto).

Perry, Jeffrey B, 2009, *Hubert Harrison: The Voice of Harlem Radicalism, 1883-1918* (Colombia University Press).

Robinson, Cedric J, 1997, *Black Movements in America* (Routledge).

Robinson, Cedric J, 2000 [1983], *Black Marxism: The Making of the Black Radical Tradition* (University of North Carolina).

Robinson, Cedric J, 2012, *Forgeries of Memory and Meaning: Blacks and the Regimes of Race in American Theater and Film before World War II* (University of North Carolina).

Robinson, Cedric J, 2016 [1980], *The Terms of Order: Political Science and the Myth of Leadership* (University of North Carolina).

Robinson, Cedric J, 2019a, *On Racial Capitalism, Black Internationalism, and Cultures of Resistance* (Pluto Press).

Robinson, Cedric J, 2019b [2001], *An Anthropology of Marxism* (Pluto Press).

Sivanandan, Ambalavaner, 1990, *Communities of Resistance* (Verso).

Sullivan, Terry, and Donny Gluckstein, 2020, *Hegel and Revolution* (Bookmarks).

Taylor, Keeanga-Yamahtta, 2016, From #BlackLivesMatter to Black Liberation (Haymarket).

Thomas, Darryl C, 2005, "The Black Radical Tradition. Theory and Practice: Black Studies and the Scholarship of Cedric Robinson", *Race & Class*, volume 47, issue 2.

Thomas, Darryl C, 2017, "Cedric J Robinson's Meditation on Malcolm X's Black Internationalism and the Future of the Black Radical Tradition", in Gaye Theresa Johnson and Alex Lubin (eds), Futures of Black Radicalism (Verso).

Trotsky, Leon, 1938, "The Chinese Revolution", www.marxists.org/archive/trotsky/1938/xx/china.htm

Williams, Eric, 1964 [1944], *Capitalism and Slavery* (Andre Deutsch).

Glossary of musical terms

Allegro Brisk and lively movement.

Chromaticism Use of "semi-tones" or intervals or notes outside the diatonic scale.

Counterpoint One or more independent melodies added to or below a given melody.

Development The second of three parts of a movement in sonata style, in which the main theme is divided up and elaborated.

Diatonic System of major or minor scales of 8 notes each without chromatic deviation.

Dominant Fifth note of the diatonic scale or a chord beginning on the fifth note.

Dynamics Variation and contrast in sound volume.

Exposition First part of usually three parts of a composition in sonata form in which the theme is presented in two contrasting keys.

Figuration Embellishment/ornamentation of a passage using musical figures.

Finale The last movement of an orchestral compostion.

Fugue Composition in which one or two themes are repeated or imitated by successive instruments or voices in a continuous interweaving of the parts.

Hemiola Rhythmic alteration consisting of three beats instead of two or vice versa.

Interval Difference in pitch between two notes.

Lied German song, especially a 19th century setting of a lyrical poem for solo voice and piano.

Mediant Third note of a diatonic scale.

Metre Basic recurrent rhythmical pattern of accents and beats per bar.

Modulation Moving through a succession of keys, often to express sudden emotional shifts.

Motif/motive Recurrent phrase, figure or theme developed through the course of a composition.

Scherzo Lively, instrumental composition or movement in quick, usually triple, time.

Subdominant Fourth note of the diatonic scale.

Tempo Speed of a piece or passage indicated by a series of directions, often by an exact metronome marking.

Texture How the tempo, melodic, and harmonic materials are combined in a composition, thus determining the overall quality of the sound.

Tonality Organisation of notes and chords of a piece in relation to the tonic.

Tonic First note of the diatonic scale.

Ludwig van Beethoven: Revolutionary Composer
Sabby Sagall

December 2020 marks the 250th anniversary of the birth of Ludwig van Beethoven, one of Europe's greatest composers, a musician of a revolutionary era who revolutionised music.[1] Why should socialists be interested? The answer is twofold. Firstly, the need for music and the ability to produce and enjoy it, is an essential element in human nature: every human society known to our history has produced some characteristic musical style.

Secondly, the confinement of classical musical education to the children of the elite and the middle class, and the termination of musical education or the reduced opportunity for under-privileged children to enjoy many kinds of "art-music", is an expression of profound deprivation, rooted in capitalist alienation, exploitation and oppression.

Thirdly, art is not merely a "mirror" of the world, but a practical intervention into it. Music, like the other arts, tells us truths about the world through its impact on our emotional life. As the Russian revolutionary and art theorist Leon Trotsky put it, art helps us orient ourselves in the world. Yet it also does more than that. The music of Beethoven, for example, did not merely reflect revolutionary Europe

1   I would like to thank the following people who read this article and gave me valuable comments: Bob Carter, Joseph Choonara, Barry Cooper, Martin Empson, Tom Hickey, Rob Hoveman, John Rose, Luca Salice, Alison Sealey and Hilary Westlake.

and North America in the late 18th and early 19th centuries, but helped to shape that world.

Importantly, there is a certain homology or structural correspondence between society and music. For example, the 18th century classical style's bass line has become the treble line's equal partner in melodic development; the French Revolution's values of "liberty, equality and fraternity" seem to liberate the bass from its role of service to the upper instruments, a process already evident in Johann Sebastian Bach's late baroque style.[2]

Beethoven had famously dedicated his Third or "Eroica" Symphony to Napoleon, whom he believed to be a great revolutionary, democratic leader. However, when Napoleon declared himself Emperor of the French in 1804, Beethoven, republican and democrat that he was, scratched out the dedication, writing, "Now he too will trample on the rights of man!" Beethoven is the classical composer whose work immediately conjures up both political and musical revolutionary ideas. He was strongly attracted to the ideals and values of the Enlightenment and scorned traditional authority and social rank. He admired the British system of government and its two-party system, which he saw as democratic.[3] The influence of French revolutionary music on, for example, his Fifth Symphony, has been frequently remarked on. In general, he seems to have had republican sympathies. According to musical historian John Clubbe, "Beethoven's ideal for Austrian society would have been a republic." He adds, "Admittedly, Beethoven did regard republics as the best solution." Clubbe also quotes a letter to Theodora Johanna Vocke in Nuremberg, dated 22 May 1793. There, Beethoven writes, in a clear indication of his opposition to the Austrian monarchy, "Love liberty above all else".[4] Also relevant is his "Wellingtons Sieg" (Wellington's Victory), which celebrates the British victory over the French at Vitoria in 1813, as is his use of "God Save the King" and "Rule Britannia" as themes for variations; all these perhaps testify to his admiration for the British parliamentary system.[5] Despite his later conservatism, he seemed convinced, early on, of the revolution's ideals. The musicologist Hugo concluded that "spiritually, he is a son of the French Revolution".[6]

Unlike Joseph Haydn and Wolfgang Amadeus Mozart, Beethoven refused to be ranked as a servant to noble families, considering himself socially their equal, and spiritually their superior by dint of his genius. He was once walking in a park in

---

2   The historical development of classical music is typically broken up into a number of distinct periods: the baroque (1600-1750), classical (1750-1820) and romantic (1810-1910) eras.
3   Cooper, 2013, p70.
4   Clubbe, 2019, pp50, 66.
5   Cooper, 2013, pp70-1.
6   Leichtentritt, 1957, p183.

the Bohemian city of Teplice with the great German writer Johann Wolfgang von Goethe when the imperial family approached; Goethe bowed respectfully, infuriating Beethoven who stormed off in the opposite direction.[7] Of course, Beethoven had to be careful as censorship was becoming increasingly harsh, and he depended on his aristocratic patrons.[8] As a young man in Vienna, studying with Haydn, he was already aware of his artistic capabilities, showing a lack of respect for the established powers. He had "a proud demeanour, and a self-assertiveness that shocked the modest Haydn", who dubbed him the "Turkish pasha".[9] He became the darling of the Viennese nobility, a factor in his later political conservatism.

Beethoven was born in 1770 into a family of musicians in Bonn, a small town of 10,000 inhabitants, the capital of the Archbishopric of Cologne until 1794 when French revolutionary forces occupied the city. The world he was born into was that of a Germany of scattered principalities dominated by a powerful Prussian state, to be united only in 1871. In contrast to England and France, Germany did not experience a bourgeois revolution—a social transformation resulting in the bourgeoisie winning political power. Its absence can be ascribed to several factors: the defeat of the peasants' revolts in 1524-5 and the devastation caused by the Thirty Years' War (1618-48), which destroyed the cities economically and politically. Friedrich Engels remarks that "the peasants, plebeians and ruined burghers were reduced to a state of Irish misery" by these events.[10] The decline of the cities also resulted from the discovery of the Americas and the shifting focus of international trade from Central Europe and the Mediterranean to the Atlantic. These factors resulted in an economically and politically weak bourgeois class, strengthening the princes, who no longer faced a challenge to their position as great feudal landowners. The powerlessness of the German bourgeoisie and their exclusion from politics, induced a passivity which affected the entire cultural life of the period.

In Austria and Germany, the Thirty Years' War had bequeathed a legacy of destruction and chaos, as well as the dominance of a foreign power—France. Germany, especially Prussia, had been further impoverished by the Seven Years' War (1756-63). Moreover, after the death of Bach in 1750, the Saxony and Thuringia regions of Germany, having been the cradle of Protestant church music, went into decline. Berlin did become a centre of music due to the sponsorship of Prussia's King Frederick II "the Great", but he favoured Italian and French music over German work.

---

7   Suchet, 2012, pp226-227.
8   Clubbe, 2019, p50.
9   Leichtentritt, 1957, p183.
10 Engels, 1969, p126. Engels was writing at the time of the Great Hunger, a period of mass starvation and disease inflicted on Ireland by British colonial policy in the 1840s.

From feudalism to capitalism

Feudal society was based on local production and consumption. Economic and political power was decentralised and vested in the landowning nobility who exploited the peasantry, compelling them to surrender either part of their labour or their produce. Nevertheless, improved production and the growth of trade stimulated urban development. Decentralised political structures meant that towns that developed as commercial centres could achieve relative independence from the feudal lords. The town became the centre of economic activity for a new class, the bourgeoisie, ancestor of today's capitalist class. With this came new political structures and ideas, so that as the bourgeoisie's economic power grew, so did its social and political weight.[11]

These changes produced a modified form of feudal rule and the growth of centralised absolute monarchies. "Economic and social life had begun to outgrow the local horizons of feudalism. This laid the basis for the development of bigger, more unified 'national' economies and states".[12] Absolutism expressed this transformation, with kings acting to curb the independent power of local feudal lords and build a unified, centralised state.

In France, the economic rise of the bourgeoisie and the market steadily undermined the power of the monarchy and the nobility, developments which culminated in the great French Revolution of 1789. The rise of the bourgeoisie and the decline or overthrow of the feudal aristocracy found expression in many areas of social endeavour such as music and the arts, but also in science and in people's economic and political lives. The 17th and 18th centuries in Europe witnessed a historically unprecedented growth of scientific enquiry, the fruits of which were an enormous expansion of knowledge and its application to the economic development of society. By 1760, that process had changed many ordinary people from agricultural labourers into machine-builders and mechanical workers whose individual productive capacity had been multiplied many times over.[13]

In Austria and Germany, the old regimes survived, but the power of the aristocracy gradually eroded. Reforming Austrian emperor Joseph II, following in the footsteps of his mother Empress Maria Theresa, attempted to abolish serfdom but fell foul of the entrenched power of the nobility. His Patent of Toleration of 1781, a good example of "enlightened despotism", granted religious freedom of worship to Lutherans, Calvinists and Serbian Orthodox Christians. Despite opposition from the papacy, this was followed a year later by the Edict of Tolerance,

---

11   McGarr, 1991, p97.
12   McGarr, 1991, p97.
13   Downs, 1992, p111.

which extended religious freedom to Jews. Joseph II was partially motivated by economic considerations—the emigration of Austria's Protestant population would have led to a slump. Nevertheless, these measures were still pushed back upon by the Esterházy family, patrons of Joseph Haydn. Their palace, an attempt to recreate the glory of France's "Sun King", Louis XIV, in Austria, was "an oasis, even a mirage, in a desert of misery, depending on serfdom for its existence".[14] Ultimately, the outbreak of the French Revolution in 1789 prompted Joseph to reverse his reforms.

Neverthelesss, on a European scale, the days of the feudal landlords and Catholicism's ideological dominance were numbered. The feudal system and ideology were gradually undermined by the rising bourgeois class, whose mercantile and industrial system was proving to be economically superior. The waning of the old regimes, the setting of the feudal sun and the rise of the star of the bourgeoisie, could be seen even in imperial Austria. There, freemasonry—at that time, a genuinely progressive movement rather than a businessman's mutual aid society—upheld the ideals of the Enlightenment and the power of reason and science to reshape society according to the values of the French Revolution: liberty, equality, fraternity.[15]

The European political context

Between 1796 and 1815, Europe had been devastated by the French revolutionary and Napoleonic wars. From the Atlantic seaboard to Moscow, ideological conflicts had been transformed into national military clashes. The banner proclaiming "liberty, fraternity, equality" had been bloodied by The Terror of 1793-4, and with Napoleon as military leader, France embarked on a campaign that turned defence of the revolution into a cover for achieving European domination. However shocking the excesses of the infant French Republic's guillotine may have been (some 16,594 were executed), they were dwarfed by the carnage of the wars between 1796 and 1815, which killed some two and a half a million soldiers and one million civilians.[16]

After Napoleon's defeat, the Congress of Vienna sat for around a year with four key victorious nations represented—Britain, Russia, Prussia and Austria—together with the vanquished France, which was officially present only as an observer. The main concern of the principal governments was to return to the traditional "balance of power", which they believed would deter any state or alliance of states from attempts at domination.

---

14 Mellers, 1957, p7.
15 Arblaster, 1992, p37.
16 Sachs, 2010, p62.

The allies displayed great leniency towards France, restoring the Bourbon dynasty and France's 1792 boundaries (larger than those of 1789). These measures were dictated by the need to keep France's state strong enough to resist possible future revolutionary upheavals. Negotiating with France's arch-diplomat, Charles-Maurice de Talleyrand-Périgord, no reparations were demanded, on the understanding that France would support Austria and Britain and help to prevent Russia from expanding westwards and linking up with Prussia.[17] However, measures were taken to prevent renewed aggression by France.

The heart of the strategy of the great powers that united under this "congress system" was intervention and restoration. Under the leadership of Austrian chancellor Prince Klemens von Metternich, the alliance that became known as the "Concert of Europe" planned to intervene in any country threatened by liberal or bourgeois nationalist ideologies of the kind that had kindled the French Jacobins. However, despite these Herculean efforts to prevent a second French revolution or a "catastrophic" spread of revolution on the French model, they were battling against the tide. "Rarely has the incapacity of governments to hold up the course of history been more conclusively demonstrated than in the generation after 1815".[18] Throughout Europe, the revolutionary atmosphere was endemic and combustible, as likely to be ignited by a spontaneous spark as by deliberate agitation. The Marxist historian Eric Hobsbawm notes:

> The political systems reimposed on Europe were profoundly and, in a period of rapid social change, increasingly inadequate for the political conditions of the continent. The economic and social discontents were so acute as to make a series of outbreaks virtually inevitable.[19]

Moreover, as Richard Evans adds, "Napoleon had stimulated among educated elites the belief that freedom from oppression could only be achieved on the basis of national self-determination".[20]

The model of 1789 gave the discontent a focus, helping to transform unrest into revolution and, most crucially, linking European countries in a current of subversion. Political opposition in Europe was confined to small groups of the well-off or the educated. Members of the labouring poor who were consciously "left wing" accepted the classical demands of middle-class revolution, though perhaps in its radical-democratic rather than its moderate version.[21]

---

17 Sachs, 2010, p64.
18 Hobsbawm, 1962, p137.
19 Hobsbawm, 1962, p141.
20 Evans, 2017, p82.
21 Hobsbawm, 1962, p143.

A crop of revolutionary initiatives, beginning in Southern Italy after 1806 and spreading north and across the Mediterranean after 1815, came to a climax in 1820-1. This even reached Russia, where the liberal Decembrists mounted a revolt in 1825. These attempts at insurrection failed everywhere—apart from Greece, where the 1821 uprising against the Ottoman Empire inspired a generation of European liberals and nationalists, including the poet Lord Byron.[22] In 1822, Beethoven wrote a new overture and a chorus, "The Consecration of the House", for the play "The Ruins of Athens", which dramatised the destruction of Greece's capital by an occupying power.

The rise and dominance of Vienna

In the final part of the 18th century Vienna emerged as the musical capital of Europe. It became the home of the new art of the symphony and the sonata, and of Italian-style opera. Could these new forms not have succeeded equally well in the other great musical centres—Naples, Rome, London, Paris, Mannheim, Dresden and Berlin? First-class artists lived in all these cities, as did wealthy patrons of the arts. However, Vienna possessed particular social and cultural conditions that made it especially fertile soil for the emergence of great music. It became known as superior to any other city for the growth of instrumental, chamber and orchestral music.

Italy had dominated the operatic scene to the point that orchestral or chamber music never attained a similar importance. Austria was different—a country brimming with musical talent, with an atmosphere that had been saturated in music for centuries. Every noble family, not only in Vienna, had a private orchestra and even a private opera company in their castle. There was an abundance of good orchestral musicians, with every butler and manservant expected to double up as an instrumental musician. Every small town had its music master who laid on orchestral music for every occasion: parties, weddings, funerals. The great noble families rivalled one another in the musicianship of their private orchestras. Leichtentritt describes the close relationship between the aristocracy and musicians: "In summer, they lived in the country in their magnificent castles, with music as a daily pleasure. In winter, they moved to their Vienna palaces, always taking their musicians with them".[23]

By the late 18th century, Vienna had also become a major economic and political hub. It was no doubt a small city by 21st century standards and yet highly sophisticated and cosmopolitan. The city was permeated by intense musical activity. Daniel Snowman explains that "Vienna was expanding rapidly... Voluntary associations sprouted up all over—reading groups, choral societies,

---

22 Hobsbawm, 1962, pp144-145, 173.
23 Leichtentritt, 1957, p173.

the Masonic lodges".[24] In the early 19th century, Vienna's musical life was enriched by small, semi-private performances in the homes of the well-off bourgeoisie as well as in the aristocratic mansions.

Italian styles dominated the Viennese musical scene in the latter half of the 18th century. However, Vienna was gradually able to throw off the Italian influence in favour of a German style. This was characterised by a solid harmonic and "contrapuntal" texture. It also played the role of mediator between the Italian and French styles, reconciling them in a higher unity through a deliberate fusion.[25] Vienna's achievement was facilitated by the intensity of its musical life, the genius of its composers and by Italian economic and political decline.[26] In 1792, the 22 year old Beethoven left Bonn and settled in Vienna.

A central feature of the classical style developed by Haydn and Mozart is an atmosphere of dramatic tension created by abrupt shifts in melody and rhythm, an uneven rhythmic flow with frequent changes of tempo. This reflects the unceasing change, the growing unevenness and unpredictability of economic and political life in a Europe that was emerging from the dark ages, less and less subject to the control of church and monarchy. The unprecedented social change in Europe in the period leading up to the French Revolution resulted from the growing economic and social power of the bourgeois class, its intensifying challenge to the power of absolute monarchy, feudal aristocracy and the Vatican. This does not mean that classical music was determined by these social changes, but they did create a new framework that helped to shape the new style. Composers internalised, as we all do, the social institutions around them, albeit unconsciously. Society was not directly reflected in music but mediated though the composers' activity.

Also important were 18th century instrumental developments, the great increase in the size of the orchestra and the invention of the clarinet in 1700 and the piano in 1709. Hammer action gave the piano a brilliant and powerful tone, but of even greater importance was the pedal, which enabled sound to be extended. This was a device unknown in previous types of keyboard instrument, giving the piano its capacity to express colour, atmosphere, light and shade.

Beethoven's classical style

Beethoven's career is generally divided into early, middle and late periods. According to this scheme, his early period lasts until roughly 1802 and the middle period until 1811-12, with the late period beginning around 1817.

24 Snowman, 2009, p91.
25 Bukofzer, 1947, p260.
26 Hindley, 1971, p237.

Early Beethoven

In the early period, Beethoven's work bears the strong imprint of Haydn and Mozart. However, he began to explore new directions, gradually expanding the scope and ambition of his work. Between 1800 and 1803, he came to be regarded as one of the leading members of the generation of young composers who followed Haydn and Mozart. With his first six string quartets composed between 1798 and 1800, and the First and Second Symphonies first performed in 1800 and 1803, Beethoven established his early reputation. His versatility was also revealed in his piano compositions, including his first two piano concertos and a dozen early piano sonatas.

The piano trios that comprise Beethoven's opus 1, and even more the string trios of opus 3, are remarkably daring, but Haydn would have recognised their affinity with his own music. However, the piano sonatas of opus 2 inhabit a new world. In the first, Sonata Number 1 in F Minor, Beethoven differs from Haydn, and even more from Mozart. The last movement subjects the melodic element to a ferocious dynamic treatment.[27]

The second, Sonata Number 2 in A Major, is subtly subversive. According to the classical convention, the exposition of a sonata was meant to establish the basic tonalities of tonic and dominant associated with the first and second themes. Yet here, extreme modulations, normally reserved for the climax of the development section, occur in the exposition. The effect is startling, a musical counterpart to Beethoven's flouting of social etiquette—his rudeness to duchesses and his throwing crockery around.[28] Beethoven's artistic and social rebellion were rooted in his personality, which in turn was shaped by the social upheavals unfolding across Europe.

It is also significant that the most characteristic music of Beethoven's youth are his piano sonatas; for him, the piano was here a dynamic as much as a melodic instrument. This is especially evident with Beethoven's Piano Sonata Number 13 in C Minor, the "Pathetique" (1798), which is described as a "call to arms" with a tempestuous first movement that follows a slow introduction.[29] The Pathetique surpasses any of his previous compositions in strength of character, depth of emotion, level of originality, and ingenuity of thematic and tonal development. Both emotionally and technically, Beethoven was, as the musicologist Barry Cooper says, "pushing the bounds of classical convention well beyond their previous

---

27 Mellers, 1957, p56.
28 Mellers, 1957, p57.
29 Mellers, 1957, p58.

limits".[30] Though rooted in the Enlightenment, Beethoven seems to point forwards towards romanticism.

Middle Beethoven

Beethoven's middle, also known as the "heroic", period—roughly 1802 to 1814—began shortly after the onset of a personal crisis that was sparked by his growing awareness of encroaching deafness. This period saw many large-scale works that express heroism and struggle. Examples include the Third to the Eighth Symphonies, the last three piano concertos (including the heroic Fifth Concerto), the Triple Concerto, String Quartets Numbers 7-11, several piano sonatas such as the "Waldstein" and "Appassionata", the "Kreutzer" Violin Sonata and his only opera, "Fidelio". Beethoven seemed to be pitting himself against the dark forces of a malevolent fate.[31]

Beethoven's first two symphonies, although anticipating his later technique, are based on classical principles but do not attain the level of Haydn's and Mozart's greatest works. They are significant largely as the music of a revolutionary genius composing within the established tradition. But the Third, "Eroica" Symphony (1803) represents a new chapter in music, the first movement opening with two "hammerblows". The opening theme enters: an arpeggio that sounds like a challenge and climaxes in conflict. The symphony has many difficulties for instrumentalists, such as hemiola and modulations to strange keys "that would catch players unawares at the first attempt, as well as tricky and rapid figuration that would require careful practice".[32] The power of the whole orchestra is displayed in a fortissimo F-major chord, with the second (E) added to the F. The strings modulate to E minor and to the first development theme that is introduced on the oboes. The work was published in 1806 and, in a swipe at Emperor Napoleon, he dedicated it to "the memory of a great man".

Beethoven had long been attracted to the idea of heroism—his "heroic" ballet "Prometheus" (1801) was an early example. The importance of the Greek mythological figure is that he challenged the gods, offering humankind the gift of fire and thus the potential to control their own destiny. Beethoven's hero is "the man of strife who is the architect of a new world".[33] Yet Beethoven himself is also a hero of the symphony in his solitary battle—revealed in his "Heiligenstadt Testament"—to pit his genius against his affliction.[34] Indeed,

---

30 Cooper, 2013, p48.
31 Mellers, 1957, p61.
32 Cooper, 2013, p71.
33 Mellers, 1957, p64.
34 The Heiligenstadt testament is a letter penned by Beethoven to his brothers in 1802 in which he despairs at his loss of hearing.

he believed that the battles for Europe's and his own salvation were very closely intertwined.

In Beethoven's sole opera "Fidelio" (1803), Florestan, wrongfully imprisoned by the wicked jailer Pizzaro, is rescued by his wife Leonora who has disguised herself as a boy (Fidelio) and obtained a job as Pizarro's assistant. The "Prisoners' Chorus" is a magnificent hymn to freedom. Beethoven was attracted to this theme for three reasons. Firstly, he had always hated all forms of despotism and arbitrary power. Secondly, he could empathise with Florestan's isolation, which reflect his own felt isolation, caused by his deafness. Thirdly, Leonora's heroism, risking death to save her husband, conjured up the kind of woman he had long hoped to find. "Fidelio" contains much music of the heroic kind.[35] The Marxist philosopher and musicologist Theodor Adorno observed the opera's invocation of the French Revolution, which "is not depicted but re-enacted as in a ritual".[36] As Clubbe suggests, it can thus be interpreted as "celebrating the anniversary of the Bastille".[37]

Beethoven's Fifth Symphony in C Minor is the natural successor to the "Eroica" because it develops still further the technique of "thematic transformation", a key feature of the classical style.[38] The first movement begins by stating a distinctive four-note "short-short-short-long" motif twice. Referred to as the "Schicksals-Motiv" (theme of detiny), it is one of the most famous motifs in Western music. There is an assertion of the will in the "Eroica" which required a great expansion in the dimensions of the classical symphony. In the Fifth, Beethoven concentrates and intensifies his power. There are aggressive patterns of tempo and rhythm and contrasts of tonality, making it a vehement conflict piece that reflects Beethoven's struggle to overcome a dogged destiny and a hostile world. Moreover, Beethoven's orchestral arrangement was unprecedented: no composer had used trombones in the way he did in the finale. Beethoven also added a contrabassoon and piccolo for the movement, thus creating "a sense of climactic power that was quite overwhelming".[39]

On completing the Fifth, Beethoven wrote its companion piece, the Sixth or "Pastoral" Symphony. This is one of his few explicitly programmatic works, "a perfect musical representation of the countryside and the feelings associated with it".[40] It is a harbinger of the romantics' preoccupation with nature. Both the Fifth and Sixth Symphonies display Beethoven's ability to create the dramatic tension mentioned earlier. Moreover, the listener is forced to appreciate his

---

35 Cooper, 2013, p73.
36 Adorno, 1998, p164.
37 Clubbe, 2019, p319.
38 Mellers, 1957, p64.
39 Cooper, 2013, p77.
40 Cooper, 2013, p78.

extraordinary melodic gift, prominent throughout his music, the primacy of melody being another central feature of the classical style.

The year 1809 falls close to the end of Beethoven's middle period, and might thus be expected to witness consolidation rather than innovation. However, this year marked a turning-point in his life. He completed the Fifth Piano Concerto in E Flat—the "Emperor"—early that year, having composed six symphonies and five concertos over the previous decade. In the remaining 18 years of his life, such large-scale orchestral works all but disappeared. He wrote only three more symphonies, one of which was also a choral work. His "heroic" period ended around 1811-12 as he embarked on smaller forms, notably lieder, and on settings of (mostly British) folk-songs.[41] Beethoven's powerful Seventh Symphony (1811-12) arguably marks the transition between the middle and late periods. The fourth movement consists of a relentlessly repeated rhythmic pattern, unlike anything in the classical symphonic tradition. It expresses his rage, perhaps, at the war-torn state of Europe, and it is the bridge taking Beethoven to the glory of his final works.

Late Beethoven

The late period—roughly 1817 to 1827—contains works of an unprecedented intellectual and emotional depth, a formal and thematic innovativeness, and a profundity of personal expression.

For about five years (1812-17), Beethoven composed fewer works. He nevertheless produced important pieces such as the Eighth Symphony and a massive cantata, "Der Glorreiche Augenblick" (The Glorious Moment). But his late period was marked by radically different music, finding initial expression in the "Hammerklavier" (Pianoforte) Sonata. Written in 1817 and 1818, this is a work that enables us "to cross the threshold into Beethoven's reborn world".[42] The piece contains four movements, a structure often used by Beethoven and imitated by contemporaries such as Franz Schubert, in contrast to the usual three movements of Haydn and Mozart sonatas. The first movement is one of Beethoven's most titanic conflict pieces, with assertive metre and modulation.

The final three sonatas, especially Sonata 32 in C Minor (1821-22), represent the climax of what Beethoven strove for in the Hammerklavier Sonata. Beethoven worked out the plan for these three sonatas during the summer of 1820 while he worked on his "Missa Solemnis" (Solemn Mass), or Mass in D Major, in which the "late" Beethoven attains his most monumental expression. He repeatedly described it as his "greatest work", even after completing the lauded Ninth

---

41 Cooper, 2013, p91.
42 Mellers, 1957, p70.

Symphony.[43] It is a work of great sophistication and profundity in which the music operates on several levels, "ranging from...directness of expression...to amazing technical complexity in the fugue".[44]

The "Missa Solemnis" is generally considered one of Beethoven's supreme achievements, and together with Bach's "Mass in B Minor" one of the most profound mass settings. It is a choral composition that sets the eucharistic liturgy to music of the "common practice period", that is, the era between the formation of the tonal system around 1680 until its dissolution around 1900. It was dedicated to Archduke Rudolph of Austria, Beethoven's principal patron, pupil and friend. The mass illustrates Beethoven's characteristic disregard for the performer; in several places, it is technically and physically exacting, with many sudden changes of dynamics, metre and tempo. There is no choral and no orchestral writing, earlier or later, that shows a more thrilling sense of the individual colour of every chord. Adorno describes it as characterised by:

> Certain archaicising moments of harmony—church modes—rather than by the advanced compositional daring of the "Große Fuge"... Altogether it reveals a sensuous aspect quite opposed to the intellectualised late style, an inclintion to splendidness and tonal monumentality...usually lacking in that late style.[45]

The massive fugues at the end of the "Gloria" and "Credo" have the mark of Beethoven's late period but absent are the sustained exploration of themes through development and also his simultaneous interest in the theme and variations form.

Adorno also suggests in his typically enigmatic style that Beethoven had become mistrustful of:

> The unity of subjectivity and objectivity, the roundness of symphonic successes... of everything that gave authenticity up to now of the works of his middle period... At this moment, he transcended the bourgeois spirit whose highest musical manifestation was his own work.[46]

Adorno seems to be suggesting that the Missa Solemnis with its "modal archaicism" looks beyond the "bourgeois spirit", which had ceased to be revolutionary but still contained within itself the seed of its own transcendence. The Missa Solemnis perhaps looks both backwards and forward—back to an idealised, harmonious, pre-capitalist community and forward, beyond the bourgeois world with its materialism and individualism, to a society based on solidarity.

---

43 Cooper, 2013, p119.
44 Cooper, 2013, p121.
45 Adorno, 2002, pp572-3.
46 Adorno, 2002, p580.

It is uncertain whether Beethoven himself was a practising Catholic. His secretary Anton Schindler suggested that he inclined to Deism, which rejects revelation, asserting that reason and observation of the natural world are sufficient to establish the existence of a supreme being. Beethoven was also interested in Eastern religions, especially Hinduism and Egyptian polytheism. Nevertheless, the Missa Solemnis's upward surges and downward leaps seem to deny a connection between man and God, instead suggesting a desire to create heaven on earth. The Mass is perhaps contradictory: a theological work with a secular dimension.

The string quartet is the most quintessential medium of Beethoven's late years, as the piano was of his youth and the symphony orchestra of his middle period. Earlier, he had not devoted much attention to the quartet which, "as a concourse of equal-voiced instruments, did not naturally lend itself to his dynamic style".[47] Nevertheless, his three middle-period "Rasumovsky" quartets are undoubtedly major works.

The cycle of late quartets begins with Number 12 in E Flat Major and ends with Number 16 in F Major. Arguably, the most comprehensive and certainly the most complicated of Beethoven's last works is the C sharp minor quartet, Number 14, which he also believed to be among his greatest works.[48]

The Große Fuge (Great Fugue) in B Flat was originally composed as the finale of a quartet. However, the audience found it so impenetrable and bewildering that he wrote a new finale, and the Große Fuge was published as a separate work. There is a brief introduction, marked "Overtura", which is followed by three main sections. The fugue theme, first heard in the "Overtura", reappears rhythmically altered in each of the three sections. Cooper explains that "the overall impression is one of overwhelming size and power—a Mount Everest among quartet movements".[49] Stravinsky described it as "an absolutely contemporary piece of music that will be contemporary forever".[50]

A key feature of Beethoven's late style is his retention of "out of date formulas" and the success with which he rehabilitated them through a technique that was uniquely his. This is exemplified, for example, throughout the Hammerklavier Sonata and most strikingly at the end of the development of its opening movement.[51] Beethoven returned, in his final phase, to his early stylistic technique, launching an amazing expansion of that style beginning with the Hammerklavier Sonata, revolutionising modulation and traditional harmony.[52]

47 Mellers, 1957, p75.
48 Mellers, 1957, p76.
49 From Cooper's introduction to the "Beethoven: Complete String Quartets" recording.
50 Stravinsky and Craft, 1963, p24.
51 Rosen, 1971, p484.
52 Rosen, 1971, p487.

Beethoven's world was clearly no longer that of Haydn and Mozart. However, he continued to use the stylistic conventions that he had learned as a child even as he expanded them beyond recognition, aware of their energy and the depth of their expressive power. So much of Beethoven seems incompatible with 18th century style that it is difficult to see how much of his greatest work synthesises late 18th century ideals.[53] He maintained his belief in the basic power of the dominant; even when using mediants within the sonata form, he prepared them with a strong dominant introduction, even though younger contemporaries preferred chromatic shifts. He preserved the classical balance between dominant and subdominant—a "dead letter" to subsequent generations—and never discarded the long final section in the tonic leading to the final resolution. Arguably, his greatest achievement was understanding the latent potential of the contemporary tonal language and greatly enlarging its expressive capacity.[54] Beethoven's paradox is that, although steeped in the classical tradition, he inaugurated a new era. Basing himself on the rational tonal system, whose climax found expression in Haydn and Mozart, he developed it as the musical foundation of a possible new world inspired by the ideals of the French Revolution.

The movements of the Ninth Symphony are not in the traditional order. He does begin with an allegro, albeit a weighty one, but puts the scherzo before the slow movement. From the opening rumbles of the first movement, Beethoven takes us through the frantic conflict of the scherzo, then on to the sublime, prayer-like lyricism of the slow movement. He then concluding with the joyful explosion and triumphant vision of the finale. The exultant finale, with its four vocal soloists and chorus, which break all musical conventions, uses the text of Friedrich Schiller's 1785 poem, "Ode to Joy". Beethoven had discovered this poem in his youth and been intoxicated with its romantic vision of liberty and fraternity. Sachs vividly describes the flow of the Ninth Symphony from the vantage point of the finale:

> We have survived the first movement's brutality and despair, participated in the second's harsh struggle and been purified by the third's glowing acceptance of life as it is. What Beethoven wants us now to experience with the fourth movement is all-embracing joy. For this is the moment in the work in which Beethoven most unequivocally declares his aim of helping to liberate mankind through art.[55]

The Ninth Symphony is one of the crowning achievements of European culture. Its premiere involved the largest orchestra ever assembled by Beethoven.[56]

---

53   Rosen, 1971, pp508-509.
54   Rosen, 1971, p508.
55   Sachs, 2010, p154.
56   Sachs, 2010, p19.

Social and political influences

The most characteristic works of Beethoven's middle period—the Third ("Eroica") and Fifth symphonies and the "Emperor" Piano Concerto—express the urge to change the world. The Eroica's assertion of the will described above; the Fifth's famous opening four notes, "knocking on the door of history"; the Emperor Concerto's heroic exhortation and the way the soloist opens with a cadenza followed by a propulsive, thrusting opening theme: all seem to communicate a longing to sweep away the old order and usher in the new.[57] These works reflect the profound influence on Beethoven of the French Revolution and its democratic, republican ideals. Haydn and Mozart had not been politically engaged, at least at a formal or conscious level. Yet as the musical embodiment of the ideals of the French Revolution, Beethoven reaches the heights of our potential for self-liberation and solidarity. Adorno wrote that "the din of the bourgeois revolution rumbles in Beethoven".[58]

One possible explanation for the decline in Beethoven's creativity during the so-called "fallow" years of 1812-16 might therefore be disappointment in the failure of the French Revolution. The revolution failed to result in liberation for humanity as a whole. Although the French bourgeoisie had inscribed on their banner "Liberty, Equality, Fraternity", they meant it only for themselves. Having won political power, they chose to consolidate it. The mantle of the struggle to extend the boundaries of freedom and democracy beyond the limits laid down by the bourgeoisie fell onto the shoulders of other social forces.

Nevertheless, the French Revolution retained a powerful influence on Beethoven. The late works—his late quartets and piano sonatas, the "Missa Solemnis" and the Ninth Symphony—combine sadness and anger at the failure of humanity to break free from the shackles of oppression with optimism that future generations would achieve this, perhaps driven by the fresh wave of revolutionary outbursts. As we saw, the key stylistic features of these works—for example, preserving the classical balance between dominant and subdominant, not discarding the last section in the tonic leading to the final resolution—express the late classical style reworked into a new, revolutionary idiom. As US writer and musician Charles Rosen explains:

> Beethoven's originality reveals itself most often not by frustrating the conventions that he learned as a child, but by magnifying them beyond the experience or expectations of any of his contemporaries... At the end of his life, he was alone in

57 Rosen, 1971, p391.
58 Adorno, 1989, p211.

continuing a late 18th century style that he so transformed into the sensibility of a new age that he seemed to have reinvented it.[59]

Beethoven in his late works expresses, doubtless unconsciously, his anger and sorrow at the burden re-imposed on Europe by Napoleon's defeat and the victorious monarchies. Yet these works also reassert his faith in the capacity of future generations to rise up against servitude. The third, slow movement of the Ninth Symphony embodies a tragic lyricism that mourns the failure of the French Revolution to fulfil its promise of liberation. However, the fourth, choral movement reasserts a belief in humanity's long-term capacity to usher in such a world. As Sachs explains, "Beethoven...wanted to help light the way for humanity; he wanted human beings to realise their high ethical potential... The uniquely expressive power of the Ninth Symphony...is one of the most striking products of human beings' attempts to continue the struggle." Moreover, for Beethoven, it is not only heroes but also "common people" who are included among the "all men" in Schiller's poem who one day "will be brothers".[60]

Central to Beethoven's existence was the longing "to help mankind raise itself out of the muck of ignorance and pain".[61] In his final decade, this moral imperative became increasingly pressing, linked as it was to his "strange and acute personal misery." It elevated Beethoven "to levels of abstract expression and of rarefied, distilled emotion that no one else in the history of Western music has reached".[62] He had a unique ability to channel his most intimate experience into sounds that also expressed his powerful drive to transform humanity's condition.

Beethoven, like Haydn and Mozart, was dependent on the Viennese nobility. However, unlike his predecessors, he also pitted himself against them—not just in his music but in his ideas too. The English musicologist Wilfrid Mellers writes, "Haydn and Mozart were incipiently revolutionary composers, but Beethoven is overtly so".[63] Beethoven was the first great composer who consciously desired to build a new and different world, and he saw music as a means to that end.

Conclusion

In one of those strange historical coincidences, two German cultural giants—Beethoven and G W F Hegel—were born in the same year. Hegel was writing at the time when Beethoven composed his Ninth Symphony, arguing that "philosophy has the universal for its object, and, in so far as we think, we

59 Rosen, 1971, p460.
60 Sachs, 2010, pp87, 111, 158.
61 Sachs, 2010, p129.
62 Sachs, 2010, p129.
63 Quoted in Neunzig, 1981, p1.

are universal ourselves".[64] Hegel saw his work as the culmination of Western philosophy, as humanity's realisation of its possibilities, its achievement of self-consciousness, the fulfilment of the "absolute idea".

Adorno drew a parallel between Beethoven and Hegel, saying that "his music expressed the same experiences which inspired Hegel's concept of the 'world spirit'".[65] There is a sense in which Beethoven is Hegel's musical counterpart. If Hegel represents a high point of bourgeois philosophy, Beethoven marks the culmination of the line of development that begins with the invention of tonality around 1680, mainly through Arcangelo Corelli's work, and journeys through the late baroque and classical eras. Perhaps the dialectic is present within his own work: the early period being the thesis, the middle period the antithesis and the late period absorbing and synthesising elements of both. His music expresses one of the peaks of bourgeois artistic creativity but also looks forward to a different society. In a world torn apart by racism, economic crisis, climate change and pandemic, Beethoven's music inspires us to fight for a society based on solidarity.

---

64 Sachs, 2010, pp129-130.
65 Adorno, 1998, p32.

References

Adorno, Theodor W, 1998, *Beethoven: The Philosophy of Music* (Polity Press).

Adorno, Theodor W, 2002, "Alienated Masterpiece: The Missa Solemnis", in *Essays on Music* (University of California Press).

Arblaster, Anthony, 1992, *Viva La Liberta: Politics in Opera* (Verso).

Bukofzer, Manfred F, 1947, *Music in the Baroque Era: From Monteverdi to Bach* (Norton).

Clubbe, John, 2019, *Beethoven: The Relentless Revolutionary* (Norton).

Cooper, Barry, 2013, *Beethoven: An Extraordinary Life* (ABRSM).

Downs, Philip G, 1992, *Classical Music: The Era of Haydn, Mozart and Beethoven* (Norton).

Engels, Friedrich, 1969 [1850], *The Peasant War in Germany* (Lawrence and Wishart).

Evans, Richard, 2017, *The Pursuit of Power: Europe 1815-1914* (Penguin).

Hindley, Geoffrey, 1971, *The Larousse Encyclopedia of Music* (Hamlyn).

Hobsbawm, Eric, 1962, *The Age of Revolution: 1783-1815* (Weidenfeld & Nicolson).

Leichtentritt, Hugo, 1957 [1938], *Music, History and Ideas* (Harvard University Press).

McGarr, Paul, 1991, "Mozart: Overture to Revolution", *International Socialism 52*, (autumn), https://bit.ly/2LtQCpVl

Mellers, Wilfrid, 1957, *The Sonata Principle From Circa 1750* (Rockliff).

Neunzig, Hans Adolf, 1981, *Brahms* (Haus Publishing).

Rosen, Charles, 1971, *The Classical Style: Haydn, Mozart, Beethoven* (Viking Press).

Sachs, Harvey, 2010, *The Ninth: Beethoven and the World in 1824* (Random House).

Snowman, Daniel, 2009, *The Gilded Stage: A Social History of Opera* (Atlantic).

Stravinsky, Igor, and Robert Craft, 1963, *Dialogues and a Diary* (Doubleday).

Suchet, John, 2012, *Beethoven: The Man Revealed* (Atlantic Monthly Press).

Vere Gordon Childe and prehistory: a way of thinking, and much more
Judy McVey

A review of ***The Fatal Lure of Politics: The Life and Thought of Vere Gordon Childe***
Terry Irving
Monash University Publishing (2020), £25.99

World-renowned archaeologist, prehistorian and linguist Vere Gordon Childe's career spanned three decades from 1925 until 1957. He was the first exponent of Marxist archaeology in the Western world and he remains today the most widely read archaeologist. According to this new biography by Australian radical historian Terry Irving, "His concepts of the Neolithic and Urban Revolutions rank among the most important theoretical advances in the study of human cultural evolution." Childe published 21 books, 281 articles or chapters and 236 book reviews in 99 periodicals. As Irving records:

> His reputation was not confined to the English-speaking world. His books were translated into 21 languages, and he travelled widely, finding appreciative audiences in Europe, Russia, Turkey and India, as well as North America and Australia.

> He featured in two novels, three poems and even a 2008 Indiana Jones film.[1]

---

1   Irving, 2020, pix. Irving was a long-time editor of *Labour History—A Journal of Labour and Social History.* His website and blog can be found at www.terryirving.net

Yet Childe's was a controversial career. It began with innovatory ideas about cultural change and the development of European civilisation. He argued in *The Dawn of European Civilization* that the West was:

Indebted to the Orient for the rudiments of the arts and crafts that initiated man's emancipation from bondage to his environment and for the foundation of those spiritual ties that coordinate human endeavours... But the peoples of the West were not slavish imitators; they adapted the gifts of the East and united the contributions made by Africa and Asia into a new and organic whole capable of developing on its own original lines.[2]

In 1927 he became the first Abercromby Professor of Archaeology at the University of Edinburgh. He organised 20 Scottish excavation sites in the 19 years between 1927 and 1946, including the internationally famous 5,000 year old Neolithic village at Skara Brae on the Orkney Islands (1928-30). Edinburgh's elite elected him to the Royal Society of Edinburgh in 1935. In 1946, he was appointed director and professor of European prehistory at the Institute of Archaeology in London, where he remained until his retirement in 1956. According to Katie Meheux, the Institute's librarian, in the context of the Cold War:

As European archaeology expanded post-war, archaeologists became uneasy about the potential inaccuracies and inadequacies of pan-European narratives written by one man and sceptical about the survival of Childe's elaborate chronologies in the face of independent radio-carbon dating.[3]

Two earlier biographies in the early 1980s revived interest in Childe's contributions in relation to his "diffusion" model.[4] This model traced the spread of different cultures and ideas between societies via communication networks.[5] After a period of considerable controversy over his legacy, a number of conferences uncovered and clarified more details about his life and career, and his commitment to revolutionary politics.[6]

In 2016, the Institute of Archaeology (now part of University College London) renamed its annual lecture the Gordon Childe Lecture, open to both qualified and non-academic participants. In 2017, the Institute celebrated its 80th anniversary by digitising Childe's *The Dawn of European Civilization*, including

---

2   Childe, 1925, pxiii.
3   Meheux, 2017.
4   These two books are archeologist Bruce Trigger's *Gordon Childe: Revolutions in Archaeology* (1980) and Sally Green's more personal text, *Prehistorian: A Biography of V Gordon Childe* (1981).
5   For more on the diffusion method, see Tringham, 1983.
6   Derricourt, 2014. A conference on Childe's life and thought, held at the University of Queensland, is reported in Gathercole, Irving and Melleuish, 1995.

each of its six editions that were published over 30 years, from 1925 onwards, reflecting developments in archaeology and in Childe's theories. The book remains an "ancestral text" for the study of European prehistory and is widely used today.[7] Childe would have approved. He democratised archaeology, making certain published works accessible to laypeople, starting with *Man Makes Himself* (1936). This was followed by *What Happened in History* (1942), which sold 300,000 copies in its first 15 years. Both are still in print.

The fatal lure of politics

Childe actually had two careers: the first was as a labour intellectual in Australia and Britain until 1924. Irving's biography brings to life the whole person, exploring a complex intellectual and personal life, and unequivocally confirming Childe's place in left politics.[8] It recognises his historical materialist "way of thinking", which provides an unorthodox Marxist thread linking his practice as an archaeologist to that as a socialist campaigning against war and racism.

Childe was born on 14 April 1892 in Sydney into a conservative Christian family; his father was an Anglican Minister and Childe attended an elite school. He began to develop his version of Marxism from 1913 when, at the University of Sydney, he was a student of Francis Anderson, a Hegelian professor of philosophy. He achieved excellent results during his education in classics at the University of Sydney (1911-13) and won a scholarship to Oxford University. There he studied classics and archaeology (1914-17), achieving a Bachelor of Letters for his thesis, "The Influence of Indo-Europeans in Prehistoric Greece".

Childe cut his radical teeth as a supporter of 2,000 gas workers who took illegal, unofficial strike action against the Australian Labor Party (ALP) government in New South Wales, when many students scabbed. The period leading up to the First World War is part of the somewhat hidden history of Australia's working-class militants, which is unearthed by Irving's other works. Rank and file rebelliousness, combined with political experience in the labour movement, would shape Childe's thinking. In Oxford, Childe learnt about guild socialism, a movement advocating workers' control of industry and cooperatives, from its most well-known advocate, libertarian socialist G D H Cole. He became a close life-long friend of Rajani Palme Dutt, founder and long-standing leader of the Communist Party of Great Britain (CPGB). He joined the revolutionary wing of a socialist club, whose

---

7   Meheux, 2017.
8   Irving was part of the New Left of the 1960s, helping to set up the Free University outside Sydney University in 1967. His first book, with Raewyn Connell, *Class Structure in Australian History* (1980), is now a classic. Recently, he has written about 19th and early 20th century workers' struggles, including *The Southern Tree of Liberty: The Democratic Movement in New South Wales before 1856* (2006).

members, such as Raymond Postgate, broke with Fabianism during the war and also went on to become founders of the CPGB. These relationships deepened Childe's Marxism; he defended jailed conscientious objectors during the First World War and took part in supporting the strikes by 200,000 engineering workers across Britain in May 1917.

A Home Office report to MI5 declared Childe "thoroughly perverted and probably a very dangerous person".[9] He paid a high price for his radical ideas and activity and was effectively blacklisted and unable to find paid work in academia before 1925, living in the shadow of state surveillance in Australia and Britain for his entire political life. He returned to Australia, where he stayed until late 1921, now a recognised labour intellectual and ALP member. In 1919, he witnessed a massive strike wave during the influenza pandemic and became adviser to Labor leader John Storey, who became the New South Wales premier from March 1920. He also heard about the revolutionary waves in Europe, with Britain itself on the brink of revolution in 1919.

"A movement that will have to go further"

In 1923 Childe published the most authoritative analysis of the Australian instantiation of what socialists today would call parliamentarism and labourism. *How Labour Governs: A Study of Workers' Representatives in Australia* remains available in print and online. It offers a forensic study of the ALP and trade union movement, showing the need for revolution to build a "proletarian democracy" to end the "exploitation and enslavement of the workers".[10] It also castigates the failure of "politicalism", a term he coined to criticise the experience of labour movement representation. Although Irving does not explore this, *How Labour Governs* also opposed racial prejudice, and the nationalism and jingoism of the times, which, Childe wrote, "found its natural political exponent in the Labor Party".[11] The book sympathetically analyses the radical syndicalist Industrial Workers of the World (IWW) and the One Big Union movement, which attracted tens of thousands of working-class people during the period up to 1920. Radical workers in 1916, led mostly by the IWW, defeated a federal ALP government plebiscite supporting conscription for the British war effort. The ALP split and lost office; a second plebiscite in 1917 also lost.

In the context of discussions at a left-wing summer school in England about the failure of British workers to make revolution, which took place as *How Labour Governs* was being published, Childe developed his analysis further, recognising

---

9   Irving, 2020, p70.
10 Childe, 1964, pxi.
11 Childe, 1964, pp72-73.

the "futility of capturing 'political power'". He argued that "it was fatuous to promise, as Labor did, to transform capitalism by evolutionary means".[12] Even the most radical left-wing governments could not control the economy and the state. The movement that created the ALP with the objective of eliminating exploitation "would have to go further".[13] He did not analyse the trade union leaders as a separate bureaucratic layer with their own interests in opposition to those of the working class and, unlike Lenin or Antonio Gramsci, Childe had not participated directly in workers' revolutions or in building new revolutionary parties. However, like both, Childe developed ideas that differed with the more orthodox Marxist movements of their times. Politically, he was closer to syndicalism in his opposition to the state socialists of the social democratic parties of Germany, Britain and Australia. It is unclear whether Childe endorsed Bolshevism as appropriate for Australia. Irving writes:

> As the First World War was ending, Childe wrote to an academic mentor in Britain that he intended to return there "to escape the fatal lure of politics" in Australia. Ten years later he was well into an academic career in Britain that would bring him great esteem, but throughout that career politics continued to lure him.[14]

Revolution in archaeology

In the 12 months after May 1922, Childe began research into prehistory, visiting museums in Central Europe and writing six authoritative articles on Indo-European influences on Greek prehistory. His reputation would be established with the book, *The Dawn of European Civilization*, published in 1925.[15] That year, he was appointed the librarian at London's Royal Anthropological Institute, and in 1927 as the first Abercromby Professor of Archaeology. He went onto assume his position at the Institute of Archaeology in London in 1946.

In Marxism Childe found a "realistic" analysis of human society—based on real, rather than abstract, laws—which he applied to archaeology. Marxism had already taken an interest in these questions. Many readers of this journal will be familiar with Friedrich Engels's book *Origin of the Family, Private Property and the State* (1884) and his theory of the evolutionary development of societies. First proposed by the 19th century American anthropologist Lewis Henry Morgan, this theory envisions an evolutionary passage from foraging or hunter-gatherer societies (labelled "savagery"), through agricultural "barbarism" to

---

12 Irving, 2020, p266.
13 Irving, 2020, p267.
14 Irving, 2020, pxi.
15 Irving, 2020, p224.

the urban-based civilisation of Egypt, Mesopotamia, Greece and Rome. As archaeologist Neil Faulkner summarises:

> Childe posited two revolutionary breaks in the sequence, comparable in significance with the Industrial Revolution that had given rise to modern capitalism. These were the Neolithic Revolution, marking the transition from hunting and gathering to an existence based on cultivation and stock raising, and the Urban Revolution, marking the further transition to city-based "civilisation". The implication was that long periods of relative stagnation could be followed by sudden leaps forward. An accumulation of innovations...could provide the basis for a sudden "revolutionary" advance to a new, higher stage of society.[16]

For Childe, nothing was fixed, including human nature, and change was dialectical, and sometimes accidental, resulting from internal and external social—structural—contradictions. Childe did not theorise class struggle separately from his explanation of cultural change.[17] His theory that knowledge and culture accumulated in human societies encouraged a belief in the possibility of "progress", as a measurable expression of development. He never thought socialism was inevitable, but believed human culture would still advance:

> Progress is an indivisible whole in which the invention of a new way of hafting an axe formed a necessary prelude to the invention of the steam engine or the aeroplane...and the first steps on the path of discovery were the hardest. Thus the achievements of our nameless forerunners are in a real sense present in our cultural heritage today.[18]

His 1936 work *Man Makes Himself* popularised a non-discriminatory conception of progress. This was illustrated when he wrote about Aboriginal Australia (which he did not formally study) and asked:

> Why assume that, when the Arunta had created a material culture adapted to their environment, they at once stopped thinking altogether? They may have gone on thinking just as much as our own cultural ancestors, although their thoughts followed different lines...[19]

He wrote in 1938 that the most important task of prehistory was to "trace out in ever greater detail the paths and mechanisms whereby the great discoveries

---

16 Faulkner, 2007, pp88-89.
17 Faulkner, 2007, pp97-101.
18 Childe, 1925, p xv.
19 Childe, 2003, p46. The Arunta are the original people of what is now known as "Central Australia".

of the Ancient East...were transmitted to the savages and barbarians" of Europe south of the Alps.[20] Although he did not acknowledge the advanced cities of other continents, this was an important insight when, in the 1930s, many European scientists were embracing pseudo-scientific ideas to justify racism and white European superiority.

Irving's book outlines Childe's role, in collaboration with Communists, in attacking the British government's complicity in the eugenics movement and the rise of Hitler's Nazi regime, which championed a supposedly superior Aryan "race". Childe assisted refugee scientists fleeing Nazism. He strongly opposed false explanations of human development in terms of preserving purity of particular ethnic groups, as argued by racists and also by official archaeologists in the Soviet Union. Instead, he demonstrated societies' success in terms of the mixing of ethnic origins combined with evolutionary change.

A way of thinking

By focusing on a historical study of the role of a political intellectual, Irving allows the reader to appreciate the development of Childe's "way of thinking" and the significance of his Marxist methodology. According to Irving, Childe used the idealism of G W F Hegel, Benedetto Croce and Giovanni Gentile to help develop a non-determinist theory of history based on Marx's historical materialism. Later he moved beyond Hegel because, Childe wrote, "Hegel could conceive of the unity of the process only as transcending it... The absolute was just raised above the process like a sort of deity".[21] Childe developed a historical materialism centred on the process of human creativity—reality as a creative process.[22]

In the 1930s and 1940s he stopped short of joining the CPGB but remained a fellow traveller and collaborated on various political and theoretical projects, especially with members of the Communist Party Historians' Group. His attitude to both the Soviet Union and Stalinism was inconsistent. Childe felt he was in a different tradition and never used Stalinist jargon, although Irving does not mention any sympathy with Trotskyism, the most prominent revolutionary alternative to Stalinism. When in 1956 Stalin was denounced as a monster by the then Russian leader, Nikita Kruschev, and Russian tanks rolled into Hungary to crush a genuine workers' uprising, he responded less with outrage than resignation. He did not live to see the widespread rejection of Stalinism in the 1960s with the emergence of the New Left. Irving locates Childe within the broad tradition of Western Marxism, which consists

---

20 Irving, 2020, p280.
21 Irving, 2020, p317.
22 Irving, 2020, pp341-343.

mainly of cultural and philosophical theorists who distinguished themselves from defenders of the Soviet Union.[23] This is perhaps accurate, because Childe lacked a consistent approach to workers' revolution—something compatible with Western Marxism but not with the Bolshevism of 1917. His intellectual home was among dissident CPGB members such as Jack Lindsay, an Australian communist writer and cultural activist who lived in Britain.

Irving states:

> This is a book about the central place held by socialist politics in his life, and his contributions to the theory of history that it entailed. It is also about the conflict in socialist politics between radical revolutionary democracy and parliamentary social democracy, for Childe decided that "politicalism"...was fatal to socialism.[24]

Childe's Marxism was never just a "way of thinking"—he was part of the struggle, supporting militant workers, opposing war, racism and fascism, identifying with labour socialism, communism and the Soviet Union, albeit with an equivocal attitude towards Stalinism. Irving's book offers a comprehensive but complex account of all this, crammed full of detail. It represents 30 years mining various sources, including Peter Gathercole's uncompleted work on a political biography. Childe destroyed most of his papers in London, causing Irving to rely on a range of other sources such as friends' correspondence. A letter sent in 1919, for instance, remembered the Oxford University Socialist Society for its "recent 'rows' with government and university authorities" and Childe as "more outspoken than any other".[25] Irving has given us a valuable account, revealing Childe in a new light and rescuing the life of a "probably dangerous man" that the security services would have preferred we forget.

The most cited Australian author in the world, Childe was finally recognised at his first university in April 1957 when the chancellor bestowed on him the honorary degree of Doctor of Letters, just months before his death. Childe committed suicide on 19 October 1957 in the Blue Mountains, New South Wales, but it was not an act of despair. In a letter he requested not to be opened until January 1968, he wrote: "To end his life deliberately is in fact something that distinguishes Homo sapiens from other animals even better than ceremonial burial of the dead".[26]

In one of his final statements, published posthumously in *Antiquity* and entitled simply "Retrospect", he wrote, "The most original and useful contributions

---

23 Irving, 2020, p251.
24 Irving, 2020, pxi.
25 Irving, 2020, p79.
26 Irving, 2020, p371.

that I may have made to prehistory are certainly not novel data...nor yet well-founded chronological schemes nor freshly defined cultures, but rather interpretative concepts and methods of explanation".[27] An excellent example of Childe's method at work is in Chris Harman's *A People's History of the World*. Harman applies and critiques this "way of thinking" in parts one and two, which explore the history of the earliest human societies.[28]

Readers will be enthralled by Irving's rich investigative research. He uncovers the life of one of the world's most important intellectuals, who challenged archaeologists, historians and socialists, and defied attempts by wartime states to deny civil liberties and academic freedom. It is a remarkable and different style of biography. As the world once again moves toward reaction and social democratic parties disappoint, Childe's anti-determinist Marxism remains relevant for socialism in the 21st century.

---

27 Childe, 1958, p69.
28 Harman, 1999, pp 3-100.

References

Childe, V Gordon, 1925, *The Dawn of European Civilization* (K Paul, Trench, Trübner & Co).

Childe, V Gordon, 1958, "Retrospect", *Antiquity*, volume 32, number 126.

Childe, V Gordon, 1964 [1923], *How Labour Governs: A Study of Workers' Representation in Australia* (Melbourne University Press).

Childe, V Gordon, 2003 [1936], *Man Makes Himself* (Spokesman).

Derricourt, Robin, 2014, "The Making of a Radical Archaeologist: The Early Years of Vere Gordon Childe", *Australian Archaeology*, volume 79, number 1.

Faulkner, Neil, 2007, "Gordon Childe and Marxist Archaeology", *International Socialism* 116 (autumn), https://isj.org.uk/gordon-childe-and-marxist-archaeology

Gathercole, Peter, Terry Irving and Gregory Melleuish (eds), 1995, *Childe and Australia: Archaeology, Politics and Ideas* (University of Queensland Press).

Harman, Chris, 1999, *A People's History of the World* (Bookmarks).

Irving, Terry, 2020, *The Fatal Lure of Politics: The Life and Thought of Vere Gordon Childe* (Monash University Publishing).

Meheux, Katie, 2017, "Digitising and Re-examining Vere Gordon Childe's *Dawn of European Civilization*: A Celebration of the UCL Institute of Archaeology's 80th Anniversary", *Archaeology International*, volume 20, number 5.

Tringham, Ruth, 1983, "V Gordon Childe 25 Years after: His Relevance for the Archaeology of the Eighties", *Journal of Field Archaeology*, volume 10, number 1.

THE GHETTO FIGHTS
Warsaw 1941-43

This remarkable memoir by Marek Edelman, a member of the Warsaw Ghetto Resistance five-person command team, tells first-hand of the struggle of Warsaw's Jews against the Nazis in the spring of 1943. With a new introduction by John Rose.

A masterpiece...it gives in serious, purposeful, reticent words a record, simple and unostentatious, of a common martyrdom...an authentic document about perseverance and moral strength. From the introduction to the Jewish Socialist Bund's first edition, 1945

£7.99

Available from:
www.bookmarksbookshop.co.uk
publications@bookmarks.uk.com
+44 (0)20 7637 1848

the socialist bookshop
bookmarks

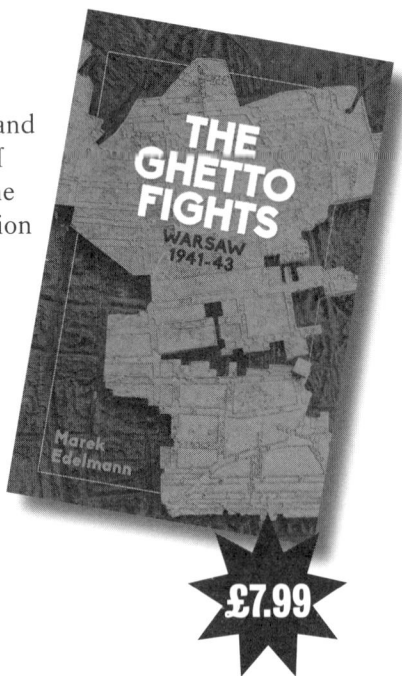

Putting the sin into syncopation
Ben Windsor

A review of *Jazz and Justice: Racism and*
the Political Economy of the Music
Gerald Horne
Monthly Review Press, £22

Jazz has an unfortunate reputation these days.[1] It is often seen as "high culture", something to be respected rather than enjoyed, with its own canon; there is a widespread belief that it belongs in the concert hall rather than on the dance floor. It's easy to forget that a hundred years ago jazz was insurgent, dangerous, sexy—and considered the lowest of low culture by its enemies.

Gerald Horne's latest book is an attempt to write a materialist history of the genre, with a focus on the racism that shaped it from the very beginning. It is quite a challenge to write about the development of such a contested and contradictory phenomenon, and one so deeply bound up with the toxic legacies of slavery. Over the years, many prominent musicians have rejected the "jazz" label, feeling that it degrades their music. One of the most outspoken was Nina Simone, who argued, "Jazz is a white term to define black people. My music is black classical music." The drummer and composer Max Roach was also unhappy with the word,

---

1   Martin, 2018. Thanks to Richard Donnelly and Dave Randall for their comments on this
     review in draft.

arguing that it evoked "the worst kind of working conditions, the worst in cultural prejudice...and the abuse and exploitation of black musicians." This distaste was not universal, but it reflected a fundamental ambivalence many performers felt about the way their music was presented to the world—and the circumstances that had forged it. As one commentator wrote, "'Jazz' was a double-edged term, sometimes representing black accomplishment and virtuosity, but sometimes a symbol of segregation and creative limitations".[2]

Right back to its origins in late 19th century New Orleans, the genre—or what some have retrospectively categorised as such—has been stamped with the brutal character of the times that it has inhabited. There are few tendencies in music that have emerged and developed in such appalling conditions. Its history is inextricably entwined with that of organised crime, prostitution, gambling, narcotics, alcoholism and—above all—the ravages of slavery and racism.

Jazz faced harsh criticism from its early days. There was even an "anti-jazz" movement, following on from an "anti-ragtime" one. This brought together a wide array of forces that were terrified at the burgeoning popularity of this low and dirty music, pulsating with the experience of black America. *The Times-Picayune* newspaper, mouthpiece of the white New Orleans establishment, led the charge; one article described jazz as "a low streak in man's tastes that has not yet come out in civilisation's wash" and demanded that it be euthanised.[3] This sentiment was echoed by the likes of Henry Ford and Thomas Edison. In 1921, a mass "crusade" was launched by the General Federation of Women's Clubs (GFWC), whose president claimed the music "was originally the accompaniment of the voodoo dance, stimulating half-crazed barbarians to the vilest deeds".[4] By the end of the decade, at least 60 communities across the US had enacted laws prohibiting jazz in public dance halls.[5]

The music conjured up all sorts of dark fantasies among the bigots, who sensed a carnivalesque element in it that threatened to turn their world upside down. Some denounced it as "musical Bolshevism, a revolt against law and order in music".[6] Others were more shocked by its tendency to induce sexy dancing. "Does jazz put the sin in syncopation?", asked one article by Anne Shaw

2   Gibb, 2002.
3   Rich, 2018.
4   Ford, a raging antisemite and fascist sympathiser, believed that jazz was a Jewish plot to infect the States with racially inferior "musical slush". In response, he poured a fortune into the promotion of country music and square dancing, which he mistakenly believed to be instrinsically "white". He had considerable success, getting almost half the country's schools to adopt it as part of their curriculum—Pennacchia, 2017.
5   www.pbs.org/wgbh/cultureshock/flashpoints/music/jazz.html
6   Street, 1922.

Faulkner, a leading member of the GFWC.[7] The BBC was little better. Its first director general, John Reith, an admirer of both Mussolini and Hitler, described it as a "filthy product of modernity" and praised the Nazis for banning it.[8] The corporation refused to broadcast jazz until the mid-1950s.

Horne rightly points out that "new musical forms are often pilloried, not least because they are misunderstood", but jazz carried the added burden of being the music of freed slaves.[9] This was music made by people whose very existence was taken as an affront by their old masters. It is thus ironic that one of the catalysts for the birth of jazz was the glut of instruments pawned by the marching bands of the defeated confederate army. Local musicians seized the opportunity to acquire these battered goods at knockdown prices.

Although several cities of the Deep South played a significant role in the development of the new music, it was in New Orleans that these influences converged and where jazz really took off. This major port at the mouth of the River Mississippi, the principal thoroughfare of the continent until the advent of railways, was a crossroads of many cultures. Despite—and even because of—its centrality to the barbaric slave economy, it developed a thriving musical culture.

Another historian of the genre, Charles Hersch, argues that jazz emerged in New Orleans because the city encapsulated the dual nature of this period in US history. Hersch observes that the music developed at the same time as a vicious counter-revolutionary wave that sought to wipe out the gains of the Civil War and Reconstruction. He writes:

> Ironically, a music that represented a joyous assertion of black culture...arose during the nadir of post-Civil War racial oppression... But what if this simultaneity is not ironic? What if the birth of jazz was both a response to and result of such racial politics?[10]

For years the city had a large, confident and well-established population of free African Americans, and many were part of a militant working class—the "vanguard of US labor".[11] As early as 1865 dockworkers launched an interracial strike. This movement reached it peak in 1892 with a city-wide general strike that brought out 25,000 black and white workers. However, its defeat was a turning point. Jim Crow bit hard, shrinking the black share of the Louisiana

---

7   Quoted in Horne, 2019, p42.
8   See the BBC website's own biography of Reith—www.bbc.com/historyofthebbc/research/ john-reith/corporation-man
9   It is perhaps more accurate to say that it was the music of the descendants of freed slaves, but this was a minor detail in the eyes of the planter class.
10 Hersch, 2007, p24.
11 Sustar, 1994.

electorate from 44% to 0.6%.[12] As a wedge was driven between them and the poor whites, one response of the black population was to "assert their pride and identity, carving out their own cultural spaces".[13]

Jazz alarmed the local ruling class. Its sexual energy threatened to undermine their authority and to seduce "their" women and "their" youth. The editorial of a New Orleans rag expressed these anxieties candidly, lamenting that jazz led "male and female, black and yellow, and even white to meet on terms of equality and abandon themselves to the extreme limit of obscenity and lasciviousness".[14]

One enduring influence on jazz was the nature of the venues where it was performed. Alongside the new music a large sex industry flourished in New Orleans. As early as 1850, it was considered the "red-light capital" of the US. The brothels became the principal employer of the town's black musicians, who were frequently shut out of more "respectable" jobs due to the colour of their skin. This shaped the performances (and the lives) of these artists in various ways. It meant difficult, dangerous and unstable working conditions, an intimate relationship with organised crime, the constant temptation of addictive substances, and an immersion in a particularly misogynist culture.

The popularity of jazz grew exponentially. It could thank some key technical innovations of the period for extending its reach—the juke box, the radio and the record player. Yet these developments were in themselves no guarantee that such a localised phenomenon could find a mass audience in the wider world. One of the theoreticians of the Harlem Renaissance, Joel Augustus Rogers, argues that something profound was going on, and that it was no accident that the music of freed slaves resonated with the oppressed and the exploited elsewhere:

> The true spirit of jazz is a joyful revolt from convention, custom, authority, boredom, even sorrow—from everything that would confine the soul of man... It has been such a balm for modern ennui...a release of all the suppressed emotions at once, a blowing off of the lid.[15]

As the music infected other states of the union, so did prohibition. In practice this meant that even when jazz clubs emerged in their own right, they were generally run by the mob, who favoured these establishments as a convenient way to launder money and sell alcohol. It was not much of a step

---

12 Disfranchisement was aimed at white farmers and workers as well. During this period the white vote in Louisiana dropped by 60 percent—Sustar, 1994.
13 Hersch, 2007, p24.
14 Quoted in Krist, 2014, p81.
15 Rogers, 1925.

up from performing in brothels. Some in the audience considered it sport to abuse—and even attack—the performers. Things got so bad that many carried weapons on stage for their own protection.

Musicians tried to organise to improve their lot, but they faced impossible odds, getting ripped off at every turn. When they turned to unions for help, they often found them to be corrupt, racist and mixed up with the mafia.[16] Quite a few of the most famous names in the genre, who made a fortune for their managers, agents and publishers, were living in poverty. Some gave up in despair, opting for regular jobs that would at least pay the rent. Many others escaped abroad, especially to Europe, where the chances of finding both respect and a living wage were far higher.

For most of its early life jazz was primarily experienced as dance music, attracting massive audiences. We have seen how, from the very start, the authorities were terrified by its ability to get black and white people cavorting together. It aroused their deepest fears—that "desegregation" would quickly lead to "miscegenation". This came to a head during the Second World War, when a debilitating tax on dance halls was imposed, driving many out of business.[17] This had a major impact on the nature of the music, sealing the fate of swing and facilitating the rise of (experimental and undanceable) bebop.

One of the most bizarre episodes in jazz history followed soon after, as the US state entered Cold War mode and decided to enlist the music in its propaganda efforts. The once-scorned genre now received official sponsorship and was sent on foreign tours, becoming a symbol of American freedom.[18] Willis Conover, the radio presenter at the forefront of this cultural offensive, reached a worldwide audience of 30 million listeners and was lionised as a celebrity when he visited the Eastern Bloc.[19]

However, the political highpoint for jazz came, appropriately, with the growth of the Civil Rights Movement. Although many musicians of earlier generations had been in awe of black singer, activist and Communist Party supporter Paul Robeson, few felt able to emulate him. Yet now, with the confidence that came from a movement on the rise, increasing numbers sought to turn the music on their oppressors. The likes of Nina Simone, Abbey Lincoln and Max Roach

---

16 As late as 1943, only two out of 673 branches of the American Federation of Musicians admitted black people to full membership. Horne, 2019, p25.

17 It seems likely this was in part motivated by a fear of what the wives of absent soldiers might get up to—and its potential effect on the "morale" of troops.

18 Horne, 2019, p242. This was a fate it shared with Abstract Expressionist painting, which received considerable backing from the CIA.

19 Outrageously, Conover claimed that the flowering of this music in his homeland "corrects the fiction that America is racist"—Horne, 2019, p243.

embraced the opportunity wholeheartedly, raising funds for combative organisations, composing fiercely political songs, hosting festivals, demanding more creative control, and setting up their own record labels.

There is a lot to enjoy in Horne's book, but it is ultimately a frustrating read. His shepherding of resources is half-hearted and, after a promising introduction, the book becomes increasingly incoherent and repetitive. Unfortunately, the thematic chapter titles—"Haitian Fight Song", "Song for Che" and so on—promise far more than they deliver. It feels as though the author and his editor lost interest. Nevertheless, Horne's ambition is admirable, and he has clearly read widely and sympathetically, assembling a wealth of material.

References

Gibb, Ann, 2002, "African American Musicians Reflect on *What is This Thing Called Jazz?*", University of California Santa Cruz (3 March), https://bit.ly/36lqoiG

Hersch, Charles B, 2008, *Subversive Sounds: Race and the Birth of Jazz in New Orleans* (University of Chicago Press)

Horne, Gerald, 2019, *Jazz and Justice: Racism and the Political Economy of the Music* (Monthly Review Press).

Krist, Gary, 2014, *Empire of Sin: A Story of Sex, Jazz, Murder and the Battle for Modern New Orleans* (Broadway Books)

Martin, Rachel, 2018, "Jazz In The 21st Century Is All About 'Playing Changes'", NPR Music (14 August), https://n.pr/33EUZ7L

Pennacchia, Robyn, 2017, "America's Wholesome Square Dancing Tradition is a Tool of White Supremacy", Quartz (12 December), https://bit.ly/3lD4jPq

Rich, Nathaniel, 2018, "When Jazz was Dangerous", *The Paris Review* (24 January), www.theparisreview.org/blog/2018/01/24/when-jazz-was-dangerous

Rogers, Joel Augustus, 1925, "Jazz at Home", *Survey Graphic Harlem* (March), volume 6, number 6.

Street, Julian, 1922, "The Jazz Baby", *Saturday Evening Post* (15 July).

Sustar, Lee, 1994, "The Roots of Multi-Racial Labour Unity in the United States", *International Socialism* 63 (summer), www.marxists.org/history/etol/newspape/isj2/1994/isj2-063/sustar.htm

Watson, Amy, 2019, "Music Album Consumption US 2018, by Genre", Statista (9 August), www.statista.com/statistics/310746/share-music-album-sales-us-genre

Marxism beyond the binaries
Paul Simpson

A review of *Transgender Resistance: Socialism and the Fight for Trans Liberation*
Laura Miles
Bookmarks (2020), £10

It is rare indeed to get an extended, detailed account of the challenges that are faced by a highly marginalised social group across various societies and regions. It is rarer still today for such an account to be linked to socialism. The central argument of *Transgender Resistance* is that trans liberation is dependent on radical social, economic and political transformation. It makes the case that although huge challenges lie ahead, trans and non-binary individuals, their organisations and their allies have agency and the power to fight oppression.[1]

Transgender Resistance is well researched, well evidenced and well argued. It is highly engaging, clearly written and skilfully structured. The book proceeds from

---

1   The term "trans" itself is used to denote a spectrum of gender expressions ranging from self-declaration in a non-given gender to those who have undergone full reassignment. "Non-binary" refers to people who describe themselves neither as cisgender (in line with given gender) nor as trans but of another kind. There are various expressions of this. Some people may describe themselves as "agender"—a category through which they resist being reduced to a social "type" according to their reproductive potential.

an analysis of the varying fortunes of trans people (or those thought to represent non-normative genders) over time (chapters 1-5); and, thereafter, it focuses on trans people in different places and cultures (chapters 6–9). It will be accessible to politically engaged readers and those prepared to extend their thinking and vocabulary, though a glossary of key terms is also helpfully provided. This is a book that writes to persuade, through evidence, argumentation and analysis. As befits its title, chapters 10 and 11 are devoted to political strategy. They develop an agenda for action, grounded in everyday material existence, that can move us beyond transphobia and the socio-economic inequalities that produce it.

Although the author claims that the countries and regions reviewed within the book are but a "snapshot", readers are nonetheless given an interesting analysis of the various factors that make transphobia endemic—both in liberal democracies and more clearly authoritarian societies. We gain insight into how the global drive for economic exploitation (including neo-imperialist military intervention), buttressed by state legislation and conservative forces within organised religion, breed violence and hostility. In turn, these conditions restrict opportunities for transitioning and access to healthcare, as well as equal citizenship and social participation.

Chapter 6 draws attention to the oppressive effects of the medicalisation of trans people. Medicalisation contributes towards pathologisation of trans people as abnormal, ignoring the social provenance of oppression. Despite equalities legislation since 2010, transphobia remains endemic in Britain's (partially) socialised health system. The author discusses issues that have been made controversial such as the ability of trans people to self-declare as the gender they feel describes them rather than having to depend on the decision of medical experts. Also discussed are children seeking help with gender identity, trans women and women-only spaces, and who counts as a woman. These concerns are usefully clarified and analysed in chapter 9. This chapter also deftly dismantles some of the most contradictory and egregious anti-trans views, and shows how they are premised on an ideology that both marginalises trans people and naturalises elite rule by the capitalist class.

It is no wonder that in many countries and regions, where authoritarian populist governments are in power, where socialised healthcare is lacking and where "alt-right" ideology and anti-LGBT+ vigilante groups are legitimised, that trans women are effectively forced into sex-work to survive or to support their transitioning process. Transitioning is sometimes highly restricted by either law or economic obstacles in countries such as the United States and South Korea. It is outlawed in countries such as Gambia, Malaysia, Nigeria and Uganda. Even where trans people are afforded some limited legal protection, they can be subject to widespread, and sometimes murderous, public hostility in countries such as

Bangladesh, Brazil, Columbia, India, Pakistan and South Africa. Such public hostility and violence is also a part of the oppression that faces trans people in Britain, Europe and the US.

Transgender Resistance is a timely work. Trans and non-binary people face attacks from the left, right and centre of the political spectrum, including from some of those who describe themselves as "radical" or "socialist feminists". Indeed, anti-trans prejudice has forged an unholy alliance between religious conservatives, the secular right and radical feminists. Their attacks are based on an essentialism that assumes that what we understand as gender is hard-wired. Some have questioned whether trans women are "real" women or a pathological category that risks erasing lesbians.[2] Others have wondered whether they are, in reality, male sexual predators seeking access to women's bodies in public toilets and other single-sex spaces.[3] Whatever the accusations, as Miles argues in chapter 2, we have witnessed a backlash against trans people's autonomy and their right to transition to the gender that is right for them.

Miles's book is valuable for its critical examination of the many instances of biologically reductionist and transphobic rhetoric, myths and bogus claims. The author calmly rebuts these with clear, rational and well-supported arguments, especially in chapters 3 and 7. Miles also clarifies the complexities of biology as they affect gender. Proponents of transphobia miss these complexities due to their commitment to a simplistic biological determinism, in which biological sex is thought to determine who counts as a "real" man or woman and how we are expected to behave.

Miles also delivers a much needed challenge to two opposing groups of theories of gender. The first group argues that one's gender is innate and solely a result of biology. The second claims that gender is a totally social or cultural construction—a human invention, informed by our understanding of "types" of people, that we have internalised. Miles argues that a Marxist position transcends this biology/social construction binary, and that each group of theories is inadequate by itself. These polarised, binary positions are at best unhelpful to our understandings of gender, and at worst both can legitimate oppression of trans people. Miles believes that biological science—itself not completely fixed because of ongoing advances in medical technologies—partially provides a material basis for gender. However, she argues that these factors need to be understood alongside an analysis of the social relations of production, and that social constructionist theories can provide an explanation of the historicity of gender—the way that it varies across time, place and culture. Social

2   The transgender feminist Julia Serano has responded to these arguments—see Serano, 2007.
3   For an account of these accusations, see Earles, 2019.

constructionist theory, as Miles indicates, began with Marxism and its theorising of historical variability. It provides insight into how the gender binary is much less natural than is claimed by the dominant ideology. That ideology stresses the centrality of the heteronormative family, which places constraints on women and excludes trans women. Moving beyond the biology/social construction dichotomy points towards a dialectical relationship between the material forces of biology and production relations on the one hand and the effects of culture and ideas on the other hand. This can also be conceptualised as the relationship between the material, economic basis of society and its political and cultural superstructure.

It is refreshing to engage with a book that recognises the fluidity of gender constructions in relation to trans and non-binary people and yet does not locate these constructions in free-floating ideas or "discourses". Instead, Miles roots them firmly within a historical materialist analysis. This sort of approach has been sadly lacking over the past 30 years in academic studies and other professional forms of writing on gender and sexuality. By drawing attention to the different ways that trans people have been regarded across time, the book underlines the explanatory power of historical materialism. Miles's work reminds us of the value of Marxist theory for dismantling the bourgeois explanation of history and the myth that societal development is set on a linear path towards ever-unfolding progress.

In fact we learn from Miles that hostility towards and oppression of sexually variant and gender-variant people has intensified under capitalism.[4] That said, the book recognises that this oppression also increased under the totalitarian homophobia of the Stalinist Soviet Union, with its intolerance of "perversions". Chapter 4 illustrates a range of class-based experiences of being trans that are uniquely contemporary, as well as forms of trans resistance that only students of history would encounter.

As an academic sociologist attracted to the discipline in the 1980s by the socialist critiques it offered of capitalism and LGBT+ oppression, I have been disappointed to witness the almost total dominance of neo-idealist, post-structuralist theories of gender and sexuality. These theories have been used especially to explain trans and non-binary experiences. Post-structuralist theorists tend to see the internalisation of ideology or "discourse" as animating subconscious behaviour but deny the effects of social structures and hierarchies that constrain expressions of gender and sexuality such as the class system.[5] Although post-structuralism is very supportive of trans people, the only strategy it offers is endless self-referential transgression

---

4   See also McIntosh, 1981.
5   See Fraser, 1997.

of gender, and it lacks a credible agenda for change. Miles presents a well argued alternative to such ways of thinking and could contribute to the reassertion of the value of structuralist, socialist analysis in studies of gender and sexuality.

Importantly, Miles uses the tools of Marxist analysis to understand trans and non-binary oppression as linked to political economy, class and race. This allows her to draw connections between trans liberation and other struggles such as those against austerity and the global rise of populism amid the failure of a centrist politics that has abandoned working-class communities. Because it makes links between trans oppression and these broader issues of socio-economic organisation, Miles's analysis could help take discussions of gender, sexuality and trans and non-binary people out of their current intellectual ghetto. With its arcane, exclusionary language, this is a ghetto that post-structuralism has had a big hand in creating.

The last two chapters are particularly enlightening. They argue that an adequate theory of oppression is a necessary starting point for practical socialist politics. Chapter 10 provides a very thoughtful critique of various theories that suggest a path to a more egalitarian society that values difference. Miles analytically works through the false promises and failures of identity politics, post-modernist thought, queer theory, privilege theory and intersectional theory. Clearly explaining all of these theories, Miles stresses that although such ideas are supportive of trans people, they tend to de-emphasise the centrality of class in producing oppression and lack a theory of social and political transformation and a corresponding praxis. For instance, post-modernism has much to say about the transgressive character of trans and its capacity to trouble or de-naturalise the gender binary. However, it can also tend to erase the everyday brutalities that trans people have to face, from hostility and violence to lack of access to services. It is thus questionable how useful such thinking is to working-class people who are struggling to navigate a complex health system in order to begin the process of transitioning, with all the surveillance and intrusion by state agencies that this involves. As Miles argues, theories that overlook the material conditions of existence and relations of production can only provide ideas for action based on localised, individualistic forms of resistance that cannot deliver collective emancipation.

I have only one minor criticism of the book. Miles could have employed the Marxist analysis elaborated by the Italian revolutionary and theorist Antonio Gramsci. Gramsci maintained that the ruling elite needs to constantly manufacture the consent of subordinated classes in order to rule. Gramsci referred to this ideological domination as "hegemony". Hegemony is secured through constant persuasion that there is no alternative to capitalism and through the masking of exploitative relations of production and marginalisation of oppressed people. Gramsci's analysis could have been deployed to explain how capitalist social organisation perpetuates and normalises transphobia through elite ownership and control of the media and culture industries. It might also have helped to explain why, despite a few attempts at positive representation, cultural institutions tend to neglect the issue of trans and non-binary people, thus failing to confront ignorance and hostility.

In summary, this is an engaging and thought-provoking book that reasserts the value of structuralist analysis of gender and sexuality. It sees that social organisation produces oppression and draws a radical implication from this: that social reorganisation could end oppression. It provides a thorough histori-cal materialist analysis of the variable fortunes of those thought to represent non-normative genders and sexualities across time and place. The book will be an invaluable resource for trans people and anyone wishing to support them through work, activism or friendship. It is a tool for those who want to rebut transphobic hostility. Chapters 8–10 offer a resource for political activists to think with, even if they do not identify as socialists. Miles extends and deepens our knowledge of transphobia and trans resistance, and she expands Marxist theory to a realm that it has largely overlooked.

References
Earles, Jennifer, 2019, "The 'Penis Police': Lesbian and Feminist Spaces, Trans Women, and the Maintenance of the Sex/Gender/Sexuality System", *Journal of Lesbian Studies*, volume 23, issue 2.

Fraser, Nancy, 1997, "Heterosexism, Misrecognition and Capitalism: A Response to Judith Butler", *Social Text*, issues 52-53.

McIntosh, Mary, 1981, "The Homosexual Role", in Ken Plummer (ed), *The Making of the Modern* (Hutchinson).

Serano, Julia, 2007, *Whipping Girl: A Transsexual Woman on Sexism and the Scapegoating of Femininity* (Seal Press).

Book reviews

Revisiting non-violence
Colette Wymer

Mohandas Gandhi: Experiments in Civil Disobedience
Talat Ahmed
Pluto (2019), £12.99

For readers who know little of India's history and its "founding father", *Mohandas Gandhi: Experiments in Civil Disobedience* is an excellent choice. Talat Ahmed provides a detailed and comprehensive, yet accessible narrative that weaves together an account of Gandhi's life with the historical, cultural, political, social and economic realities of his time. This creates a multilayered tapestry that chronicles the events and ideas that shaped Gandhi's life. Importantly, Ahmed both defends and challenges aspects of his legacy.

Gandhi has been heroised, romanticised and sanitised. He has been called a father, a leader, a saint and a revolutionary. It is this final claim that Ahmed addresses and counters most clearly. She traces Gandhi's life from his birth in 1869 to his assassination in 1948. In a set of rich early chapters, Ahmed tells the story of how Gandhi was born a "middle-class and middle-caste Hindu", before studying law in London and going on to practice in South Africa. There, he first experienced systemic racism and began his life as an activist. In 1915 he returned to India as the "champion of the oppressed" (p56).

Despite his privileged upbringing, Gandhi is often remembered as "a man of the people". Certainly his dedication to challenging the oppression of the "dalits" or "untouchables"—the lowest caste in India—justifies this to some degree. Nevertheless, there were always limitations on Gandhi's activism, some of which flowed from his class status. However, these limitations were also related to those who influenced his ideas: the Russian author and Christian pacificist Leo Tolstoy, the prominent social thinker and philanthropist John Ruskin and the US philosopher Henry David Thoreau, who wrote the seminal 1849 essay *Civil Disobedience*.

Coupled with his Hindu theology, these influences shaped an approach that was more philosophical and moralistic than socialist and revolutionary.

This showed, for example, in Gandhi's rejection of movements that directly challenged capitalist interests. For him, working-class projects such as the All-India Trade Union Congress "antagonised employers by preaching class warfare" (p94). Ahmed's book highlights the contradictions that Gandhi was consistently faced with as he attempted to unite the forces of national liberation in the absence of an analysis of the relationships between classes in Indian society.

As the book's title suggests, Ahmed pays particular attention to Gandhi's theory of non-violence, analysing its effectiveness and limitations. This is timely. Non-violent resistance strategies have enjoyed a resurgence in popularity through movements such as Extinction Rebellion. Moreover, discussions of violence and non-violence expose fundamental questions about the tactics that are needed today in the struggles taking place around the globe. The Black Lives Matter movement in the United States, for example, has thrown up debates about the legitimacy and effectiveness of rioting as a tactic and how it is possible to resist armed fascist groups. These themes have been developed in this journal by Martin Empson's detailed and excellent "Non-violence, Social Change and Revolution" (*International Socialism 165*), which draws on Ahmed's work.

Civil disobedience and non-compliance can play an important role in resistance, and Ahmed provides many inspiring examples of the effective use of Gandhi's methods. Principled defiance of the law is difficult and courageous. Nevertheless, throughout history, these weapons alone have fallen short. As Ahmed illustrates, civil disobedience and non-compliance can only take us so far because the enemy will always refuse to play by the same rules.

Under Gandhi's instruction, followers were forbidden from even defending themselves. Many died as a result. Others fought back. Gandhi believed that this was a moral issue. He saw the capacity of an individual to engage in non-violent action in a disciplined fashion as tied up with their understanding of "satyagraha", one's ability to "hold to the truth".

When movements went beyond his control, Gandhi called them to an end. For instance, he halted the national non-cooperation movement of 1922, suspending disobedience and beginning a personal hunger strike as penance for the violence that had been "used in his name". Unfortunately, he failed to condemn the state for its violence against protesters. Ahmed explains, "Gandhi's position was always to condemn violence, but he was particular about who was to blame for it" (p91).

Perhaps the clearest revelation of the limits of Gandhi's political methods occurred during the mutiny of the Royal Indian Navy in Mumbai in 1946. Ahmed's account of the events is electric. The mutineer's militancy, the breadth of their support and the defiance of Indian workers created a powerful uprising.

Vitally, it was rooted in class unity and cut across religious divides between Hindus, Muslims and Sikhs. It was also incredibly effective. Ahmed argues that the mutiny was the decisive event in forcing the British out and a defining moment in realising an Independent India. Yet despite the importance of the mutiny, it was not supported, let alone led, by Gandhi.

Ahmed also takes us through fascinating accounts of Gandhi's life that reveal some of his less than admirable positions on race and religion, women, poverty and oppression, as well as his insights into patriotism and imperialism.

The issue of religion is particularly pertinent in India today. Religion had not historically been a defining, let alone dividing feature in India. Often identity has been dominated by other factors such as region and language or dialect. It was during the the 20th century that religion became an increasing source of tensions. Many Muslims fought for British imperial interests in the First or Second World Wars, and yet would still be denied equal rights when they returned home to India. The minority Muslim population responded by reasserting themselves through organisations such as the Khilafat movement and the Muslim League. By the mid-1920s religion was firmly planted on the political agenda.

Ahmed explains that Gandhi "held all faiths to be equal, believing that they were different paths to the one god and salvation" (p84):

> The championing of oppressed groups was essential to Gandhi's prognosis for Indian nationalism and so Hindu-Muslim unity was a central objective. He understood that a united front against the British Empire had to be fought for. (p85)

This led Gandhi to support Muslim groups that fought religious oppression. Nevertheless, he failed to challenge his own party, the Indian National Congress (INC), as it shifted from cross-communal unity towards a more nationalistic, anti-Muslim position. This repositioning paved the way for the partition of India and Pakistan in 1947 and the explosion of brutal religious violence that followed. Displacing some 10-12 million people along religious lines, partition continues to provide the backdrop for the tensions between Hindus and Muslims in India today.

Although the INC went on to rule India for 55 of the 73 years since independence in 1947, today they have been displaced as the largest party in the Lok Sabha, the directly elected house of the Indian parliament. Instead it is the Bharatiya Janata Party (Indian People's Party, BJP) and its prime minister Narendra Modi who run the Indian federal state today. The BJP is a pro-business Hindu nationalist party and its national election victories in 2014 and 2019 relied heavily on anti-Muslim propaganda. Modi's celebrity-like status and popularity, as well as the enormous donations that he attracts, have boosted the BJP's membership to more than 110 million. Today, it is the largest political party in the world.

Modi's early allegiance was to the Rashtriya Swayamsevak Sangh (RSS), a fascist paramilitary organisation that promotes the "Hindutva" Hindu nationalist ideology and sees the BJP as its political arm. Although there is a tension between Modi's RSS membership and his role as prime minister, he has nevertheless used his position to push the Hindutva agenda. A recent example of this is his introduction of the Citizenship (Amendment) Act, which extended citizenship to Hindu and Buddhist migrants from Bangladesh but denied the same rights to Muslims. Modi's desire to marginalise Muslims and promote an ethno-nationalist vision of India's future has drawn comparisions with Zionism. Likewise the subjugation of the Muslim-majority territory of Jammu and Kashmir has led some to compare Modi's India with the Israeli apartheid state. As Raju Das suggested in a recent article in this journal, the "supremacist zeal" of the BJP's Hindutva means:

> There will be deeper connections between India and Israel. India will fast become like Israel. We might see the emergence of an "Indian Zionism"... Jammu and Kashmir is fast becoming a South Asian Palestine. Without any consent from Kashmiris at all, the BJP government has taken away their legal autonomy.

Opportunities exist for the Indian left, but it remains weak. Partition and religious turmoil has left a deep scar on Indian society. Some of these problems are rooted partially in the sort of movement that Gandhi built and the type of society that emerged from the independence struggles that he was so central to. Of course, it is right to recognise the truly inspiring contribution of Gandhi, but an honest critique is also necessary. Ahmed does this with sensitivity but without sentiment.

Nonetheless, this is no time to dismiss non-compliance. The collective refusal to return to unsafe workplaces or to send children into unsafe schools has been a feature of popular resistance to governments that have mishandled the Covid-19 crisis. However, neither is it a time to limit our expectations for a better world. The people of India have independence, but they are not truly liberated. Inequality and poverty reign. Extreme nationalism, rooted in the powerful fascist RSS organisation, is a part of mainstream politics, and the everyday horrors of capitalism continue. Marxists understand that any effective attempts to challenge or undermine the current capitalist system will be met with the severest response from the state. Age old tactics of divide and rule are used as much today, in the face of the crisis of neoliberalism, as they ever were. Brutal state repression continues to suppress uprisings across the globe, and a creeping authoritarianism can be discerned as the system reels from the shock of coronavirus.

If we are to apply the lessons of history and thus avoid repeating its darkest moments, an earnest and honest critique of figures such as Gandhi is vital. Ahmed has provided a detailed and balanced account of his life and thought from a Marxist perspective. This is a worthy read for anyone grappling with a way forward today.

Pick of the quarter

International Socialism has, over recent issues, argued that the world is in a grip of a "triple crisis"—expressed through the pandemic, economic disorder and ecological destruction. Across the Atlantic, John Bellamy Foster, the editor of the United States-based *Monthly Review*, has presented a similar position. In a piece entitled "The Renewal of the Socialist Ideal" (https://monthlyreview.org/2020/09/01/the-renewal-of-the-socialist-ideal), published in the September issue, he argues: "Catastrophe capitalism...is manifested today in the convergence of (1) the planetary ecological crisis, (2) the global epidemiological crisis, and (3) the unending world economic crisis."

Foster charts deepening class polarisation and the re-emergence of the idea of socialism in the US, but notes that the socialism on offer is often of a social democratic variety, which is tested harshly in this context of crisis. Alongside this left revival comes broader mass struggle, focused outside the electoral terrain, which can lay the basis for a revival of the "communist" ideal (in the sense advocated by Karl Marx and Friedrich Engels). Some of Foster's strategic conclusions—for instance, the scope for left-nationalist projects in countries such as Cuba or Venezuela under former president Hugo Chávez to challenge capitalism—are certainly arguable, but the article represents an interesting intervention in discussions about the strategy of the left today.

Meanwhile, across the Irish Sea, issue 28 of *Irish Marxist Review* contains an excellent piece entitled "The (Ongoing) Crisis of Global Capitalism" by Brian O'Boyle (www.irishmarxistreview.net/index.php/imr/article/view/383). This analyses both the immediate impact of Covid-19 on the economy and the longer term problems faced by the capitalist system. One of the themes of O'Boyle's analysis, and that of many authors in this journal, is that capitalism is in the grip of an extended crisis of profitability. *The Review of Radical Political Economics* has just published the online version of an article on this theme by Adalmir Antonio Marquetti, Catari Vilela Chaves, Leonardo Costa Ribeiro and Eduardo da Motta e Albuquerque. The authors consider the rate of profit in the US and

China, using the Orbis database of information on private sector companies for 2007-14. Their research shows that the US rate of profit was low but fairly stable throughout this period, other than a brief V-shaped drop in 2008, whereas the Chinese rate of profit was higher, but declined fairly sharply from 2010 to 2014.

They also look at the rate of profit within particular sectors of these economies. This helps to open up new ways to think about the flow of capital through the world economy, and the complex shifts in profitability in particular countries and sectors that might result from the combination of crises and competition. For instance, they show how the dispersion of profit rates grew during the 2008-9 crisis, as some firms went under and others used the failure of their rivals to grasp new opportunities.

Finally, political scientist Jon Wittrock has written a provocative essay for *Rethinking Marxism*, entitled "All That Is Holy: The Role of Religion in Postcapitalist Communities" (www.tandfonline.com/doi/full/10.1080/089356 96.2020.1809836). Although his argument is solidly based in Marxism, he also utilises the notion of "family resemblance" developed by Ludwig Wittgenstein, the great philosopher of language. Wittgenstein argued against the common idea that concepts connect distinct things through identifying some essential characteristic that they all share. Instead, he claimed, concepts express a set of overlapping similarities between these things. Wittrock argues that religion is best understood as such a collection of overlapping ideas and practices, rather than any sort of unitary phenomenon.

Of course, the concept of religion does encompass institutionalised forms of ritual that are bound up with the functioning of capitalist states and the propagation of ruling-class ideology. Nevertheless, it can also include "practices of asceticism and meditation, ecstatic drumming and dancing, and phenomenological explorations of overwhelming states of consciousness" that are divorced from such institutional forms. Wittrock speculates, against the traditional Marxist view, that this means some aspects of religion could survive the overthrow of capitalism—and might even be renewed and transformed by their implantation in new forms of communal life.

JC & RD